THE ROUGH GUIDE

THAI

PHRASEBOOK

Compiled by

LEXUS

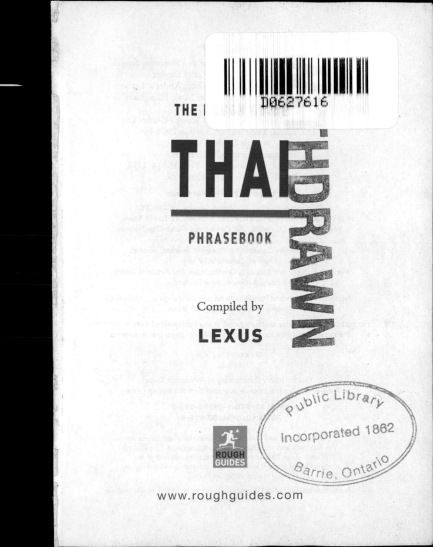

www.roughguides.com

Credits

Compiled by Lexus with David and Somsong Smyth
Lexus Series Editor: Sally Davies
Rough Guides Reference Director: Andrew Lockett
Rough Guides Series Editor: Mark Ellingham

First edition published in 1999 by Rough Guides Ltd.
This updated edition published in 2006 by
Rough Guides Ltd,
80 Strand, London WC2R 0RL
345 Hudson St, 4th Floor, New York 10014, USA
Email: mail@roughguides.co.uk.

Distributed by the Penguin Group.

Penguin Books Ltd, 80 Strand, London WC2R 0RL
Penguin Putnam, Inc., 375 Hudson Street, NY 10014, USA
Penguin Group (Australia), 250 Camberwell Road, Camberwell, Victoria 3124, Australia
Penguin Books Canada Ltd, 10 Alcorn Avenue, Toronto, Ontario, Canada M4V 1E4
Penguin Group (New Zealand), Cnr Rosedale and Airborne Roads, Albany, Auckland, New Zealand

Typeset in Bembo and Helvetica to an original design by Henry Iles.
Printed in Italy by LegoPrint S.p.A

288pp.

British Library Cataloguing in Publication Data
A catalogue for this book is available from the British Library.

ISBN 13: 978-1-84353-622-2
ISBN 10: 1-84353-622-6

Online information about Rough Guides can be found at our website www.roughguides.com

CONTENTS

Introduction 5

Basic Phrases 5

Scenarios 13

English - Thai 31

Thai - English 182

Thai - English: Signs and Notices 223

Menu Reader
- Food 246
- Drink 260

How the Language Works
- Pronunciation 265
- Tones 267
- The Thai alphabet 269
- Articles / Nouns / Classifiers 271
- Adjectives and adverbs 274
- Pronouns 276
- Possessives 277
- Verbs 278
- Questions, answers, yes and no 280
- Polite particles: krúp, kâ, ká 282
- Dates / Days 283
- Months / Time 284
- Numbers 286
- Conversion Tables 288

Introduction

The Rough Guide Thai dictionary phrasebook is a highly practical introduction to the contemporary language. Laid out in clear A-Z style, it uses key-word referencing to lead you straight to the words and phrases you want – so if you need to book a room, just look up 'room'. The Rough Guide gets straight to the point in every situation, in bars and shops, on trains and buses, and in hotels and banks.

The main part of the Rough Guide is a double dictionary: English-Thai then Thai-English. Before that, there's a section called **Basic Phrases** and to get you involved in two-way communication, the Rough Guide includes, in this new edition, a set of **Scenario** dialogues illustrating questions and responses in key situations such as renting a car and asking directions. You can hear these and then download them free from **www.roughguides.com/phrasebooks** for use on your computer or MP3 player.

Forming the heart of the guide, the **English-Thai** section gives easy-to-use transliterations of the Thai words wherever pronunciation might be a problem. Throughout this section, cross-references enable you to pinpoint key facts and phrases, while asterisked words indicate where further information can be found in a section at the end of the book called **How the Language Works**. This section sets out the fundamental rules of the language, with plenty of practical examples. You'll also find here other essentials like numbers, dates, telling the time and basic phrases. The **Thai-English** section is in two parts: a dictionary, arranged phonetically, of all the words and phrases you're likely to hear (starting with a section of slang and colloquialisms); then a compilation, arranged by subject, of various signs, labels, instructions and other basic words you may come across in print or in public places.

Near the back of the book too the Rough Guide offers an extensive **Menu Reader**. Consisting of food and drink sections (each starting with a list of essential terms), it's indispensable whether you're eating out, stopping for a quick drink, or browsing through a local food market.

เที่ยวให้สนุกนะ
têe-o hâi sa-nòok ná!
have a good trip!

Introduction

The Rough Guide Thai dictionary phrasebook is a highly practical introduction to the contemporary language. Laid out in clear A–Z style, it uses key-word referencing to lead you straight to the words and phrases you want – so if you need to book a room, just look up "room". The Rough Guide gets straight to the point in every situation, in bars and shops, on trains and buses, and in hotels and banks.

The main part of the Rough Guide is a double dictionary: English–Thai then Thai–English. Before that, there's a section called Basic Phrases and to get you involved in two-way communication, the Rough Guide includes, in this new edition, a set of Scenario dialogues illustrating questions and responses in key situations such as renting a car and asking directions. You can hear these and then download them free from www.roughguides.com/phrasebooks for use on your computer or MP3 player.

Forming the heart of the guide, the English–Thai section gives easy-to-use transliterations of the Thai words wherever pronunciation might be a problem. Throughout this section, cross-references enable you to pinpoint key facts and phrases, while asterisked words indicate where further information can be found in a section at the end of the book called **How the Language Works**. This section sets out the fundamental rules of the language, with plenty of practical examples. You'll also find here other essentials like numbers, dates, telling the time and basic phrases. The Thai–English section is in two parts: a dictionary, arranged phonetically, of all the words and phrases you're likely to hear (starting with a section of slang and colloquialisms), then an compilation, arranged by subject, of various signs, labels, instructions and other basic words you may come across in print or in public places.

Near the back of the book too the Rough Guide offers an extensive **Menu Reader**. Consisting of food and drink sections (each starting with a list of essential terms), it's indispensable whether you're eating out, stopping for a quick drink, or browsing through a local food market.

[illegible]

Basic Phrases

yes
krúp (kâ); châi
ครับ(คะ) ใช่

no
mâi
ไม่

OK
oh-kay
โอเค

bye
lah gòrn
ลาก่อน

see you!
jer gun mài ná!
เจอกันใหม่นะ

see you later
děe-o jer gun èek
เดี๋ยวเจอกันอีก

hello
sa-wùt dee
สวัสดี

hi!
bpai năi?
ไปไหน

good morning
sa-wùt dee krúp (kâ)
สวัสดีครับ(ค่ะ)

good evening
sa-wùt dee krúp (kâ)
สวัสดีครับ(ค่ะ)

good night
sa-wùt dee krúp (kâ)
สวัสดีครับ(ค่ะ)

goodbye
lah gòrn ná
ลาก่อนนะ

please
(requesting something)
kŏr ...
ขอ ...

(offering)
chern krúp (kâ)
เชิญครับ(ค่ะ)

(could you) please ...?
chôo-ay ... nòy dâi mái?
ช่วย ... หน่อยได้ไหม

yes please
ao krúp (kâ)
เอาครับ(ค่ะ)

thanks, thank you
kòrp-koon
ขอบคุณ

no thanks, no thank you
mâi ao kòrp-koon
ไม่เอาขอบคุณ

thank you very much
kòrp-koon mâhk
ขอบคุณมาก

don't mention it
mâi bpen rai
ไม่เป็นไร

how do you do?
sa-wùt dee krúp (kâ)
สวัสดีครับ(ค่ะ)

how are you?
bpen yung-ngai bâhng?
เป็นอย่างไรบ้าง

fine, thanks
sa-bai dee krúp (kâ)
สบายดีครับ(ค่ะ)

nice to meet you
yin dee têe dâi róo-jùk gun
ยินดีที่ได้รู้จักกัน

excuse me
(to get past, to say sorry) kŏr-tôht
ขอโทษ
(to get attention) koon krúp (kâ)
คุณครับ (ค่ะ)
(to say pardon?) a-rai ná?
อะไรนะ

I'm sorry
pŏm (chún) sĕe-a jai
ผม(ฉัน)เสียใจ

sorry?/pardon (me)?
(didn't understand) a-rai ná krúp (ká)?
อะไรนะครับ(คะ)

I see/I understand
kâo jai láir-o
เข้าใจแล้ว

I don't understand
pŏm (chún) mâi kâo jai
ผม(ฉัน)ไม่เข้าใจ

do you speak English?
koon pôot pah-săh ung-grìt bpen mái?
คุณพูดภาษาอังกฤษเป็นไหม

I don't speak Thai
pŏm (chún) pôot pah-săh tai mâi bpen
ผม(ฉัน)พูดภาษาไทยไม่เป็น

could you speak more slowly?
pôot cháh cháh nòy!
พูดช้า ๆ หน่อย

could you repeat that?
pôot èek tee dâi mái?
พูดอีกทีได้ไหม

could you write it down?
chôo-ay kěe-un long hâi nòy, dâi mái?
ช่วยเขียนลงให้หน่อยได้ไหม

I'd like a ...
pǒm (chún) ao ...
ผม(ฉัน)เอา ...

I'd like to ...
pǒm (chún) yàhk ...
ผม(ฉัน)อยาก ...

can I have ...?
kǒr ... dâi mái?
ขอ ... ได้ไหม

how much is it?
tâo-rài?
เท่าไร

it is ...
bpen ...
เป็น ...

where is it?
yòo têe nǎi?
อยู่ที่ไหน

is it far?
yòo glai mái?
อยู่ไกลไหม

Scenarios

1. Accommodation

is there an inexpensive hotel you can recommend?
▶ chôo-ay náir-num rohng rairm rah-kah tòok, hâi nòy kâ?

kŏr-tôht krúp, dtem mòt láir-o ◀
I'm sorry, they all seem to be fully booked

can you give me the name of a good middle-range hotel?
▶ kòr chêu rohng rairm têe dee bpahn glahng, dâi mái ká?

wŏr doo gòrn ná krúp, dtôrng gahn púk jai glahng meu-ung châi mái krúp? ◀
let me have a look; do you want to be in the centre?

if possible
▶ tâh bpen bpai dâi

▶ têe púk glai nít-nòy, mâi bpen rai châi mái krúp?
do you mind being a little way out of town?

not too far out
▶ mâi koo-un glai gern bpai kâ

where is it on the map?
▶ yòo dtrong năi bon păirn-têe ká?

can you write the name and address down?
▶ kĕe-an chêu têe yòo hâi nòy dâi mái ká?

I'm looking for a room in a private house
▶ gum-lung hăh hôrng púk hôrng nèung, nai bâhn púk sòo-an dtoo-a kâ

2. Banks

bank account	bun-chee ta-nah-kahn
to change money	lâirk ngern
cheque	chék
to deposit money	fàhk ngern
pin number	mái lâyk ra-hùt
pound	bporn
to withdraw money	tŏrn ngern

can you change this into baht?
▸ rúp lâirk bpen ngern baht mái krúp?

dtôrng-gahn lâirk ngern bàirp năi ká? ◂
how would you like the money?

small notes
▸ bairng yôy

big notes
▸ báirng yài

do you have information in English about opening an account?
▸ mee kôr moon gahn bpèrt bun-chee bpen pah-săh ung-grìt mái krúp?

mee kâ. dtôrng-gahn bpèrt bun-chee bàirp năi ká? ◂
yes, what sort of account do you want?

I'd like a current account
▸ dtôrng-gahn bpèrt bun-chee gra-sàir rai wun krúp

kŏr doo núng-sĕu dern tahng nòy kâ? ◂
your passport, please

can I use this card to draw some cash?
▸ chái bùt née tŏrn ngern dâi mái krúp?

dtôrng bpai têe kairt-chee-a kâ ◂
you have to go to the cashier's desk

I want to transfer this to my account at Bangkok Bank
▸ dtôrng-gahn ohn ngern kâo bun-chee ta-nah-kahn grOOng-tâyp krúp

dâi kâ, dtàir dtôrng kít ngern kâh toh-ra-sùp ná ká ◂
OK, but we'll have to charge you for the phonecall

download these scenarios as MP3s from:

3. Booking a room

shower	hôrng núm fùk boo-a
telephone in the room	toh-ra-sùp nai hôrng púk
payphone in the lobby	toh-ra-sùp săh-tah-ra-ná têe lorp-bêe

do you have any rooms?
▶ mee hôrng púk wâhng mái krúp?

sŭm-rup gèe kon ká? ◀
for how many people?

for one/for two
▶ sŭm-rup kon dee-o/sŭm-rùp sŏrng kon

mee kâ, mee hôrng wâhng ◀
yes, we have rooms free

ja púk gèe keun ka? ◀
for how many nights?

just for one night
▶ keun dee-o krúp

how much is it?
▶ tâo-rài krúp?

hôrng púk mee hôrng núm róy hâh-sìp bàht, hôrng púk mâi mee hôrng núm roy bàht kâ ◀
150 baht with bathroom and 100 baht without bathroom

does that include breakfast?
▶ roo-um ah-hăhn cháo dôo-ay mái krúp?

can I see a room with bathroom?
▶ kŏr doo hôrng púk mee hôrng núm dâi mái krúp?

ok, I'll take it
▶ dtòk-long ao hôrng née krúp

when do I have to check out?
▶ dtôrng chék-áo gèe mohng krúp?

is there anywhere I can leave luggage?
▶ fàhk gra-bpăo têe năi krúp?

Scenarios → Thai

4. Car hire

automatic	gee-a ùt-dta-noh-mút
full tank	dtem tüng
manual	gee-a meu
rented car	rót chăo

I'd like to rent a car
▶ kŏr chăo rót nèung kun krúp

▶ chăo nahn tâo-rài ká?
for how long?

two days
▶ sŏrng wun

I'll take the ...
▶ pŏm ao...

is that with unlimited mileage?
▶ mâi jum-gùt ra-ya tahng châi mái krúp?

châi kâ ◀
it is

kŏr doo bai kùp kèe nòy kâ? ◀
can I see your driving licence, please?

núng-sěu dern tahng dôo-ay kâ ◀
and your passport

is insurance included?
▶ roo-um bpra-gun mái krúp?

roo-um kâ. dtàir dtôrng jài ngern sòo-un râirk pun bàht ayng ◀
yes, but you have to pay the first 1000 baht

wahng ngern mút jum pun bàht. dâi mái ká? ◀
can you leave a deposit of 1000 baht?

and if this office is closed, where do I leave the keys?
▶ tâh órp-fít bpìt láir-o, keun gOOn-jair têe năi krúp?

yòrn mun long nai glòrng nún kâ ◀
you drop them in that box

5. Communications

ADSL modem	moh-dem ay dee áyt airn
at	airt
dial-up modem	moh-dem rêe-uk pàhn mài lâyk toh-ra-sùp
dot	dòrt
Internet	in-dter-nèt
mobile (phone)	toh-ra-sùp meu tĕu
password	ra-hùt pàhn
telephone socket adaptor	dtâo sèe-ap toh-ra-sùp
wireless hotspot	bor-ri-gahn in-dter-nèt rai săi kwahm ray-o soong

is there an Internet café around here?
▸ mee ráhn in-dter-nèt täir-o née mái ká?

can I send email from here?
▸ têe nêe, sòng ee-may-o dâi mái ká?

where's the at sign on the keyboard?
▸ krèu-ung măi àirt yòo dtrong năi bon kee-bòrt ká?

can you switch this to a UK keyboard?
▸ chôo-ay bplèe-un kee-bòrt bpen pah-săh ung-grìt, dâi mái ká?

can you help me log on?
▸ chôo-ay lórk-orn dâi mái ká?

I'm not getting a connection, can you help?
▸ dtòr săi sŭn-yahn mâi dâi, chôo-ay nòy dâi mái ká?

where can I get a top-up card for my mobile?
▸ séu bùt dterm ngern toh-ra sùp meu tĕu dâi têe năi ká?

can you put me through to ...?
▸ chôo-ay dtòr ... hâi nòy kâ?

zero	sŏon	five	hâh
one	nèung	six	hòk
two	sŏrng	seven	jèt
three	săhm	eight	bpàirt
four	sèe	nine	gâo

Scenarios → Thai

6. Directions

where? têe năi?	which direction? tahng năi?

hi, I'm looking for Yaowarat Road
▸ sa-wùt dee krúp, pŏm gum-lung hăh ta-nŏn yao-wa-râht

kŏr-tôht kâ, mâi ker-ee dâi yin mah gòrn ler-ee ◂
sorry, never heard of it

---

hi, can you tell me where Yaowarat Road is?
▸ sa-wùt dee krúp, bòrk nòy dâi mái wâh ta-nŏn yao-wa-râht yòo têe năi krúp?

---

chún gôr mâi châi kon têe nêe kâ ◂
I'm a stranger here too

---

hi, Yaowarat Road, do you know where it is?
▸ sa-wùt dee krúp, sâhp mái wâh, ta-nŏn yao-wa-râht yòo têe năi krúp?

---

lée-o dtrong hòo-a mOOm ◂
around the corner

lée-o sái têe sùn-yahn fai têe sŏrng ◂
left at the second traffic lights

lŭng jàhk nún, ta-nŏn râirk tahng kwăh keu ta-nŏn yao-wa-râht kâ ◂
then it's the first street on the right

dtrong bpai straight ahead	kâhng nâh in front of	por pàhn just after	têe nôhn over there
dtrong kâhm opposite	ler-ee bpai further	tahng kwăh on the right	tùt bpai next
glâi near	lée-o turn off	tahng sái on the left	
kâhng lŭng back	pàhn ... bpai past the ...	ta-nŏn street	

download these scenarios as MP3s from:

7. Emergencies

accident	OO-bùt-dti-hàyt
ambulance	rót pa-yah-bahn
consul	sa-tăhn gong-sŏOn
embassy	sa-tăhn tôot
fire brigade	nòo-ay dùp plerng
police	dtum-roo-ut

help!
▸ chôo-ay dôo-ay!

can you help me?
▸ chôo-ay nòy dâi mái ká?

please come with me! it's really very urgent
▸ mah gùp chún nòy kâ! mee rêu-ung dòo-un mâhk jing jing

I've lost (my keys)
▸ chún tum (gOOn-jair) hăi

(my car) is not working
▸ (rót chún) sēe-a

(my purse) has been stolen
▸ chún dohn ka-moy-ee (gra-bpăo sa-dtahng)

I've been mugged
▸ chún dohn jêe

---

chêu a-rai krúp? ◂
what's your name?

kŏr doo núng-sĕu dern tahng nòy krúp ◂
I need to see your passport

I'm sorry, all my papers have been stolen
▸ kŏr-tôht kâ, àyk-ga-săhn túng-mòt dohn ka-moy-ee kâ

Scenarios → Thai

8. Friends

hi, how're you doing?
▶ sa-wùt dee, sa-bai dee mái?

---

sa-bai dee, lâir-o koon lâ? ◀
OK, and you?

yeah, fine
▶ sa-bai dee

not bad
▶ gôr dee

---

d'you know Pairot?
▶ róo-jùk pai-róht mái?

and this is Suchada
▶ láir nêe sòo-chah-dah

hây, róo-jùk gun lâir-o ◀
yeah, we know each other

where do you know each other from?
▶ róo-jùk gun têe nái?

jer gun têe bâhn sùk-dah ◀
we met at Sukda's place

---

that was some party, eh?
▶ mee bpah-dtêe rèr?

---

yêe-um mâhk ◀
the best

---

are you guys coming for a beer?
▶ bpai gin bee-a mái?

▶ dee, bpai gun tèr
cool, let's go

mâi bpai ná, dèe-o bpai jer a-lí-sà ◀
no, I'm meeting Alisa

---

see you at Sukda's place tonight
▶ keun née jer gun têe bâhn sùk-dah ná

---

lâir-o jer gun ná ◀
see you

9. Health

I'm not feeling very well
▶ chún róo-sèuk mâi sa-bai kâ

can you get a doctor?
▶ chôo-ay dtahm mŏr dâi mái ká?

jèp têe năi krúp? ▶
where does it hurt?

it hurts here
▶ jèp têe nêe ká

jèp dta-lòrt mái krúp? ◀
is the pain constant?

it's not a constant pain
▶ mâi kâ, mâi jèp dta lòrt

can I make an appointment?
▶ kòr nút dâi mái ká?

can you give me something for ...?
▶ hâi yah gâir ... dâi mái ká?

yes, I have insurance
▶ kâ. chún mee bpra-gun sÒOk-ka-pâhp

antibiotics	yah bpa-dti-chee-wa-ná
antiseptic ointment	yah tah kâh chéu-a
cystitis	gra-pór bpùt-sa-wa ùk-sàyp
dentist	mŏr fun
diarrhoea	tórng sèe-a
doctor	mŏr
hospital	rohng pa-yah-bahn
ill	mâi sa-bai
medicine	yah
painkillers	yah gâir bpòo-ut
pharmacy	ráhn kăi yah
to prescribe	sùng yah
thrush	ah-gahn ùk-sàyp chéu-a rah

10. Language difficulties

a few words	sŏrng săhm kum
interpreter	lâhm
to translate	bplair

bùt kray-dìt kOOn, tòok ra-ngúp chái krúp ◀
your credit card has been refused

---

what, I don't understand; do you speak English?
▶ a-rai ná-ká, mâi kâo jai kâ, kOOn pôot pah-săh ung-grìt dâi mái ká?

---

kOOn chái bùt kray-dìt née, mâi dâi láir-o krúp ◀
you can't use this credit card any more

---

could you say that again?
▶ chôo-ay pôot èek krúng dâi mái ká?

slowly
▶ cháh cháh

I understand very little Thai
▶ chún kâo jai pah-săh tai dâi nít-nòy kâ

I speak Thai very badly
▶ pôot pah-săh tai dâi mâi dee ler-ee

---

kOOn jài ngern dôo-ay bùt née, mâi dâi krúp ◀
you can't use this card to pay

---

kâo jai mái krúp? ▶
do you understand?

sorry, no
▶ mâi kâo jai kâ, kòr-tôht kâ

---

is there someone who speaks English?
▶ mee krai pôot pah-săh ung-grìt dâi mái ká?

oh, now I understand
▶ ŏr, kâo jai láir-o kâ

is that ok now?
▶ rêe-up róy rèu yung ká?

download these scenarios as MP3s from:

11. Meeting people

hello
▶ sa-wùt dee krúp

---

sa-wùt dee kâ, chún chêu nin-da kâ ◀
hello, my name's Ninda

Graham, from England, Thirsk
▶ pŏm chêu graham, mah jàhk thirsk, bpra-tâyt ung-grìt

---

mâi róo-jùk kâ, meu-ung nóe yòo têe năi ká? ◀
don't know that, where is it?

---

not far from York, in the North; and you?
▶ mâi glai jàhk york, tang pâhk nĕu-a, láir-o koon lâ?

---

chún mah jàhk chee-ang mài, mah kon dee-o rĕu ká? ◀
I'm from Chiangmai; here by yourself?

---

no, I'm with my wife and two kids
▶ bplào krúp, mah gùp pun-ra-yah láir lôok sŏrng kon

---

what do you do?
▶ tum ngahn a-rai krúp?

---

dâhn korm-pew-dtêr kâ ◀
I'm in computers

---

me too
▶ pŏm gôr mĕu-un gun

here's my wife now
▶ nêe pun-ra-yah pŏm krúp

---

yin dee têe dâi róo-jùk kâ ◀
nice to meet you

12. Post offices

airmail	air may-o
post card	bprai-sa-nee-ya-bùt
post office	bprai-sa-nee
stamp	sa-dtairm

what time does the post office close?
▶ bprai-sa-nee bpìt gèe mohng ká?

---

tóok wun jun tèung wun sòok dtorn hâh mohng yen krúp ◀
five o'clock weekdays

---

is the post office open on Saturdays?
▶ bprai-sa-nee bpèrt wun săo rěu bplào ká?

bpèrt těung têe-ang krúp ◀
until midday

I'd like to send this registered to England
▶ yàhk long ta-bee-an un née láir sòng bpai ung-grìt kâ

---

dâi krúp, túng-mòt hâh-sìp bàht ◀
certainly, that will cost 50 baht

---

and also two stamps for England, please
▶ lair kŏr sa-dtairm sŏrng doo-ung sŭm-rùp bpra-tâyt ung-grìt kâ

do you have some airmail stickers?
▶ mee sa-tík-gêr air may-o mái ká?

do you have any mail for me?
▶ mee jòt-mài sùm-rùp chún mah mái ká?

ต่างประเทศ dtàhng bpra-tâyt international	จดหมาย jòt-măi letters	ภายในประเทศ pai nai bpra-tâyt domestic
บริการไปรษณีย์รอจ่าย bor-ri-gahn bprai-sa-nee ror jài poste restante		พัสดุ put-sa-doo parcels

download these scenarios as MP3s from:

13. Restaurants

bill	bin
menu	may-noo
table	dtó

can we have a non-smoking table?
▶ kŏr dtó têe mâi sòop boo-rèe dâi mái krúp?

there are two of us
▶ sŭm-rùp sŏrng kon krúp

there are four of us
▶ sŭm-rùp sèe kon krúp

what's this?
▶ nêe a-rai krúp?

bplah cha-nít nèung kâ ◀
it's a type of fish

bpen ah-hăhn pi-sàyt pra-jum tórng tìn kâ ◀
it's a local speciality

kâo mah kâhng nai si kâ, ja hâi doo ◀
come inside and I'll show you

we would like two of these, one of these, and one of those
▶ kŏr un née sŏrng têe, un née nèung têe, láir un nóhn nèung têe krúp

dèum a-rai ká? ◀
and to drink?

red wine
▶ wai dairng

white wine
▶ wai kăo

a beer and two orange juices
▶ kŏr bee-a nèung gâir-o láir núm sôm sŏrng gâir-o krúp

some more bread please
▶ kŏr ka-nŏm bpung èek krúp

ah-hăhn a-ròy mái ká? ◀
how was your meal?

excellent!, very nice!
▶ a-ròy mâhk krúp!

ja rúp a-rai èek mái ká? ◀
anything else?

just the bill thanks
▶ chék bin ler-ee, kòrp-kOOn krúp

14. Shopping

hâi chôo-ay mái ká?
can I help you?

can I just have a look around?
kŏr doo gorn krúp

yes, I'm looking for ...
krúp, pŏm gum-lung hăh ...

how much is this?
un née tâo-rài krúp?

nèung pun bàht kâ
one thousand baht

OK, I think I'll have to leave it; it's a little too expensive for me
rĕr krúp. mâi séu ròrk krúp. mun pairng bpai

un née lâ ká?
how about this?

can I pay by credit card?
jài dôo-ay bùt kray-dìt dâi mái?

it's too big
yài gern bpai krúp

it's too small
lék gern bpai krúp

it's for my son – he's about this high
dtoo-a née sŭm-rùp lôok chai pŏm – sŏong bpra-mahn née krúp

rúp a-rai èek mái ká?
will there be anything else?

that's all thanks
króp láir-o, kòrp-kOOn krúp

make it six hundred and I'll take it
hâi rah-kah hòk róy bàht. láir-o ja séu

fine, I'll take it
dee. ao krúp

เปิด bpèrt open	ปิด bpìt closed	โต๊ะจ่ายเงิน dtó jài ngern cash desk
ขายลดราคา kăi lót rah-kah sale	แลกเปลี่ยน lâirk bplèe-un to exchange	

download these scenarios as MP3s from:

15. Sightseeing

art gallery	hŏr sĭn
bus tour	rót too-a num têe-o
city centre	jai glahng meu-ung
closed	bpìt
guide	múk-koo-tâyt
museum	pí-pít-ta-pun
open	bpèrt

I'm interested in seeing the old town
▶ yahk bpai têe-o meu-ung gào

are there guided tours?
▶ mee too-a têe mee múk koo-tâyt mái ká?

kŏr-tôht krúp, dtem mòt láir-o ◀
I'm sorry, it's fully booked

how much would you charge to drive us around for four hours?
▶ kùp rót pah têe-o, sùk sèe chôo-a mohng, ja kít ngern tâo-rài ká?

can we book tickets for the concert here?
▶ jorng dtŏo-a korn-sèrt têe nêe dâi mái ká?

▶ dâi krúp, chêu a-rai krúp?
yes, in what name?

▶ kray-dìt gáht bàirp năi krúp?
which credit card?

where do we get the tickets?
▶ rúp dtŏo-a têe năi ká?

rúp têe bpra-dtoo tahng kâo krúp ◀
just pick them up at the entrance

is it open on Sundays?
▶ wun ah-tít bpèrt mái ká?

how much is it to get in?
▶ kâh kâo tâo-rài ká?

are there reductions for groups of 6?
▶ lót rah-kah săm-rùp glOOm mah dôo-ay gun hòk kon mái ká?

that was really impressive!
▶ nâh bpra-túp jai jing jing!

16. Trains

to change trains	dtor rót fai
platform	chahn chah-lah
return	dtŏo-a bpai glùp
single	dtŏo-a têe-o dee-o
station	sa-tăh-nee rót fai
stop	jòrt
ticket	dtŏo-a

how much is ...?
▸ ... rah-kah tâo-rài ká?

---

a single, second class to ...
▸ dtŏo-a têe-o dee-o, chún sŏrng nèung bai bpai ...

---

two returns, second class to ...
▸ dtŏo-a bpai glùp, chún sŏrng sŏrng bai bpai ...

---

for today
▸ sŭm-rùp wun née

for tomorrow
▸ sŭm-rùp wun prÔOng-née

for next Tuesday
▸ sŭm-rùp wun ung-kahn nâh

---

dtôrng jài kâh bor-ri-gahn pi-sàyt, sŭm-rùp rót fai sa-bprin-dtêr krúp ◂
there's a supplement for the Sprinter Train

dtôrng-gahn jorng têe nûng mái krúp? ◂
do you want to make a seat reservation?

kOOn dtôrng dtòr rót fai têe sa-tăh-nee dorn meu-ung krúp ◂
you have to change at Don Muang Station

---

what time is the last train to Chiangmai?
▸ rót fai bpai chee-ung mài, têe-o sÒOt tái, òrk gèe mohng ká?

is this seat free?
▸ têe nêe wâhng mái ká?

excuse me, which station are we at?
▸ kŏr-tôht kâ, têe nêe sa-tăh-nee a-rai ká?

is this where I change for Chiangmai?
▸ têe nêe, dtòr rót fai bpai chee-ung mài châi mái ká?

English → Thai

A

a, an*

about: about 20 bpra-mahn yêe-sìp
ประมาณยี่สิบ

it's about 5 o'clock **bpra-mahn** hâh mohng yen
ประมาณห้าโมงเย็น

a film about Thailand nǔng rêu-ung meu-ung tai
หนังเรื่องเมืองไทย

above kâhng bon
ข้างบน

abroad dtàhng bpra-tâyt
ต่างประเทศ

absolutely (I agree) nâir-norn
แน่นอน

absorbent cotton sǔm-lee
สำลี

accelerator kun rêng
คันเร่ง

accept rúp
รับ

accident OO-bùt-dti-hàyt
อุบัติเหตุ

there's been an accident mee OO-bùt-dti-hàyt
มีอุบัติเหตุ

accommodation têe púk
ที่พัก

accurate tòok-dtôrng
ถูกต้อง

ache bpòo-ut
ปวด

my back aches bpòo-ut lǔng
ปวดหลัง

across: across the ... kâhm ...
ข้าม ...

adapter (for voltage) krêu-ung bplairng fai fáh
เครื่องแปลงไฟฟ้า

(plug) bplúk
ปลั๊ก

address têe-yòo
ที่อยู่

what's your address? kOOn púk yòo têe-nǎi?
คุณพักอยู่ที่ไหน

address book sa-mòOt têe-yòo
สมุดที่อยู่

admission charge kâh kâo
ค่าเข้า

adult pôo-yài
ผู้ใหญ่

advance: in advance lôo-ung nâh
ล่วงหน้า

aeroplane krêu-ung bin
เครื่องบิน

after lŭng
หลัง
after you chern gòrn
เชิญก่อน
after lunch lŭng ah-hăhn glahng wun
หลังอาหารกลางวัน
afternoon dtorn bài
ตอนบ่าย
in the afternoon dtorn bài
ตอนบ่าย
this afternoon bài née
บ่ายนี้
aftershave yah tah lŭng gohn nòo-ut
ยาทาหลังโกนหนวด
aftersun cream yah tah lŭng àhp dàirt
ยาทาหลังอาบแดด
afterwards tee lŭng
ทีหลัง
again èek
อีก
against: I'm against it pŏm (chún) mâi hĕn dôo-ay
ผม(ฉัน)ไม่เห็นด้วย
age ah-yóo
อายุ
ago: a week ago ah-tít nèung mah láir-o
อาทิตย์หนึ่งมาแล้ว
an hour ago chôo-a mohng nèung mah láir-o
ชั่วโมงหนึ่งมาแล้ว
agree: I agree pŏm (chún) hĕn dôo-ay
ผม(ฉัน)เห็นด้วย
AIDS rôhk áyd
โรคเอดส์
air ah-gàht
อากาศ
by air tahng ah-gàht
ทางอากาศ
air-conditioning krêu-ung air
เครื่องแอร์
airmail: by airmail sòng tahng ah-gàht
ส่งทางอากาศ
airmail envelope sorng jòt-măi ah-gàht
ซองจดหมายอากาศ
airport sa-năhm bin
สนามบิน
to the airport, please bpai sa-năhm bin
ไปสนามบิน
airport bus rót sa-năhm bin
รถสนามบิน
aisle seat têe nûng dtìt tahng dern
ที่นั่งติดทางเดิน
alarm clock nah-li-gah bplòok
นาฬิกาปลุก

alcohol lâo
เหล้า
alcoholic kon kêe lâo mao yah
คนขี้เหล้าเมายา
all: all the boys pôo-chai tóok kon
ผู้ชายทุกคน
all the girls pôo-yĭng tóok kon
ผู้หญิงทุกคน
all of it túng mòt
ทั้งหมด
all of them tóok kon
ทุกคน
that's all, thanks sèt láir-o kòrp-koon
เสร็จแล้วขอบคุณ
allergic: I'm allergic to ... pŏm (chún) páir ...
ผม(ฉัน)แพ้ ...
allowed: is it allowed? un-nóo-yâht mái?
อนุญาตไหม
all right mâi bpen rai
ไม่เป็นไร
I'm all right pŏm (chún) sa-bai dee
ผม(ฉัน)สบายดี
are you all right? bpen yung-ngai bâhng?
เป็นอย่างไรบ้าง
almost gèu-up
เกือบ
alone kon dee-o
คนเดียว
alphabet dtoo-a uk-sŏrn
ตัวอักษร
already ... láir-o
... แล้ว
also dôo-ay
ด้วย
although máir wâh
แม้ว่า
altogether túng mòt
ทั้งหมด
always sa-mĕr
เสมอ
am*: I am ... pŏm (chún) bpen ...
ผม(ฉัน)เป็น ...
a.m.: at six/seven a.m. hòk/jèt mohng cháo
หก/เจ็ดโมงเช้า
amazing (surprising) mâi nâh chêu-a
ไม่น่าเชื่อ
(very good) wi-sàyt
วิเศษ
ambulance rót pa-yah-bahn
รถพยาบาล
call an ambulance! rêe-uk rót pa-yah-bahn!
เรียกรถพยาบาล

America a-may-ri-gah
อเมริกา
American (adj) a-may-ri-gun
อเมริกัน
I'm American pŏm (chún) bpen kon a-may-ri-gun
ผม(ฉัน)เป็นคนอเมริกัน
among nai ra-wàhng
ในระหว่าง
amount jum-noo-un
จำนวน
amp: a 13-amp fuse few sìp săhm airm
ฟิวส์สิบสามแอมป์
and láir
และ
angry gròht
โกรธ
animal sùt
สัตว์
ankle kôr táo
ข้อเท้า
anniversary (wedding) wun cha-lŏrng króp rôrp
วันฉลองครบรอบ
annoy: this man's annoying me kon née tum hâi pŏm (chún) rum-kahn
คนนี้ทำให้ผม(ฉัน)รำคาญ
annoying nâh rum-kahn
น่ารำคาญ
another èek
อีก
can we have another room? kŏr bplèe-un hôrng nòy dâi mái?
ขอเปลี่ยนห้องหน่อยได้ไหม
another beer, please kŏr bee-a èek kòo-ut nèung
ขอเบียร์อีกขวดหนึ่ง
antibiotics yah bpùti-chee-wa-ná
ยาปฏิชีวนะ
antihistamines yah airn-dtêe hít-dta-meen
ยาแอนตีฮิสตะมีน
antique: is it an antique? bpen kŏrng gào taír táir rĕu bplào?
เป็นของเก่าแท้ ๆ หรือเปล่า
antique shop ráhn kăi kŏrng gào
ร้านขายของเก่า
antiseptic yah kâh chéu-a
ยาฆ่าเชื้อ
any: have you got any bread/tomatoes? mee ka-nŏm-bpung/ma-kĕu-a-tâyt mái?
มีขนมปัง/มะเขือเทศไหม
do you have any change? mee sàyt sa-dtahng mái?
มีเศษสตางค์ไหม
sorry, I don't have any kŏr-tôht pŏm (chún) mâi mee
ขอโทษผม(ฉัน)ไม่มี

anybody krai gôr dâi
ใครก็ได้
does anybody speak English? mee **krai** pôot pah-săh ung-grìt dâi?
มีใครพูดภาษาอังกฤษได้
there wasn't anybody there mâi mee **krai** yòo têe nûn
ไม่มีใครอยู่ที่นั่น

anything a-rai gôr dâi
อะไรก็ได้

dialogues

anything else? ao a-rai èek mái?
nothing else, thanks mâi ao krúp (kâ)

would you like anything to drink? dèum a-rai mái?
I don't want anything, thanks mâi krúp (kâ)

apart from nôrk jàhk
นอกจาก
apartment a-páht-mén
อพาร์ตเม้นท์
apartment block dtèuk a-páht-mén
ตึกอพาร์ตเม้นท์
apologize kŏr-tôht
ขอโทษ
appendicitis rôhk sâi dtìng
โรคไส้ติ่ง
apple air-bpêrn
แอปเปิล
appointment nút
นัด

dialogue

good morning, how can I help you? sa-wùt dee krúp mee a-rai ja hâi chôo-ay mái krúp?
I'd like to make an appointment with ... yàhk nút póp gùp ...
what time would you like? yàhk dâi way-lah tâo-rài?
three o'clock bài săhm mohng
I'm afraid that's not possible, is four o'clock all right? kít wâh kong mâi dâi ao bpen way-lah sèe mohng dâi mái?
yes, that will be fine krúp dtòk-long
the name was? chêu a-rai krúp?

apricot ay-pri-kort
เอพริคอท

April may-săh-yon
เมษายน

are*: we are rao bpen
เราเป็น

you are kOOn bpen
คุณเป็น

they are káo bpen
เขาเป็น

area bor-ri-wayn
บริเวณ

area code ra-hùt
รหัส

arm kăirn
แขน

arrange: will you arrange it for us? chôo-ay **jùt gahn** hâi nòy dâi mái?
ช่วยจัดการให้หน่อยได้ไหม

arrival gahn mah tĕung
การมาถึง

arrive mah tĕung
มาถึง

when do we arrive? rao ja **tĕung** mêu-a rài?
เราจะถึงเมื่อไร

has my fax arrived yet? fairks kŏrng pŏm (chún) **mah** rĕu yung?
แฟกซ์ของผม(ฉัน)มาหรือยัง

we arrived today rao **mah tĕung** wun née
เรามาถึงวันนี้

art sĭn-la-bpà
ศิลป

art gallery ráhn kăi pâhp kĕe-un
ร้านขายภาพเขียน

artist sĭn-la-bpin
ศิลปิน

as: as big as yài tâo gùp
ใหญ่เท่ากับ

as soon as possible yàhng ray-o têe sòOt têe ja ray-o dâi
อย่างเร็วที่สุดที่จะเร็วได้

ashtray têe kèe-a bOO-rèe
ที่เขี่ยบุหรี่

Asia ay-see-a
เอเซีย

ask tăhm
ถาม

I didn't ask for this pŏm (chún) mâi dâi **kŏr** ao un née
ผม(ฉัน)ไม่ได้ขอเอาอันนี้

could you ask him to ...? chôo-ay **bòrk hâi** káo ... dâi mái?
ช่วยบอกให้เขา ... ได้ไหม

asleep: she's asleep káo norn lùp yòo
เขานอนหลับอยู่

aspirin airt-pai-rin
แอสไพริน

asthma rôhk hèut
โรคหืด
astonishing nâh bpra-làht jai
น่าประหลาดใจ
at: at the hotel **têe** rohng rairm
ที่โรงแรม
at the station **têe** sa-tăh-nee rót fai
ที่สถานีรถไฟ
at six o'clock **way-lah** hòk mohng
เวลาหกโมง
at Noi's **têe** bâhn koon nói
ที่บ้านคุณน้อย
athletics gree-tah
กรีฑา
attractive sŏo-ay
สวย
aubergine ma-kĕu-a
มะเขือ
August sĭng-hăh-kom
สิงหาคม
aunt (elder sister of mother/father) bpâh
ป้า
(younger sister of father) ah
อา
(younger sister of mother) náh
น้า
Australia órt-sa-tray-lee-a
ออสเตรเลีย
Australian (adj) órt-sa-tray-lee-a
ออสเตรเลีย
I'm Australian pŏm (chún) bpen kon órt-sa-tray-lee-a
ผม(ฉัน)เป็นคนออสเตรเลีย
automatic ùt-dta-noh-mút
อัตโนมัติ
(car) rót ùt-dta-noh-mút
รถอัตโนมัติ
automatic teller bor-ri-gahn ngern dòo-un
บริการเงินด่วน
autumn réu-doo bai-mái rôo-ung
ฤดูใบไม้ร่วง
in the autumn dtorn réu-doo bai-mái rôo-ung
ตอนฤดูใบไม้ร่วง
average tum-ma-dah
ธรรมดา
on average doy-ee cha-lèe-a
โดยเฉลี่ย
awake: is he awake? káo **dtèun** láir-o rĕu yung?
เขาตื่นแล้วหรือยัง
away: go away! bpái!
ไป
is it far away? yòo glai mái?
อยู่ไกลไหม
awful yâir mâhk
แย่มาก

axle plao
เพลา

B

baby dèk òrn
เด็กอ่อน
baby food ah-hăhn dèk
อาหารเด็ก
baby's bottle kòo-ut nom
ขวดนม
baby-sitter kon fâo dèk
คนเฝ้าเด็ก
back (of body) lŭng
หลัง
(back part) kâhng lŭng
ข้างหลัง
at the back kâhng lŭng
ข้างหลัง
can I have my money back? kŏr ngern keun dâi mái?
ขอเงินคืนได้ไหม
to come/go back glùp mah/glùp bpai
กลับมา/กลับไป
backache bpòo-ut lŭng
ปวดหลัง
bacon mŏo bay-korn
หมูเบคอน
bad mâi dee
ไม่ดี
a bad headache bpòo-ut hŏo-a mâhk
ปวดหัวมาก
badly mâi dee
ไม่ดี
bag tŏong
ถุง
(handbag) gra-bpăo tĕu
กระเป๋าถือ
(suitcase) gra-bpăo dern tahng
กระเป๋าเดินทาง
baggage gra-bpăo
กระเป๋า
baggage check têe fâhk gra-bpăo
ที่ฝากกระเป๋า
baggage claim săi pahn lum-lee-ung gra-bpăo
สายพานลำเลียงกระเป๋า
bakery ráhn tum ka-nŏm-bpung
ร้านทำขนมปัง
balcony ra-bee-ung
ระเบียง
a room with a balcony hôrng mee ra-bee-ung
ห้องมีระเบียง
ball lôok born
ลูกบอล
ballpoint pen bpàhk-gah lôok lêun
ปากกาลูกลื่น

bamboo mái pài
ไม้ไผ่
bamboo shoot(s) nòr mái
หน่อไม้
banana glôo-ay
กล้วย
band (musical) wong don-dtree
วงดนตรี
bandage pâh pun plǎir
ผ้าพันแผล
Bandaids® plah-sa-dter
พลาสเตอร์
Bangkok grOOng-tâyp
กรุงเทพฯ
bank (money) ta-nah-kahn
ธนาคาร
bank account bun-chee ngern fàhk ta-nah-kahn
ปัญชีเงินฝากธนาคาร
bar bah
บาร์
barber's châhng dtùt pǒm
ช่างตัดผม
bargaining gahn dtòr rah-kah
การต่อราคา

dialogue

how much is this? nêe tâo-rài?
500 baht hâh ròy bàht
that's too expensive pairng bpai nòy
how about 400? sèe róy dâi mái?
I'll let you have it for 450 kít sèe róy hâh sìp gôr láir-o gun
can't you reduce it a bit more?/OK, it's a deal lót èek mâi dâi lěu?/oh kay, dtòk long

basket dta-grâh
ตะกร้า
bath àhng àhp náhm
อ่างอาบน้ำ
can I have a bath? kǒr àhp náhm dâi mái?
ขออาบน้ำได้ไหม
bathroom hôrng náhm
ห้องน้ำ
with a private bathroom hôrng norn têe mee hôrng náhm dôo-ay
ห้องนอนที่มีห้องน้ำด้วย
bath towel pâh chét dtoo-a
ผ้าเช็ดตัว
bathtub àhng àhp náhm
อ่างอาบน้ำ
battery bair-dta-rêe
แบตเตอรี
bay ào
อ่าว

be* bpen
เป็น
beach chai hàht
ชายหาด
on the beach tee chai haht
ที่ชายหาด
beach mat sèu-a bpoo chai-hàht
เสื่อปูชายหาด
beach umbrella rôm gun dàirt
ร่มกันแดด
beans tòo-a
ถั่ว
beansprouts tòo-a ngôrk
ถั่วงอก
beard krao
เครา
beautiful sŏo-ay
สวย
because prór
เพราะ
because of ... neû-ung jàhk ...
เนื่องจาก ...
bed dtee-ung
เตียง
I'm going to bed now pŏm (chún) bpai norn
ผม(ฉัน)ไปนอน
bedroom hôrng norn
ห้องนอน

beef néu-a woo-a
เนื้อวัว
beer bee-a
เบียร์
two beers, please kŏr bee-a sŏrng kòo-ut
ขอเบียร์สองขวด
before gòrn
ก่อน
begin rêrm
เริ่ม
when does it begin? rêrm mêu-a rài?
เริ่มเมื่อไร
beginner pôo rêrm ree-un
ผู้เริ่มเรียน
beginning: at the beginning dtorn dtôn
ตอนต้น
behind kâhng lŭng
ข้างหลัง
behind me kâhng lŭng pŏm (chún)
ข้างหลังผม(ฉัน)
Belgian (adj) bayl-yee-um
เบลเยียม
Belgium bpra-tâyt bayl-yee-um
ประเทศเบลเยียม
below dtâi
ใต้
belt kĕm kùt
เข็มขัด

bend (in road) tahng kóhng
ทางโค้ง
berth (on ship) têe-norn
ที่นอน
beside: beside the ... kâhng kâhng ...
ข้างๆ ...
best dee têe sòot
ดีที่สุด
better dee gwàh
ดีกว่า
are you feeling better? kôy yung chôo-a mái?
ค่อยยังชั่วไหม
between ra-wàhng
ระหว่าง
beyond ler-ee bpai
เลยไป
bicycle jùk-gra-yahn
จักรยาน
big yài
ใหญ่
too big yài gern bpai
ใหญ่เกินไป
it's not big enough yài mâi por
ใหญ่ไม่พอ
bike jùk-gra-yahn
จักรยาน
(motorbike) jùk-gra-yahn-yon
จักรยานยนตร์
bikini bi-gi-nee
บิกินี
bill bin
บิล
(US) bai báirng
ใบแบ๊งค์
could I have the bill, please? chék bin
เช็คบิล
bin tǔng ka-yà
ถังขยะ
bin liners tǒong ka-yà
ถุงขยะ
bird nók
นก
birthday wun gèrt
วันเกิด
happy birthday! oo-ay-porn wun gèrt!
อวยพรวันเกิด
biscuit kóok-gêe
คุกกี้
bit: a little bit nít-nòy
นิดหน่อย
a big bit chín yài
ชิ้นใหญ่
a bit of ... ... chín nèung
... ชิ้นหนึ่ง
a bit expensive pairng bpai nòy
แพงไปหน่อย
bite (by insect, dog) gùt
กัด
bitter (taste etc) kǒm
ขม

black sěe dum
สีดำ
blanket pâh hòm
ผ้าห่ม
bleach (for toilet) yah láhng hôrng náhm
ยาล้างห้องน้ำ
blind dtah bòrt
ตาบอด
blinds môo-lêe
มู่ลี่
blister plăir porng
แผลพอง
blocked (road, pipe, sink) dtun
ตัน
blond (adj) pŏm sěe torng
ผมสีทอง
blood lêu-ut
เลือด
high blood pressure kwahm dun loh-hìt sŏong
ความดันโลหิตสูง
blouse sêu-a pôo-yĭng
เสื้อผู้หญิง
blow-dry bpào pŏm
เป่าผม
I'd like a cut and blow-dry yàhk hâi dtùt láir bpào pŏm
อยากให้ตัดและเป่าผม
blue sěe núm ngern
สีน้ำเงิน
boarding pass bùt têe-nûng
บัตรที่นั่ง
boat reu-a
เรือ
body râhng-gai
ร่างกาย
boiled egg kài dtôm
ไข่ต้ม
boiled rice kâo sŏo-ay
ข้าวสวย
boiler môr náhm
หม้อน้ำ
bone gra-dòok
กระดูก
bonnet (of car) gra-bprohng rót
กระโปรงรถ
book (noun) núng-sěu
หนังสือ
(verb) jorng
จอง
can I book a seat? kŏr jorng têe-nûng dâi mái?
ขอจองที่นั่งได้ไหม

dialogue

I'd like to book a table for two yàhk jorng dtó sŭm-rùp sŏrng kon
what time would you like it booked for? ja jorng way-lah tâo-rài?

half past seven tôom krêung
that's fine dâi krúp
and your name? chêu a-rai krúp?

bookshop, bookstore ráhn kăi núng-sĕu
ร้านขายหนังสือ
boot (footwear) rorng-táo
รองเท้า
(of car) gra-bprohng tái rót
กระโปรงท้ายรถ
border (of country) chai dairn
ชายแดน
bored: I'm bored pŏm (chún) bèu-a
ผม(ฉัน)เบื่อ
boring nâh bèu-a
น่าเบื่อ
born: I was born in Manchester pŏm (chún) **gèrt** têe Manchester
ผม(ฉัน)เกิดที่ Manchester
I was born in 1960 pŏm (chún) **gèrt** bpee nèung pun gâo róy hòk sìp
ผม(ฉัน)เกิดปีหนึ่งพันเก้าร้อยหกสิบ
borrow yeum
ยืม
may I borrow ...? kŏr yeum ... dâi mái?
ขอยืม ... ได้ไหม
both túng sŏrng
ทั้งสอง
bother: sorry to bother you kŏr-tôht têe róp-goo-un
ขอโทษที่รบกวน
bottle kòo-ut
ขวด
bottle-opener têe bpèrt kòo-ut
ที่เปิดขวด
bottom (of person) gôn
ก้น
at the bottom of the hill cherng kăo
เชิงเขา
at the bottom of the street bplai ta-nŏn
ปลายถนน
bowl chahm
ชาม
box hèep
หีบ
box office hôrng kăi dtŏo-a
ห้องขายตั๋ว
boy pôo-chai
ผู้ชาย
boyfriend fairn
แฟน
bra sêu-a yók song
เสื้อยกทรง

bracelet gum-lai meu
กำไลมือ
brake bràyk
เบรค
brandy lâo brùn-dee
เหล้าบรั่นดี
bread ka-nŏm-bpung
ขนมปัง
break (verb) dtàirk
แตก
I've broken the ... pŏm (chún) tum ... dtàirk
ผม(ฉัน)ทำ ... แตก
I think I've broken my wrist pŏm (chún) kít wâh kôr meu **hùk**
ผม(ฉัน)คิดว่าข้อมือหัก
break down sěe-a
เสีย
I've broken down (car) rót pŏm (chún) sěe-a
รถผม(ฉัน)เสีย
breakdown service bor-ri-gahn sôrm
บริการซ่อม
breakfast ah-hăhn cháo
อาหารเช้า
break-in: I've had a break-in mee ka-moy-ee kâo bâhn
มีขโมยเข้าบ้าน
breast nom
นม
breathe hăi jai
หายใจ
breeze lom òrn òrn
ลมอ่อนๆ
bridge (over river) sa-pahn
สะพาน
brief sûn
สั้น
briefcase gra-bpăo
กระเป๋า
bright (light etc) sa-wàhng
สว่าง
bright red dairng jùt
แดงจัด
brilliant (idea) yêe-um
เยี่ยม
bring ao ... mah
เอา ... มา
I'll bring it back later ja keun hâi tee lŭng
จะคืนให้ทีหลัง
Britain bpra-tâyt ung-grìt
ประเทศอังกฤษ
British ung-grìt
อังกฤษ
brochure rai la-èe-ut
รายละเอียด
broken dtàirk láir-o
แตกแล้ว
bronchitis lòrt lom ùk-sàyp
หลอดลมอักเสบ

brooch kĕm glùt sêu-a
เข็มกลัดเสื้อ
broom mái gwàht
ไม้กวาด
brother (older) pêe chai
พี่ชาย
(younger) nórng chai
น้องชาย
brother-in-law (older) pêe kĕr-ee
พี่เขย
(younger) nórng kĕr-ee
น้องเขย
brown sĕe núm dtahn
สีน้ำตาล
bruise fók-chúm
ฟกช้ำ
brush (for hair) bprairng pŏm
แปรงผม
(artist's) bprairng
แปรง
(for cleaning) mái gwàht
ไม้กวาด
bucket tŭng
ถัง
Buddha prá-pÓOt-ta-jâo
พระพุทธเจ้า
Buddhism sàh-sa-năh pÓOt
ศาสนาพุทธ
Buddhist (noun) chao pÓOt
ชาวพุทธ
buffet car rót sa-bee-ung
รถเสบียง
buggy (for child) rót kĕn dèk
รถเข็นเด็ก
building ah-kahn
อาคาร
bulb (light bulb) lòrt fai fáh
หลอดไฟฟ้า
bumper gun chon
กันชน
bungalow bung-gah-loh
บังกาโล
bureau de change bor-ri-gahn lâirk ngern
บริการแลกเงิน
burglary ka-moy-ee kâo bâhn
ขโมยเข้าบ้าน
Burma bpra-tâyt pa-mâh
ประเทศพม่า
Burmese pa-mâh
พม่า
burn (noun) plăir mâi
แผลไหม้
burnt: this is burnt un née mâi
อันนี้ไหม้
burst: a burst pipe tôr dtàirk
ท่อแตก
bus rót may
รถเมล์
what number bus is it to ...?
rót bpai ... ber tâo-rài?
รถไป ... เบอร์เท่าไร
when is the next bus to ...?
rót têe-o nâh bpai ... òrk gèe

mohng?
รถเที่ยวหน้าไป ... ออกกี่โมง
what time is the last bus? rót têe-o sòOt tái òrk gèe mohng?
รถเที่ยวสุดท้ายออกกี่โมง

dialogue

does this bus go to ...? rót kun née bpai ... mái?
no, you need a number ... mâi bpai kOOn dtôrng kêun mǎi-lâyk ...

business tÓO-rá
ธุระ
bus station sa-tǎh-nee rót may
สถานีรถเมล์
bus stop bpâi rót may
ป้ายรถเมล์
bust nâh òk
หน้าอก
busy (restaurant etc) nâirn
แน่น
I'm busy tomorrow prôOng née mee tÓO-rá
พรุ่งนี้มีธุระ
but dtàir
แต่
butcher's ráhn néu-a
ร้านเหนือ
butter ner-ee sòt
เนยสด
button gra-doOm
กระดุม
buy séu
ซื้อ
where can I buy ...? pǒm (chún) **séu** ... dâi têe nǎi?
ผม(ฉัน)ซื้อ ... ได้ที่ไหน
by: by bus/car doy-ee rót may/rót yon
โดยรถเมล์/รถยนต์
written by ... kěe-un **doy-ee** ...
เขียนโดย ...
by the window glâi nâh-dtàhng
ใกล้หน้าต่าง
by the sea chai ta-lay
ชายทะเล
by Monday gòrn wun jun
ก่อนวันจันทร์
bye lah gòrn
ลาก่อน

C

cabbage ga-lùm-bplee
กะหล่ำปลี

cake ka-nŏm káyk
ขนมเค้ก
call (verb) rêe-uk
เรียก
(to phone) toh-ra-sùp, toh
โทรศัพท์, โทร
what's it called? rêe-uk wâh a-rai?
เรียกว่าอะไร
he/she is called ... káo chêu ...
เขาชื่อ ...
please call the doctor chôo-ay rêe-uk mŏr hâi nòy
ช่วยเรียกหมอให้หน่อย
please give me a call at 7.30 a.m. chôo-ay **toh mah** way-lah jèt mohng krêung
ช่วยโทรมาเวลาเจ็ดโมงครึ่ง
please ask him to call me chôo-ay hâi káo **toh mah**
ช่วยให้เขาโทรมา
call back: I'll call back later dĕe-o ja **toh mah mài**
เดี๋ยวจะโทรมาใหม่
call round: I'll call round tomorrow prÔOng née ja **wáir** mah hăh
พรุ่งนี้จะแวะมาหา
Cambodia bpra-tâyt gum-poo-chah
ประเทศกัมพูชา
Cambodian (adj) ka-măyn
เขมร
camcorder glôrng bun-téuk pâhp
กล้องบันทึกภาพ
camera glôrng tài rôop
กล้องถ่ายรูป
camera shop ráhn kăi glôrng tài rôop
ร้านขายกล้องถ่ายรูป
can gra-bpŏrng
กระป๋อง
a can of beer bee-a gra-bpŏrng
เบียร์กระป๋อง
can*: can you ...? kOOn ... dâi mái?
คุณ ... ได้ไหม
can I have ...? kŏr ... dâi mái?
ขอ ... ได้ไหม
I can't ... pŏm (chún) ... mâi dâi
ผม(ฉัน) ... ไม่ได้
Canada bpra-tâyt kairn-nah-dah
ประเทศแคนาดา
Canadian (adj) kair-nah-dah
แคนาดา
I'm Canadian pŏm (chún)

bpen kon kair-nah-dah
ผม(ฉัน)เป็นคนแคนาดา
canal klorng
คลอง
cancel ngót
งด
candies tórp-fêe
ท๊อฟฟี่
candle tee-un
เทียน
can-opener têe bpèrt gra-bpŏrng
ที่เปิดกระป๋อง
cap (hat) mòo-uk
หมวก
car rót yon
รถยนต์
by car doy-ee rót yon
โดยรถยนต์
carburettor kah-ber-ret-dtêr
คาร์บูเรเตอร์
card (business) nahm bùt
นามบัตร
here's my card nêe nahm bùt pŏm (chún)
นี่นามบัตรผม(ฉัน)
cardigan sêu-a năo
เสื้อหนาว
careful ra-mút ra-wung
ระมัดระวัง
be careful! ra-wung ná!
ระวังนะ
caretaker kon fâo bâhn
คนเฝ้าบ้าน
car ferry pair chái bun-tóok rót-yon kâhm fâhk
แพใช้บรรทุกรถยนต์ข้ามฟาก
car hire bor-ri-gahn rót châo
บริการรถเช่า
carnival ngahn
งาน
car park têe jòrt rót
ที่จอดรถ
carpet prom
พรม
car rental bor-ri-gahn rót châo
บริการรถเช่า
carriage (of train) dtôo rót fai
ตู้รถไฟ
carrier bag tŏong hêw
ถุงหิ้ว
carrot hŏo-a pùk-gàht dairng
หัวผักกาดแดง
carry (something in the hands) tĕu
ถือ
(something by a handle) hêw
หิ้ว
(a heavy load on the back or shoulder) bàirk
แบก
(a child, in one's arms) ôom
อุ้ม

carry-cot dta-grâh sài dèk
ตะกร้าใส่เด็ก
carton glòrng
กล่อง
carwash bor-ri-gahn láhng rót
บริการล้างรถ
case (suitcase) gra-bpăo dern tahng
กระเป๋าเดินทาง
cash (noun) ngern sòt
เงินสด
(verb) kêun ngern
ขึ้นเงิน
will you cash this for me?
chôo ay bpai **kêun ngern** hâi nòy dâi mái?
ช่วยไปขึ้นเงินให้หน่อยได้ไหม
cash desk dtó jài ngern
โต๊ะจ่ายเงิน
cash dispenser bor-ri-gahn ngern dòo-un
บริการเงินด่วน
cassette móo-un tâyp kah-set
ม้วนเทปคาสเซ็ท
cassette recorder krêu-ung lên tâyp kah-set
เครื่องเล่นเทปคาสเซ็ท
castle bprah-sàht
ปราสาท
casualty department pa-nàirk oo-bùt-dti-hàyt chòok chĕrn
แผนกอุบัติเหตุฉุกเฉิน
cat mair-o
แมว
catch (verb) jùp
จับ
where do we catch the bus to ...? rao kêun rót may bpai ... têe năi?
เราขึ้นรถเมล์ไป ... ที่ไหน
Catholic (adj) káirt-oh-lík
แคโทลิค
cauliflower dòrk ga-lùm-bplee
ดอกกะหล่ำปลี
cave tûm
ถ้ำ
ceiling pay-dahn
เพดาน
cemetery bpàh cháh
ป่าช้า
centigrade* sen-dti-gràyd
เซ็นติเกรด
centimetre* sen-dti-mét
เซ็นติเมตร
central glahng
กลาง
centre sŏon glahng
ศูนย์กลาง
how do we get to the city centre? bpai sŏon glahng meu-ung yung-ngai?
ไปศูนย์กลางเมืองอย่างไร
certainly nâir-norn
แน่นอน

certainly not! mâi ròrk!
ไม่หรอก

chair gâo êe
เก้าอี้

champagne chairm-bpayn
แชมเปญ

change (noun: money) sàyt sa-dtahng
เศษสตางค์

change (verb: money)
bplèe-un
เปลี่ยน

can I change this for ...? kŏr **lâirk** âi nêe bpen ... dâi mái?
ขอแลกไอ้นี่เป็น ... ได้ไหม

I don't have any change pŏm (chún) mâi mee **báirnk yôy yôy**
ผม(ฉัน)ไม่มีแบงค์ย่อยๆ

can you give me change for a 100 baht note? kŏr dtàirk bai la róy nòy, dâi mái?
ขอแตกใบละร้อยหน่อยได้ไหม

dialogue

do we have to change (trains)? dtôrng **bplèe-un** rót fai rĕu bplào?
yes, change at Bang Krathum/no it's a direct train dtôrng, dtôrng **bplèe-un** têe bahng gra-tOOm/mâi dtôrng, bpen rót dtrong

changed: to get changed bplèe-un sêu-a
เปลี่ยนเสื้อ

charge (noun) kâh
ค่า
(verb) kít kâh
คิดค่า

cheap tòok
ถูก

do you have anything cheaper? mee a-rai tòok gwàh rĕu bplào?
มีอะไรถูกกว่าหรือเปล่า

check (verb) chék doo
เช็คดู

could you check the ..., please? chôo-ay chék doo ... nòy, dâi mái?
ช่วยเช็คดู ... หน่อยได้ไหม

check (US: noun) chék
เช็ค
(US: bill) bin
บิล
see **cheque** and **bill**

check book sa-mòOt chék
สมุดเช็ค

check-in dtròo-ut chûng

núm-nùk
ตรวจชั่งน้ำหนัก
check in: where do we have to check in? rao dtôrng 'check in' têe năi?
เราต้อง 'check in' ที่ไหน
cheek (on face) gâirm
แก้ม
cheerio! wùt dee hâ!
วัสดีฮ่ะ
cheese ner-ee kăirng
เนยแข็ง
chemist's ráhn kăi yah
ร้านขายยา
cheque chék
เช็ค
do you take cheques? jai bpen chék, dâi mái?
จ่ายเป็นเช็คได้ไหม
cheque book sa-mòot chék
สมุดเช็ค
cheque card bùt chék
บัตรเช็ค
cherry cher-rêe
เชอร์รี่
chess màhk róok
หมากรุก
chest nâh òk
หน้าอก
chewing gum màhk fa-rùng
หมากฝรั่ง
Chiangmai chee-ung mài
เชียงใหม่
chicken gài
ไก่
chickenpox ee-sòok ee-săi
อีสุกอีใส
child dèk
เด็ก
child minder kon lée-ung doo dèk
คนเลี้ยงดูเด็ก
children's pool sà wâi náhm dèk
สระว่ายน้ำเด็ก
chilli prík
พริก
chin kahng
คาง
Chinese (adj) jeen
จีน
chips mun fa-rùng tôrt
มันฝรั่งทอด
chocolate chork-goh-lairt
ช็อกโกเลต
choose lêu-uk
เลือก
chopsticks dta-gèe-up
ตะเกียบ
Christian name chêu
ชื่อ

Christmas krít-sa-maht
คริสต์มาส
church bòht
โบสถ์
cigar si-gah
ซิการ์
cigarette boo-rèe
บุหรี่
cigarette lighter fai cháirk
ไฟแช็ค
cinema rohng nŭng
โรงหนัง
circle wong glom
วงกลม
city meu-ung
เมือง
city centre jai glahng meu-ung
ใจกลางเมือง
clean (adj) sa-àht
สะอาด
can you clean these for me?
tum kwahm sa-àht nêe hâi nòy dâi mái?
ทำความสะอาดนี่ให้หน่อยได้ไหม
cleaning solution (for contact lenses) núm yah tum kwahm sa-àht
น้ำยาทำความสะอาด
cleansing lotion núm yah tum kwahm sa-àht
น้ำยาทำความสะอาด
clear chút
ชัด
(obvious) hĕn dâi chút
เห็นได้ชัด
clever cha-làht
ฉลาด
cliff nâh păh
หน้าผา
clinic klee-ník
คลีนิค
cloakroom têe fàhk kŏrng
ที่ฝากของ
clock nah-li-gah
นาฬิกา
close (verb) bpìt
ปิด

dialogue

what time do you close?
kOOn bpìt gèe mohng?
we close at 8 p.m. on weekdays and 6 p.m. on Saturdays rao bpìt way-lah sŏrng tÔOm ra-wàhng wun jun wun sÒOk láir hòk mohng wun săo
do you close for lunch?
bpìt way-lah ah-hăhn glahng wun rĕu bplào?
yes, between 1 and 3.30 p.m. krúp ra-wàhng way-

lah bài mohng tĕung săhm mohng krêung

closed bpìt
ปิด

cloth (fabric) pâh
ผ้า

(for cleaning etc) pâh kêe réw
ผ้าขี้ริ้ว

clothes sêu-a pâh
เสื้อผ้า

clothes line rao dtàhk pâh
ราวตากผ้า

clothes peg mái nèep pâh
ไม้หนีบผ้า

cloud mâyk
เมฆ

cloudy mâyk kréum
เมฆครึ้ม

clutch klút
คลัทช์

coach (bus) rót too-a
รถทัวร์

(on train) dtôo rót fai
ตู้รถไฟ

coach station sa-tăhn-nee rót may
สถานีรถเมล์

coach trip rót num têe-o
รถนำเที่ยว

coast chai ta-lay
ชายทะเล

on the coast chai ta-lay
ชายทะเล

coat (long coat) sêu-a kloom
เสื้อคลุม

(jacket) sêu-a nôrk
เสื้อนอก

coathanger mái kwăirn sêu-a
ไม้แขวนเสื้อ

cockroach ma-lairng sàhp
แมลงสาบ

cocoa goh-gôh
โกโก้

coconut ma-práo
มะพร้าว

coconut milk núm ma-práo
น้ำมะพร้าว

code (for phoning) ra-hùt
รหัส

what's the (dialling) code for Chiangmai? ra-hùt chee-ung mài ber a-rai?
รหัสเชียงใหม่เบอร์อะไร

coffee gah-fair
กาแฟ

two coffees, please kŏr gah-fair sŏrng tôo-ay
ขอกาแฟสองถ้วย

coffee shop kòrp-fêe chórp
คอฟฟี่ช๊อบ

coin ngern rĕe-un
เงินเหรียญ

Coke® koh-lâh
โคล่า
cold (adj) nǎo
หนาว
I'm cold pŏm (chún) nǎo
ผม(ฉัน)หนาว
I have a cold pŏm (chún) bpen wùt
ผม(ฉัน)เป็นหวัด
collapse: he's collapsed káo mòt sa-dtì
เขาหมดสติ
collar kor bpòk sêu-a
คอปกเสื้อ
collect gèp
เก็บ
I've come to collect ... pŏm (chún) mah gèp ...
ผม(ฉัน)มาเก็บ ...
collect call toh-ra-sùp gèp ngern bplai tahng
โทรศัพท์เก็บเงินปลายทาง
college wít-ta-yah-lai
วิทยาลัย
colour sěe
สี
do you have this in other colours? mee sěe èun mái?
มีสีอื่นไหม
colour film feem sěe
ฟิล์มสี
comb (noun) wěe
หวี
come mah
มา

dialogue

where do you come from?
koon mah jàhk nǎi krúp (ká)?
I come from Edinburgh
pŏm (chún) mah jàhk Edinburgh

come back glùp mah
กลับมา
I'll come back tomorrow prôong née glùp mah mài
พรุ่งนี้กลับมาใหม่
come in chern kâo mah
เชิญเข้ามา
comfortable sa-dòo-uk
สะดวก
compact disc pàirn see dee
แผ่นซีดี
company (business) bor-ri-sùt
บริษัท
compartment (on train) hôrng pôo doy-ee săhn
ห้องผู้โดยสาร
compass kěm-tít
เข็มทิศ

complain bòn
บ่น
complaint rêu-ung rórng ree-un
เรื่องร้องเรียน
I have a complaint pŏm (chún) mee rêu-ung rórng ree-un
ผม(ฉัน)มีเรื่องร้องเรียน
completely túng mòt
ทั้งหมด
computer korm-pew-dter
คอมพิวเตอร์
concert gahn sa-dairng don-dtree
การแสดงดนตรี
concussion sa-mŏrng tòok gra-tóp gra-teu-un
สมองถูกกระทบกระเทือน
conditioner (for hair) kreem nôo-ut pŏm
ครีมนวดผม
condom tŏong yahng
ถุงยาง
conference gahn bpra-choom
การประชุม
confirm rúp-rorng
รับรอง
congratulations! kŏr sa-dairng kwahm yin dee!
ขอแสดงความยินดี
connecting flight têe-o bin dtòr
เที่ยวบินต่อ
connection dtòr
ต่อ
conscious mee sa-dtì
มีสติ
constipation tórng pòok
ท้องผูก
consulate sa-tăhn gong-sŏon
สถานกงสุล
contact (verb) dtìt dtòr
ติดต่อ
contact lenses korn-táirk layn
คอนแทคเล็นซ์
contraceptive krêu-ung koom gum-nèrt
เครื่องคุมกำเนิด
convenient sa-dòo-uk
สะดวก
that's not convenient nûn mâi kôy sa-dòo-uk
นั่นไม่ค่อยสะดวก
cook (verb) tum ah-hăhn
ทำอาหาร
not cooked dìp dìp
ดิบๆ
cooker dtao
เตา
cookie kóok-gêe
คุกกี้
cooking utensils krêu-ung

chái nai kroo-a
เครื่องใช้ในครัว

cool yen
เย็น

cork jòok kòo-ut
จุกขวด

corkscrew têe bpèrt kòo-ut
ที่เปิดขวด

corner: on the corner têe moom
ที่มุม

in the corner yòo dtrong hŏo-a mum
อยู่ตรงหัวมุม

correct (right) tòok
ถูก

corridor tahng dern
ทางเดิน

cosmetics krêu-ung sŭm-ahng
เครื่องสำอาง

cost (noun) rah-kah
ราคา

how much does it cost? rah-kah tâo-rài?
ราคาเท่าไร

cot bplay
เปล

cotton fâi
ฝ้าย

cotton wool sŭm-lee
สำลี

couch (sofa) têe nûng rúp kàirk
ที่นั่งรับแขก

cough ai
ไอ

cough medicine yah gâir ai
ยาแก้ไอ

could: could you ...? kOOn ... dâi mái?
คุณ ... ได้ไหม

could I have ...? kŏr ... dâi mái?
ขอ ... ได้ไหม

I couldn't ... pŏm (chún) ... mâi dâi
ผม(ฉัน) ... ไม่ได้

country (nation) bpra-tâyt
ประเทศ

countryside chon-na-bòt
ชนบท

couple (two people) kôo
คู่

a couple of ... sŏrng săhm ...
สองสาม ...

courier múk-kOO-tâyt
มัคคุเทศก์

course (main course etc) chóOt ah-hăhn
ชุดอาหาร

of course nâir-norn
แน่นอน

of course not mâi ròrk
ไม่หรอก

cousin lôok pêe lôok nórng
ลูกพี่ลูกน้อง

cow woo-a
วัว

crab bpoo
ปู

crash (noun) rót chon
รถชน

I've had a crash pŏm (chún) gèrt rót chon
ผม(ฉัน)เกิดรถชน

crazy bâh
บ้า

cream kreem
ครีม

credit card bùt kray-dìt
บัตรเครดิต

can I pay by credit card? jài doy-ee bùt kray-dìt dâi mái?
จ่ายโดยบัตรเครดิตได้ไหม

dialogue

can I pay by credit card? jài doy-ee bùt kray-dìt dâi mái?
which card do you want to use? ja chái bùt a-rai krúp?
Access/Visa
yes, sir dâi krúp
what's the number? ber a-rai krúp?
and the expiry date? láir-o bùt mòt ah-yóo mêu-rai?

crisps mun fa-rùng tôrt
มันฝรั่งทอด

crockery tôo-ay chahm
ถ้วยชาม

crossing (by sea) kâhm ta-lay
ข้ามทะเล

crossroads sèe yâirk
สี่แยก

crowd fŏong kon
ฝูงคน

crowded kon nâirn
คนแน่น

crown (on tooth) lèe-um fun
เหลี่ยมฟัน

cruise lôrng reu-a
ล่องเรือ

crutches mái yun rúk ráir
ไม้ยันรักแร้

cry (verb) rórng hâi
ร้องไห้

cucumber dtairng gwah
แตงกวา

cup tôo-ay
ถ้วย

a cup of ..., please kŏr ... tôo-ay nèung
ขอ ... ถ้วยหนึ่ง

cupboard dtôo
ตู้
cure (verb) gâir
แก้
curly pŏm yìk
ผมหยิก
current (electrical) gra-săir fai fáh
กระแสไฟฟ้า
(in water) gra-săir náhm
กระแสน้ำ
curtains mâhn
ม่าน
cushion mŏrn
หมอน
custom bpra-pay-nee
ประเพณี
Customs sŏon-la-gah-gorn
ศุลกากร
cut (noun) dtùt
ตัด
(verb) roy bàht
รอยบาด
I've cut myself pŏm (chún) mee roy bàht
ผม(ฉัน)มีรอยบาด
cutlery chórn sôrm
ช้อนส้อม
cycling gahn tèep jùk-ra-yahn
การถีบจักรยาน
cyclist kon tèep jùk-ra-yahn
คนถีบจักรยาน

D

dad pôr
พ่อ
daily bpra-jum wun
ประจำวัน
damage (verb) kwahm sĕe-a hăi
ความเสียหาย
damaged sĕe-a láir-o
เสียแล้ว
I'm sorry, I've damaged this kŏr-tôht pŏm (chún) tum hâi sĕe-a
ขอโทษผม(ฉัน)ทำให้เสีย
damn! chìp-hăi!
ฉิบหาย
damp (adj) chéun
ชื้น
dance (noun) ra-bum
ระบำ
(verb) dtên rum
เต้นรำ
would you like to dance? yàhk dtên rum mái?
อยากเต้นรำไหม
dangerous un-dta-rai
อันตราย

Danish den-mahk
เดนมาร์ก

dark (adj: colour) gàir
แก่
(hair) dum
ดำ
it's getting dark mêut láir-o
มืดแล้ว

date*: what's the date today?
wun née wun têe tâo-rài?
วันนี้วันที่เท่าไร
let's make a date for next Monday nút póp gun wun jun nâh
นัดพบกันวันจันทร์หน้า

dates (fruit) in-ta-pa-lǔm
อินทผลัม

daughter lôok sǎo
ลูกสาว

daughter-in-law lôok sa-pái
ลูกสะใภ้

dawn (noun) rôong
รุ่ง
at dawn rôong cháo
รุ่งเช้า

day wun
วัน
the day after tomorrow wun ma-reun née
วันมะรืนนี้
the day before wun gòrn
วันก่อน
the day before yesterday mêu-a wun seun née
เมื่อวานวันซืนนี้
every day tóok wun
ทุกวัน
all day túng wun
ทั้งวัน
in two days' time èek sǒrng wun
อีกสองวัน

day trip bpai glùp wun dee-o
ไปกลับวันเดียว

dead dtai
ตาย

deaf hǒo nòo-uk
หูหนวก

deal (business) tÓO-ra-gìt
ธุรกิจ
it's a deal dtòk long láir-o
ตกลงแล้ว

death gahn dtai
การตาย

decaffeinated coffee gah-fair mâi mee kah-fay-in
กาแฟไม่มีคาเฟอิน

December tun-wah-kom
ธันวาคม

decide dtùt sǐn jai
ตัดสินใจ
we haven't decided yet rao yung mâi dâi dtùt sǐn jai
เรายังไม่ได้ตัดสินใจ

decision gahn dtùt sĭn jai
การตัดสินใจ
deck (on ship) dàht fáh
ดาดฟ้า
deckchair gâo êe pâh bai
เก้าอี้ผ้าใบ
deep léuk
ลึก
definitely nâir-norn
แน่นอน
definitely not! mâi ròrk!
ไม่หรอก
degree (qualification) bpa-rin-yah
ปริญญา
delay (noun) kwahm chúk cháh
ความชักช้า
deliberately doy-ee ay-dta-nah
โดยเจตนา
delicatessen ráhn kăi ah-hăhn sŭm-rèt rôop
ร้านขายอาหารสำเร็จรูป
delicious a-ròy
อร่อย
deliver sòng
ส่ง
delivery (of mail) gahn sòng jòt-măi
การส่งจดหมาย
Denmark bpra-tâyt den-mahk
ประเทศเดนมาร์ก
dentist mŏr fun
หมอฟัน

dialogue

it's this one here un nêe ná
this one? un née, châi mái?
no that one mâi châi, un nún
here? un nêe, châi mái?
yes châi

dentures chóot fun tee-um
ชุดฟันเทียม
deodorant yah dùp glìn dtoo-a
ยาดับกลิ่นตัว
department pa-nàirk
แผนก
department store hâhng
ห้าง
departure kăh òrk
ขาออก
departure lounge hôrng pôo doy-ee săhn kăh òrk
ห้องผู้โดยสารขาออก
depend: it depends láir-o dtàir
แล้วแต่
it depends on ... láir-o dtàir ...
แล้วแต่ ...
deposit (as security) ngern fàhk
เงินฝาก

(as part payment) kâh mút-jum
ค่ามัดจำ

description kum ùt-ti-bai
คำอธิบาย

dessert kŏrng wăhn
ของหวาน

destination jòot-măi bplai tahng
จุดหมายปลายทาง

develop (film) láhng
ล้าง

dialogue

could you develop these films? láhng feem née dâi mái?
yes, certainly dâi krúp
when will they be ready? sèt mêu-rai?
tomorrow afternoon prôong née bài
how much is the four-hour service? bor-ri-gahn sèe chôo-a mohng tâo-rài?

diabetic (noun) bpen rôhk bao wăhn
เป็นโรคเบาหวาน

dial (verb) mŏon
หมุน

dialling code ra-hùt toh-ra-sùp
รหัสโทรศัพท์

diamond pét
เพชร

diaper pâh ôrm
ผ้าอ้อม

diarrhoea tórng sĕe-a
ท้องเสีย

do you have something for diarrhoea? mee yah gâir tórng sĕe-a mái?
มียาแก้ท้องเสียไหม

diary sa-mòot bun-téuk bpra-jum wun
สมุดบันทึกประจำวัน

dictionary pót-ja-nah-nóo-grom
พจนานุกรม

didn't* mâi dâi ...
ไม่ได้ ...

see not

die dtai
ตาย

diesel núm mun rót dee-sen
น้ำมันรถดีเซล

diet ah-hăhn pi-sàyt
อาหารพิเศษ

I'm on a diet pŏm (chún) gum-lung lót núm nùk
ผม(ฉัน)กำลังลดน้ำหนัก

I have to follow a special diet

pŏm (chún) dtôrng tahn ah-hăhn pi-sàyt
ผม(ฉัน)ต้องทานอาหารพิเศษ

difference kwahm dtàirk dtàhng
ความแตกต่าง

what's the difference? dtàirk dtàhng gun yung-ngai?
แตกต่างกันอย่างไร

different dtàhng
ต่าง

this one is different un née **dtàhng gun**
อันนี้ต่างกัน

a different table/room èek dtó/hôrng nèung
อีกโต๊ะ/ห้องหนึ่ง

difficult yâhk
ยาก

difficulty bpun-hăh
ปัญหา

dinghy reu-a bòt
เรือบด

dining room hôrng rúp-bpra-tahn ah-hăhn
ห้องรับประทานอาหาร

dinner (evening meal) ah-hăhn yen
อาหารเย็น

to have dinner tahn ah-hăhn yen
ทานอาหารเย็น

direct (adj) dtrong
ตรง

is there a direct train? mee rót fai dtrong bpai mái?
มีรถไฟตรงไปไหม

direction tahng
ทาง

which direction is it? yòo tahng năi?
อยู่ทางไหน

is it in this direction? bpai tahng née, châi mái?
ไปทางนี้ใช่ไหม

directory enquiries bor-ri-gahn sòrp tăhm ber toh-ra-sùp
บริการสอบถามเบอร์โทรศัพท์

dirt kêe fòon
ขี้ฝุ่น

dirty sòk-ga-bpròk
สกปรก

disabled pí-gahn
พิการ

disappear hăi bpai
หายไป

it's disappeared mun hăi bpai năi gôr mâi róo
มันหายไปไหนก็ไม่รู้

disappointed pìt wŭng
ผิดหวัง

disappointing mâi dee tâo têe

kít wái
ไม่ดีเท่าที่คิดไว้
disaster hăi-ya-ná
หายนะ
disco dit-sa-gôh
ดิสโก้
discount lót rah-kah
ลดราคา
is there a discount? lót rah-kah nòy dâi mái?
ลดราคาหน่อยได้ไหม
disease rôhk
โรค
disgusting nâh glèe-ut
น่าเกลียด
dish (meal) gùp kâo
กับข้าว
(bowl) chahm
ชาม
dishcloth pâh chét jahn
ผ้าเช็ดจาน
disinfectant yah kâh chéu-a rôhk
ยาฆ่าเชื้อโรค
disk (for computer) jahn bun-téuk
จานบันทึก
disposable diapers/nappies pâh ôrm sŭm-rèt rôop chái krúng dee-o
ผ้าอ้อมสำเร็จรูปใช้ครั้งเดียว
distance ra-yá tahng
ระยะทาง
in the distance yòo nai ra-yá glai
อยู่ในระยะไกล
district kàyt
เขต
disturb róp-goo-un
รบกวน
diversion (detour) bplèe-un sên tahng dern
เปลี่ยนเส้นทางเดิน
diving board têe gra-dòht náhm
ที่กระโดดน้ำ
divorced yàh gun láir-o
หย่ากันแล้ว
dizzy: I feel dizzy pŏm (chún) wee-un hŏo-a
ผม(ฉัน)เวียนหัว
do (verb) tum
ทำ
what shall we do? rao ja tum yung-ngai?
เราจะทำอย่างไร
how do you do it? tum yung-ngai?
ทำอย่างไร
will you do it for me? chôo-ay tum hâi nòy, dâi mái?
ช่วยทำให้หน่อยได้ไหม

dialogues

how do you do? sa-wùt dee krúp (kâ)
nice to meet you yin dee têe dâi róo-jùk gun
what do you do? (work) koon tum ngahn a-rai krúp (ká)?
I'm a teacher, and you? bpen kroo, láir-o koon lâ?
I'm a student bpen núk sèuk-săh
what are you doing this evening? yen née bpai năi?
we're going out for a drink, do you want to join us? rao bpai gin lâo, bpai dôo-ay gun mái?

do you want fish sauce? sài núm bplah mái?
I do, but she doesn't mâi sài dtàir káo gôr sài

doctor mŏr
หมอ
we need a doctor rao dtôrng gahn hăh mŏr
เราต้องการหาหมอ
please call a doctor chôo-ay rêe-uk mŏr
ช่วยเรียกหมอ

dialogue

where does it hurt? jèp dtrong năi?
right here dtrong née
does that hurt now? yung jèp yòo rĕu bplào?
yes jèp
take this to the pharmacy ao nêe bpai ráhn kăi yah

document àyk-ga-săhn
เอกสาร
dog măh
หมา
doll dtóok-ga-dtah
ตุ๊กตา
domestic flight têe-o bin pai nai
เที่ยวบินภายใน
don't!* yàh!
อย่า
don't do that! yàh tum yàhng nún!
อย่าทำอย่างนั้น
door bpra-dtoo
ประตู
doorman kon fâo bpra-dtoo
คนเฝ้าประตู

double kôo
คู่
double bed dtee-ung yày
เตียงใหญ่
double room hôrng kôo
ห้องคู่
doughnut doh-nút
โดนัท
down: down here yòo têe nêe
อยู่ที่นี่
put it down over there wahng bpai têe nôhn
วางไปที่โน่น
it's down there on the right lur-ee bpai kâhng nâh tahng dâhn kwǎh meu
เลยไปข้างหน้าทางด้านขวามือ
it's further down the road bpai dtahm ta-nǒn kâhng nâh
ไปตามถนนข้างหน้า
downmarket (restaurant etc) rah-kah tòok
ราคาถูก
downstairs kâhng lâhng
ข้างล่าง
dozen lǒh
โหล
half a dozen krêung lǒh
ครึ่งโหล
drain (in sink, in street) tôr ra-bai
ท่อระบาย
draughty: it's draughty mee lom yen kâo
มีลมเย็นเข้า
draw wâht
วาด
drawer lín-chúk
ลิ้นชัก
drawing rôop wâht
รูปวาด
dreadful yâir
แย่
dream (noun) kwahm fǔn
ความฝัน
dress (noun) sêu-a chóot
เสื้อชุด
dressed: to get dressed dtàirng dtoo-a
แต่งตัว
dressing (for cut) pâh pun plǎir
ผ้าพันแผล
salad dressing núm (râht) sa-lùt
น้ำ(ราด)สลัด
dressing gown sêu-a kloom chóot norn
เสื้อคลุมชุดนอน
drink (noun) krêu-ung dèum
เครื่องดื่ม
(verb) dèum
ดื่ม
a cold drink krêu-ung dèum

English → Thai

Dr

yen yen
เครื่องดื่มเย็นๆ
can I get you a drink? kOOn ja dèum a-rai mái?
คุณจะดื่มอะไรไหม
what would you like (to drink)? kOOn ja dèum a-rai?
คุณจะดื่มอะไร
no thanks, I don't drink mâi krúp (kâ) pŏm (chún) mâi dèum
ไม่ครับ(ค่ะ)ผม(ฉัน)ไม่ดื่ม
I'll just have a drink of water kŏr náhm bplào tâo-nún
ขอน้ำเปล่าเท่านั้น

drinking water náhm dèum
น้ำดื่ม
is this drinking water? náhm née gin dâi mái?
น้ำนี้กินได้ไหม

drive (verb) kùp
ขับ
we drove here rao kùp rót mah
เราขับรถมา
I'll drive you home pŏm (chún) kùp rót bpai sòng
ผม(ฉัน)ขับรถไปส่ง

driver kon kùp
คนขับ

driving licence bai kùp kèe
ใบขับขี่

drop: just a drop, please (of drink) nít dee-o tâo-nún
นิดเดียวเท่านั้น

drug yah
ยา

drugs (narcotics) yah-sàyp-dtìt
ยาเสพติด

drunk (adj) mao
เมา

drunken driving kùp rót ka-nà mao
ขับรถขณะเมา

dry (adj) hâirng
แห้ง

dry-cleaner ráhn súk hâirng
ร้านซักแห้ง

duck bpèt
เป็ด

due: he was due to arrive yesterday káo koo-un ja mah mêu-a wahn née
เขาควรจะมาเมื่อวานนี้
when is the train due? rót fai mah gèe mohng?
รถไฟมากี่โมง

dull (pain) mâi rOOn rairng
ไม่รุนแรง
(weather) mêut moo-a
มืดมัว

dummy (baby's) hŏo-a nom lòrk
หัวนมหลอก

during nai ra-wàhng
ในระหว่าง

dust fòon
ฝุ่น

dustbin tǔng ka-yà
ถังขยะ

dusty mee fòon yér
มีฝุ่นเยอะ

Dutch horl-lairn
ฮอลแลนด์

duty-free (goods) mâi dtôrng sěe-a pah-sěe
ไม่ต้องเสียภาษี

duty-free shop ráhn káh sǐn-káh bplòrt pah-sěe ah-gorn
ร้านค้าสินค้าปลอดภาษีอากร

E

each (every) tóok
ทุก

how much are they each? un la tâo-rài?
อันละเท่าไร

ear hǒo
หู

earache: I have earache pǒm (chún) bpòo-ut hǒo
ผม(ฉัน)ปวดหู

early ray-o
เร็ว

early in the morning cháo dtròo
เช้าตรู่

I called by earlier pǒm (chún) mah hǎh mêu-a gòrn née
ผม(ฉัน)มาหาเมื่อก่อนนี้

earrings dtôom hǒo
ตุ้มหู

east dta-wun òrk
ตะวันออก

in the east tahng dta-wun òrk
ทางตะวันออก

Easter ee-sa-dtêr
อีสเตอร์

easy ngâi
ง่าย

eat gin kâo
กินข้าว

we've already eaten, thanks rao gin kâo láir-o
เรากินข้าวแล้ว

eau de toilette núm òp
น้ำอบ

egg kài
ไข่

egg noodles ba-mèe
บะหมี่

either: either ... or ... ... rěu ...
... หรือ ...

either of them un nǎi gôr dâi
อันไหนก็ได้

elastic (noun) săi yahng yêut
สายยางยืด
elastic band yahng rút
ยางรัด
elbow kôr sòrk
ข้อศอก
electric fai fáh
ไฟฟ้า
electrical appliances krêu-ung fai fáh
เครื่องไฟฟ้า
electrician châhng fai fáh
ช่างไฟฟ้า
electricity fai fáh
ไฟฟ้า
elephant cháhng
ช้าง
elevator líf
ลิฟท์
else: something else a-rai èek
อะไรอีก
somewhere else têe èun
ที่อื่น

dialogue

would you like anything else? ao a-rai èek mái?
no, nothing else, thanks mâi krúp (kâ), kòrp-kOOn

embassy sa-tăhn tôot
สถานทูต
emergency chÒOk chĕrn
ฉุกเฉิน
this is an emergency! bpen pah-wá chÒOk chĕrn!
เป็นภาวะฉุกเฉิน
emergency exit tahng òrk chÒOk chĕrn
ทางออกฉุกเฉิน
empty wâhng
ว่าง
end (noun) jòp
จบ
(verb) sîn sÒOt, jòp
สิ้นสุด, จบ
at the end of the soi sÒOt soy
สุดซอย
when does it end? jòp mêu-rài?
จบเมื่อไร
engaged (toilet, telephone) mâi wâhng
ไม่ว่าง
(to be married) mûn
หมั้น
engine (car) krêu-ung yon
เครื่องยนต์
England bpra-tâyt ung-grìt
ประเทศอังกฤษ
English (adj) ung-grìt
อังกฤษ

(language) pah-săh ung-grìt
ภาษาอังกฤษ
I'm English pŏm (chún) bpen kon ung-grìt
ผม(ฉัน)เป็นคนอังกฤษ
do you speak English? koon pôot pah-săh ung-grìt bpen mái?
คุณพูดภาษาอังกฤษเป็นไหม
enjoy: to enjoy oneself sa-nòok
สนุก

dialogue

how did you like the film? nŭng sa-nòok mái?
I enjoyed it very much, did you enjoy it? sa-nòok mâhk, koon kít wâh sa-nòok mái?

enjoyable sa-nòok dee
สนุกดี
enlargement (of photo) pâhp ka-yăi
ภาพขยาย
enormous yài bêr-rêr
ใหญ่เบ้อเร่อ
enough por
พอ
there's not enough mâi por
ไม่พอ
it's not big enough yài mâi por
ใหญ่ไม่พอ
that's enough por láir-o
พอแล้ว
entrance (noun) tahng kâo
ทางเข้า
envelope sorng jòt-măi
ซองจดหมาย
epileptic bpen rôhk lom bâh mŏo
เป็นโรคลมบ้าหมู
equipment òop-bpa-gorn
อุปกรณ์
error têe pìt
ที่ผิด
especially doy-ee cha-pòr
โดยเฉพาะ
essential jum-bpen
จำเป็น
it is essential that ... jum-bpen têe ...
จำเป็นที่ ...
Europe yoo-rohp
ยุโรป
European (adj) yoo-rohp
ยุโรป
even máir dtàir
แม้แต่
even if ... máir wâh ...
แม้ว่า ...

evening (early evening) dtorn yen
ตอนเย็น
(late evening) dtorn glahng keun
ตอนกลางคืน
this evening (early evening) yen née
เย็นนี้
(late evening) keun née
คืนนี้
in the evening (early evening) dtorn yen
ตอนเย็น
(late evening) dtorn glahng keun
ตอนกลางคืน
evening meal ah-hăhn yen
อาหารเย็น
eventually nai têe sÒOt
ในที่สุด
ever ker-ee
เคย

dialogue

have you ever been to Phuket? kOOn ker-ee bpai poo-gèt mái?
yes, I was there two years ago ker-ee, ker-ee bpai mêu-a sŏrng bpee gòrn

every tÓOk
ทุก
every day tÓOk wun
ทุกวัน
everyone tÓOk kon
ทุกคน
everything tÓOk yàhng
ทุกอย่าง
everywhere tôo-a bpai
ทั่วไป
exactly! châi láir-o!
ใช่แล้ว
exam gahn sòrp
การสอบ
example dtoo-a yàhng
ตัวอย่าง
for example chên ...
เช่น ...
excellent yêe-um
เยี่ยม
excellent! yêe-um ler-ee!
เยี่ยมเลย
except yók wáyn
ยกเว้น
excess baggage núm nùk gern
น้ำหนักเกิน
exchange rate ùt-dtrah lâirk bplèe-un
อัตราแลกเปลี่ยน
exciting nâh dtèun dtên
น่าตื่นเต้น

excuse me (to get past, to say sorry) kŏr-tôht
ขอโทษ
(to get attention) koon krúp (kâ)
คุณครับ (คะ)
(to say pardon?) a-rai ná?
อะไรนะ
exhaust (pipe) tôr ai sěe-a
ท่อไอเสีย
exhausted (tired) nèu-ay
เหนื่อย
exhibition ní-tá-sa-gahn
นิทรรศการ
exit tahng òrk
ทางออก
where's the nearest exit? tahng òrk glâi têe sòot yòo têe năi?
ทางออกใกล้ที่สุดอยู่ที่ไหน
expect kâht
คาด
expensive pairng
แพง
experienced mee bpra-sòp-ba-gahn
มีประสบการณ์
explain ùt-ti-bai
อธิบาย
can you explain that? chôo-ay ùt-ti-bai hâi nòy, dâi mái?
ช่วยอธิบายให้หน่อยได้ไหม
express (mail) bprai-sa-nee dòo-un
ไปรษณีย์ด่วน
(train) rót fai dòo-un
รถไฟด่วน
extension (telephone) dtòr
ต่อ
extension 341, please kŏr dtòr ber săhm sèe nèung
ขอต่อเบอร์สามสี่หนึ่ง
extension lead săi pôo-ung
สายพ่วง
extra: can we have an extra one? kŏr **èek** un nèung
ขออีกอันหนึ่ง
do you charge extra for that? kít **dtàhng hàhk** rěu bplào?
คิดต่างหากหรือเปล่า
extraordinary bplàirk mâhk
แปลกมาก
extremely mâhk lěu-a gern
มากเหลือเกิน
eye dtah
ตา
will you keep an eye on my suitcase for me? chôo-ay fâo gra-bpăo hâi nòy, dâi mái?
ช่วยเฝ้ากระเป๋าให้หน่อยได้ไหม
eyebrow pencil din-sŏr kěe-un kéw
ดินสอเขียนคิ้ว

eye drops yah yòrt dtah
ยาหยอดตา
eyeglasses (US) wâirn dtah
แว่นตา
eyeliner têe kĕe-un kòrp dtah
ที่เขียนขอบตา
eye make-up remover núm yah láhng têe kĕe-un kòrp dtah
น้ำยาล้างที่เขียนขอบตา
eye shadow kreem tah nŭng dtah
ครีมทาหนังตา

F

face nâh
หน้า
factory rohng ngahn
โรงงาน
Fahrenheit* fah-ren-háit
ฟาเร็นไฮท์
faint (verb) bpen lom
เป็นลม
she's fainted káo bpen lom
เขาเป็นลม
I feel faint pŏm (chún) róo-sèuk bpen lom
ผม(ฉัน)รู้สึกเป็นลม
fair (funfair) ngahn òrk ráhn
งานออกร้าน
(trade) ngahn sa-dairng sĭn-káh
งานแสดงสินค้า
(adj) yóot-dti-tum
ยุติธรรม
fairly kôrn-kâhng
ค่อนข้าง
fake kŏrng bplorm
ของปลอม
fall (US) réu-doo bai-mái rôo-ung
ฤดูใบไม้ร่วง
in the fall dtorn réu-doo bai-mái rôo-ung
ตอนฤดูใบไม้ร่วง
fall (verb) hòk lóm
หกลม
she's had a fall káo hòk lóm
เขาหกลม
false mâi jing
ไม่จริง
family krôrp-kroo-a
ครอบครัว
famous mee chêu sĕe-ung
มีชื่อเสียง
fan (electrical) pút lom
พัดลม
(handheld) pút
พัด
(sports) kon chôrp doo gee-lah
คนชอบดูกีฬา

fan belt săi pahn
สายพาน
fantastic yêe-um yôrt
เยี่ยมยอด
far glai
ไกล

dialogue

is it far from here? yòo glai mái?
no, not very far mâi glai
well, how far? gèe gi-loh-met?
it's about 20 kilometres bpra-mahn yêe-sìp gi-loh-met

fare kâh doy-ee săhn
ค่าโดยสาร
farm fahm
ฟาร์ม
fashionable tun sa-măi
ทันสมัย
fast ray-o
เร็ว
fat (person) ôo-un
อ้วน
(on meat) mun
มัน
father pôr
พ่อ
father-in-law (of a man) pôr dtah
พ่อตา
(of a woman) pôr pŏo-a
พ่อผัว
faucet górk náhm
ก๊อกน้ำ
fault kwahm pìt
ความผิด
sorry, it was my fault kŏr-tôht **kwahm pìt** kŏrng pŏm (chún)
ขอโทษ ความผิดของผม(ฉัน)
it's not my fault mâi châi **kwahm pìt** kŏrng pŏm (chún)
ไม่ใช่ความผิดของผม(ฉัน)
faulty pìt
ผิด
favourite bpròht
โปรด
fax (machine) krêu-ung toh-ra-săhn
เครื่องโทรสาร
(verb: person) sòng toh-ra-săhn bpai hâi
ส่งโทรสารไปให้
(document) bun-téuk toh-ra-săhn, fáirks
บันทึกโทรสาร, แฟกซ์
February gOOm-pah-pun
กุมภาพันธ์

feel róo-sèuk
รู้สึก
I feel hot pǒm (chún) róo-sèuk rórn
ผม(ฉัน)รู้สึกร้อน
I feel unwell pǒm (chún) róo-sèuk mâi sa-bai
ผม(ฉัน)รู้สึกไม่สบาย
I feel like going for a walk pǒm (chún) yàhk ja bpai dern lên
ผม(ฉัน)อยากจะไปเดินเล่น
how are you feeling? koon róo-sèuk bpen yung-ngai bâhng?
คุณรู้สึกเป็นอย่างไรบ้าง
I'm feeling better pǒm (chún) róo-sèuk kôy yung chôo-a
ผม(ฉัน)รู้สึกค่อยยังชั่ว
felt-tip (pen) bpàhk-gah may-jik
ปากกาเมจิก
fence róo-a
รั้ว
fender gun chon
กันชน
ferry reu-a kâhm fâhk
เรือข้ามฟาก
festival ngahn
งาน
fetch rúp
รับ
I'll fetch him pǒm (chún) ja bpai rúp káo
ผม(ฉัน)จะไปรับเขา
will you come and fetch me later? mah rúp pǒm (chún) tee lǔng dâi mái?
มารับผม(ฉัน)ทีหลังได้ไหม
feverish bpen kâi
เป็นไข้
few: a few sǒrng sǎhm
สองสาม
a few days sǒrng sǎhm wun
สองสามวัน
fiancé(e) kôo mûn
คู่หมั้น
field sa-nǎhm
สนาม
fight (noun) gahn chók dtòy
การชกต่อย
fill dterm
เติม
fill in gròrk
กรอก
do I have to fill this in? dtôrng gròrk un née rěu bplào?
ต้องกรอกอันนี้หรือเปล่า
fill up tum hâi dtem
ทำให้เต็ม
fill it up, please dterm núm

mun hâi dtem
เติมน้ำมันให้เต็ม
filling (in tooth) òot fun
อุดฟัน
film (movie) nǔng
หนัง
(for camera) feem
ฟิล์ม

dialogue

do you have this kind of film? mee feem bàirp née mái?
yes, how many exposures? mee, ao gèe rôop?
36 sǎhm sìp

film processing láhng feem
ล้างฟิล์ม
filthy sòk-ga-bpròk
สกปรก
find (verb) jer
เจอ
I can't find it pǒm (chún) hǎh mâi jer
ผม(ฉัน)หาไม่เจอ
I've found it pǒm (chún) jer láir-o
ผม(ฉัน)เจอแล้ว
find out hǎh rai la-êe-ut
หารายละเอียด
could you find out for me? chôo-ay hǎh rai la-êe-ut hâi nòy dâi mái?
ช่วยหารายละเอียดให้หน่อยได้ไหม
fine (weather) dee
ดี
(punishment) kâh bprùp
ค่าปรับ

dialogues

how are you? bpen yung-ngai bâhng?
I'm fine, thanks sa-bai dee kòrp koon mâhk

is that OK? oh kay mái?
that's fine thanks dee láir-o kòrp-koon

finger néw meu
นิ้วมือ
finish (verb) jòp
จบ
I haven't finished yet pǒm (chún) yung mâi sèt
ผม(ฉัน)ยังไม่เสร็จ
when does it finish? jòp gèe mohng?
จบกี่โมง

fire: fire! fai mâi!
ไฟไหม้
can we light a fire here? gòr fai dtrong née dâi mái?
ก่อไฟตรงนี้ได้ไหม
fire alarm sŭn-yahn fay mâi
สัญญาณไฟไหม้
fire brigade gorng dtum-ròo-ut dùp plerng
กองตำรวจดับเพลิง
fire escape bun-dai sŭm-rùp nĕe fai
บรรไดสำหรับหนีไฟ
fire extinguisher krêu-ung dùp plerng
เครื่องดับเพลิง
first râirk
แรก
I was first pŏm (chún) bpen kon râirk
ผม(ฉัน)เป็นคนแรก
at first tee râirk
ทีแรก
the first time krúng râirk
ครั้งแรก
first on the left lée-o sái têe tahng yâirk kâhng nâh
เลี้ยวซ้ายที่ทางแยกข้างหน้า
first aid gahn bpa-tŏm pa-yah-bahn
การปฐมพยาบาล
first-aid kit chóot bpa-thŏm pa-yah-bahn
ชุดปฐมพยาบาล
first class (travel etc) chún nèung
ชั้นหนึ่ง
first floor chún sŏrng
ชั้นสอง
(US) chún nèung
ชั้นหนึ่ง
first name chêu
ชื่อ
fish (noun) bplah
ปลา
fisherman kon jùp bplah
คนจับปลา
fishing gahn jùp bplah
การจับปลา
fishing boat reu-a bpra-mong
เรือประมง
fishing village mòo bâhn bpra-mong
หมู่บ้านประมง
fishmonger's ráhn kăi bplah
ร้านขายปลา
fit (attack) ah-gahn bpen lom
อาการเป็นลม
fit: it doesn't fit me sài mâi dâi
ใส่ไม่ได้
fitting room hôrng lorng sêu-a pâh
ห้องลองเสื้อผ้า

fix (verb: arrange) jùt
จัด
can you fix this? (repair) un née **gâir** dâi mái?
อันนี้แก้ได้ไหม
fizzy sâh
ซ่า
flag tong
ธง
flannel (facecloth) pâh chét nâh
ผ้าเช็ดหน้า
flash (for camera) fláirt
แฟลช
flat (noun: apartment) fláirt
แฟลต
(adj) bairn
แบน
I've got a flat tyre yahng bairn
ยางแบน
flavour rót
รส
flea mùt
หมัด
flight têe-o bin
เที่ยวบิน
flight number têe-o bin măi-lâyk
เที่ยวบินหมายเลข
flippers rorng táo ma-nóOt gòp
รองเท้ามนุษย์กบ
floating market dta-làht náhm
ตลาดน้ำ
flood núm tôo-um
น้ำท่วม
floor (of room) péun
พื้น
(storey) chún
ชั้น
on the floor yòo bon péun
อยู่บนพื้น
florist ráhn kăi dòrk-mái
ร้านขายดอกไม้
flour bpâirng săh-lee
แป้งสาลี
flower dòrk-mái
ดอกไม้
flu kâi wùt
ไข้หวัด
fluent: John speaks fluent Thai John pôot pah-săh tai dâi **khlôrng**
จอห์นพูดภาษาไทยได้คล่อง
fly (noun) ma-lairng wun
แมลงวัน
(verb) bin
บิน
can we fly there? bpai krêu-ung bin dâi mái?
ไปเครื่องบินได้ไหม
fly in bin kâo mah
บินเข้ามา

fly out bin òrk bpai
บินออกไป
fog mòrk long
หมอกลง
foggy: it's foggy mòrk long
หมอกลง
folk dancing gahn fórn rum péun meu-ung
การฟ้อนรำพื้นเมือง
folk music don-dtree péun meu-ung
ดนตรีพื้นเมือง
follow dtahm
ตาม
follow me dtahm pŏm (chún) mah
ตามผม(ฉัน)มา
food ah-hăhn
อาหาร
food poisoning ah-hăhn bpen pít
อาหารเป็นพิษ
food shop/store ráhn kăi kŏrng chum
ร้านขายของชำ
foot* (of person) táo
เท้า
on foot dern bpai
เดินไป
football (game) fóot-born
ฟุตบอล
(ball) lôok fóot-born
ลูกฟุตบอล
football match gahn kàirng kŭn fóot-born
การแข่งขันฟุตบอล
for: do you have something for ...? (headache/diarrhoea etc) mee a-rai gâir ... mái?
มีอะไรแก้ ... ไหม

dialogues

who's the fried rice for? kâo pùt **sŭm-rùp** krai?
that's for me **sŭm-rùp** pŏm
and this one? láir-o nêe lâ?
that's for her **sŭm-rùp** káo

where do I get the bus for Bangsaen? kêun rót bpai bahng-săirn têe-năi?
the bus for Bangsaen leaves from the central market rót bpai bahng-săirn òrk jàhk dta-làht glahng

how long have you been here for? koon yòo têe nêe nahn tâo-rài?
I've been here for two days,

how about you? yòo sŏrng wun, láir-o koon lâ?
I've been here for a week pŏm (chún) yòo têe nêe ah-tít nèung láir-o

forehead nâh pàhk
หน้าผาก
foreign dtàhng bpra-tâyt
ต่างประเทศ
foreigner chao dtàhng bpra-tâyt
ชาวต่างประเทศ
forest bpàh
ป่า
forget leum
ลืม
I forget, I've forgotten pŏm (chún) leum láir-o
ผม(ฉัน)ลืมแล้ว
fork sôrm
ส้อม
(in road) tahng yâirk
ทางแยก
form (document) bàirp form
แบบฟอร์ม
formal (dress) bpen tahng gahn
เป็นทางการ
fortnight sŏrng ah-tít
สองอาทิตย์
fortunately chôhk dee
โชคดี
forward: could you forward my mail? chôo-ay sòng jòt-măi dtòr bpai hâi dôo-ay
ช่วยส่งจดหมายต่อไปให้ด้วย
forwarding address têe yòo sŭm-rùp sòng jòt-măi bpai hâi
ที่อยู่สำหรับส่งจดหมายไปให้
foundation cream kreem rorng péun
ครีมรองพื้น
fountain núm póo
น้ำพุ
foyer (of hotel) hôrng tŏhng glahng sŭm-rùp rúp kàirk
ห้องโถงกลางสำหรับรับแขก
(of theatre) bor-ri-wayn nûng púk ror
บริเวณนั่งพักรอ
fracture (noun) gra-dòok hùk
กระดูกหัก
France bpra-tâyt fa-rùng-sàyt
ประเทศฝรั่งเศส
free ì-sa-rá
อิสระ
(no charge) free
ฟรี
is it free (of charge)? free rĕu bplào?
ฟรีหรือเปล่า
freeway tahng dòo-un
ทางด่วน

freezer dtôo châir kăirng
ตู้แช่แข็ง
French (adj) fa-rùng-sàyt
ฝรั่งเศส
(language) pah-săh fa-rùng-sàyt
ภาษาฝรั่งเศส
French fries mun fa-rùng tôrt
มันฝรั่งทอด
frequent bòy bòy
บ่อย ๆ
how frequent is the bus to Pattaya? mee rót bpai pút-ta-yah bòy kâir năi?
มีรถไปพัทยาบ่อยแค่ไหน
fresh (weather, breeze) sòt chêun
สดชื่น
(fruit etc) sòt
สด
fresh orange núm sôm kún
น้ำส้มคั้น
Friday wun sòok
วันศุกร์
fridge dtôo yen
ตู้เย็น
fried pùt
ผัด
fried egg kài dao
ไข่ดาว
fried noodles (Thai-style) pùt tai
ผัดไทย
(Chinese-style) pùt see éw
ผัดซีอิ๊ว
fried rice kâo pùt
ข้าวผัด
friend pêu-un
เพื่อน
friendly bpen pêu-un
เป็นเพื่อน
frog gòp
กบ
from jàhk
จาก
when does the next train from Ubon arrive? rót fai **jàhk** oo-bon têe-o nâh mah tĕung gèe mohng?
รถไฟจากอุบลเที่ยวหน้ามาถึงกี่โมง
from Monday to Friday dtûng dtàir wun jun jon tĕung wun sòok
ตั้งแต่วันจันทร์จนถึงวันศุกร์
from next Thursday
dtûng dtàir wun pa-réu-hùt
ตั้งแต่วันพฤหัส

dialogue

where are you from? koon **mah jàhk** năi?
I'm from Slough pŏm (chún) mah jàhk Slough

Fr

front nâh
หน้า
in front kâhng nâh
ข้างหน้า
in front of the hotel kâhng nâh rohng rairm
ข้างหน้าโรงแรม
at the front kâhng nâh
ข้างหน้า
frozen châir kǎirng
แช่แข็ง
frozen food ah-hǎhn châir kǎirng
อาหารแช่แข็ง
fruit pǒn-la-mái
ผลไม้
fruit juice núm pǒn-la-mái
น้ำผลไม้
fry (deep-fry) tôrt
ทอด
(stir-fry) pùt
ผัด
frying pan ga-tá
กะทะ
full dtem
เต็ม
it's full of ... dtem bpai dôo-ay ...
เต็มไปด้วย ...
I'm full pǒm (chún) ìm láir-o
ผม(ฉัน)อิ่มแล้ว
full board gin yòo prórm
กินอยู่พร้อม
fun: it was fun sa-nòok dee
สนุกดี
funeral ngahn sòp
งานศพ
funny (strange) bplàirk
แปลก
(amusing) dta-lòk
ตลก
furniture krêu-ung reu-un
เครื่องเรือน
further ler-ee bpai
เลยไป
it's further down the road bpai dtahm ta-nǒn kâhng nâh
ไปตามถนนข้างหน้า

dialogue

how much further is it to Hua Hin? bpai hǒo-a hǐn èek glai mái?
about 5 kilometres bpra-mahn hâh gi-loh-met

fuse few
ฟิวส์
the lights have fused few kàht
ฟิวส์ขาด

fuse box glòrng few
กล่องฟิวส์
fuse wire săi few
สายฟิวส์
future a-nah-kót
อนาคต
in future nai a-nah-kót
ในอนาคต

G

game (cards etc) gaym
เกม
(match) gahn lên
การเล่น
(meat) néu-a sùt bpàh
เนื้อสัตว์ป่า
garage (for fuel) bpúm núm mun
ปั๊มน้ำมัน
(for repairs) òo sôrm rót
อู่ซ่อมรถ
(for parking) rohng rót
โรงรถ
garbage (waste) ka-yà
ขยะ
garden sŏo-un
สวน
garlic gra-tee-um
กระเทียม
gas gáirt
แก๊ส
(US) núm mun
น้ำมัน
see **petrol**
gas cylinder (camping gas) tǔng gáirt
ถังแก๊ส
gasoline núm mun
น้ำมัน
gas station bpúm núm mun
ปั๊มน้ำมัน
gate bpra-dtoo
ประตู
(at airport) chôrng kâo
ช่องเข้า
gay gay
เกย์
gay bar bah gay
บาร์เกย์
gearbox glòrng gee-a
กล่องเกียร์
gear lever kun gee-a
คันเกียร์
gears gee-a
เกียร์
general (adj) tôo-a bpai
ทั่วไป
gents (toilet) boo-ròot
บุรุษ
genuine (antique etc) táir
แท้

German (adj) yer-ra-mun
เยอรมัน
(language) pah-săh yer-ra-mun
ภาษาเยอรมัน

German measles rôhk hùt yer-ra-mun
โรคหัดเยอรมัน

Germany bpra-tâyt yer-ra-mun
ประเทศเยอรมัน

get (fetch) dâi
ได้

will you get me another one, please? kŏr ao èek un nèung dâi mái?
ขอเอาอีกอันหนึ่งได้ไหม

how do I get to ...? bpai ... yung-ngai?
ไป ... อย่างไร

do you know where I can get them? sâhp mái wâh ja séu dâi têe năi?
ทราบไหมว่าจะซื้อได้ที่ไหน

get back (return) glùp
กลับ

get in (arrive) tĕung
ถึง

get off long
ลง

where do I get off? pŏm (chún) long têe năi?
ผม(ฉัน)ลงที่ไหน

get on (to train etc) kêun
ขึ้น

get out (of car etc) long
ลง

get up (in the morning) dtèun
ตื่น

gift kŏrng kwŭn
ของขวัญ

gin lâo yin
เหล้ายิน

a gin and tonic, please kŏr yin toh-nik
ขอยินโทนิค

girl pôo-yĭng
ผู้หญิง

girlfriend fairn
แฟน

give hâi
ให้

can you give me some change? kŏr lâirk sàyt sa-dtahng dâi mái?
ขอแลกเศษสตางค์ได้ไหม

I gave it to him pŏm (chún) hâi káo bpai láir-o
ผม(ฉัน)ให้เขาไปแล้ว

will you give this to ...? chôo-ay ao née bpai hâi ... nòy, dâi mái?
ช่วยเอานี้ไปให้ ... หน่อยได้ไหม

dialogue

how much do you want for this? nêe kít tâo-rài?
200 baht sŏrng róy bàht
I'll give you 150 baht pŏm (chún) ja hâi koon róy hâh sìp bàht

give back keun
คืน
glad yin dee
ยินดี
glass gâir-o
แก้ว
glasses (spectacles) wâirn dtah
แว่นตา
gloves tŏong meu
ถุงมือ
glue (noun) gao
กาว
go bpai
ไป
we'd like to go to the waterfalls rao yàhk ja bpai têe-o núm dtòk
เราอยากจะไปเที่ยวน้ำตก
where are you going? koon bpai năi?
คุณไปไหน
where does this bus go? rót may săi née bpai năi?
รถเมล์สายนี้ไปไหน
let's go! bpai tèr!
ไปเถอะ
she's gone (left) káo bpai láir-o
เขาไปแล้ว
where has he gone? káo bpai năi?
เขาไปไหน
I went there last week pŏm (chún) bpai têe nûn mêu-a ah-tít têe láir-o
ผม(ฉัน)ไปที่นั่นเมื่ออาทิตย์ที่แล้ว
go away bpai
ไป
go away! bpai hâi pón!
ไปให้พ้น
go back (return) glùp
กลับ
go down (the stairs etc) long bpai
ลงไป
go in (enter) kâo bpai
เข้าไป
go out (in the evening) têe-o bpai
ไปเที่ยว
do you want to go out tonight? keun née yàhk bpai têe-o mái?
คืนนี้อยากไปเที่ยวไหม

go through pàhn bpai
ผ่านไป

go up (the stairs etc) kêun bpai
ขึ้นไป

goat páir
แพะ

God pra-jâo
พระเจ้า

goggles wâirn dtah dum náhm
แว่นตาดำน้ำ

gold torng
ทอง

Golden Triangle săhm lèe-um torng kum
สามเหลี่ยมทองคำ

goldsmith châhng torng
ช่างทอง

golf górp
กอล์ฟ

golf course sa-năhm górp
สนามกอล์ฟ

good dee
ดี

good! dee láir-o!
ดีแล้ว

goodbye lah gòrn ná
ลาก่อนนะ

good evening sa-wùt dee krúp (kâ)
สวัสดีครับ(ค่ะ)

good morning sa-wùt dee krúp (kâ)
สวัสดีครับ(ค่ะ)

good night sa-wùt dee krúp (kâ)
สวัสดีครับ(ค่ะ)

goose hàhn
ห่าน

got: we've got to leave rao dtôrng bpai
เราต้องไป

have you got any ...? mee ... mái?
มี ... ไหม

government rút-ta-bahn
รัฐบาล

gradually tee la nòy
ทีละหน่อย

grammar wai-yah-gorn
ไวยากรณ์

gram(me) grum
กรัม

granddaughter lăhn săo
หลานสาว

grandfather (maternal) dtah
ตา

(paternal) bpòo
ปู่

grandmother (maternal) yai
ยาย

(paternal) yâh
ย่า

grandson lăhn chai
หลานชาย
grapefruit sôm oh
ส้มโอ
grapes a-ngòon
องุ่น
grass yâh
หญ้า
grateful róo-sèuk kòrp-koon
รู้สึกขอบคุณ
great (excellent) yôrt
ยอด
that's great! yôrt!
ยอด
Great Britain bpra-tâyt ung-grìt
ประเทศอังกฤษ
Greece bpra-tâyt greet
ประเทศกรีซ
greedy dta-glà
ตะกละ
green sĕe kĕe-o
สีเขียว
greengrocer's ráhn kăi pùk
ร้านขายผัก
grey sĕe tao
สีเทา
grill (noun) dtao bpîng
เตาปิ้ง
grilled yâhng
ย่าง
grocer's ráhn kăi kŏrng chum
ร้านขายของชำ
ground péun din
พื้นดิน
on the ground bon péun din
บนพื้นดิน
ground floor chún nèung
ชั้นหนึ่ง
group glòom
กลุ่ม
guarantee (noun) bai rúp-rorng
ใบรับรอง
is it guaranteed? mee bai rúp bpra-gun mái?
มีใบรับประกันไหม
guest kàirk
แขก
guesthouse gáyt háot
เกสต์เฮาส์
guide (noun: person) múk-koo-tâyt
มัคคุเทศก์
guidebook kôo meu num têe-o
คู่มือนำเทียว
guided tour rai-gahn num têe-o
รายการนำเที่ยว
guitar gee-dtah
กีตาร์

Gulf of Thailand ào tai
อ่าวไทย
gum (in mouth) ngèu-uk
เหงือก
gun (pistol) bpeun pók
ปืนพก
(rifle) bpeun yao
ปืนยาว
gym rohng yim
โรงยิม

H

hair pŏm
ผม
hairbrush bprairng pŏm
แปรงผม
haircut dtùt pŏm
ตัดผม
hairdresser's (men's) ráhn dtàirng pŏm chai
ร้านแตงผมชาย
(women's) ráhn tum pŏm sa-dtree
ร้านทำผมสตรี
hairdryer krêu-ung bpào pŏm
เครื่องเป่าผม
hair gel kreem sài pŏm
ครีมใส่ผม
hairgrips gíp nèep pŏm
กิ๊บหนีบผม
hair spray sa-bpray chèet pŏm
สเปรย์ฉีดผม
half* krêung
ครึ่ง
half an hour krêung chôo-a mohng
ครึ่งชั่วโมง
half a litre krêung lít
ครึ่งลิตร
about half that bpra-mahn krêung nèung
ประมาณครึ่งหนึ่ง
half-price krêung rah-kah
ครึ่งราคา
ham mŏo hairm
หมูแฮม
hamburger hairm-ber-gêr
แฮมเบอร์เกอร์
hammer (noun) kórn
ฆ้อน
hand meu
มือ
handbag gra-bpăo tĕu
กระเป๋าถือ
handbrake brayk meu
เบรคมือ
handkerchief pâh chét nâh
ผ้าเช็ดหน้า
handle (on door, suitcase) dâhm
ด้าม
hand luggage gra-bpăo tĕu
กระเป๋าถือ

hang-gliding gahn hŏhn rôrn
การโหนร่อน

hangover bpòo-ut hŏo-a
ปวดหัว

I've got a hangover pŏm (chún) bpòo-ut hŏo-a

happen gèrt kêun
เกิดขึ้น

what's happening? gèrt a-rai kêun?
เกิดอะไรขึ้น

what has happened? mee a-rai gèrt kêun?
มีอะไรเกิดขึ้น

happy dee jai
ดีใจ

I'm not happy about this rêu-ung née pŏm (chún) mâi sa-bai jai
เรื่องนี้ผม(ฉัน)ไม่สบายใจ

harbour tâh reu-a
ท่าเรือ

hard kăirng
แข็ง

(difficult) yâhk
ยาก

hard-boiled egg kài dtôm kăirng
ไข่ต้มแข็ง

hardly mâi kôy ...
ไม่ค่อย ...

hardly ever mâi kôy ...
ไม่ค่อย ...

hardware shop ráhn kăi krêu-ung lèk
ร้านขายเครื่องเหล็ก

hat mòo-uk
หมวก

hate (verb) glèe-ut
เกลียด

have* mee
มี

can I have a ...? kŏr ... nòy
ขอ ... หน่อย

do you have ...? mee ... mái?
มี ... ไหม

what'll you have? (drink) kOOn ja dèum a-rai?
คุณจะดื่มอะไร

I have to leave now pŏm (chún) **dtôrng** bpai děe-o née
ผม(ฉัน)ต้องไปเดี๋ยวนี้

do I have to ...? pŏm (chún) **dtôrng** ... rĕu bplào?
ผม(ฉัน)ต้อง ... หรือเปล่า

can we have some ...? kŏr ... nòy dâi mái?
ขอ ... หน่อยได้ไหม

hayfever rôhk hèut
โรคหืด

he* káo
เขา

head hŏo-a
หัว
headache bpòo-ut hŏo-a
ปวดหัว
headlights fai nâh rót
ไฟหน้ารถ
headphones hŏo fung
หูฟัง
healthy (person) mee sòok-ka-pâhp dee
มีสุขภาพดี
(food) bpen bpra-yòht gàir râhng-gai
เป็นประโยชน์แก่ร่างกาย
hear dâi yin
ได้ยิน

dialogue

can you hear me? dâi yin mái?
I can't hear you, could you repeat that? pŏm (chún) mâi dâi yin, pôot èek tee dâi mái?

hearing aid krêu-ung chôo-ay fung
เครื่องช่วยฟัง
heart hŏo-a jai
หัวใจ
heart attack hŏo-a jai wai
หัวใจวาย
heat kwahm rórn
ความร้อน
heating krêu-ung tum kwahm rórn
เครื่องทำความร้อน
heavy nùk
หนัก
heel (of foot) sôn táo
ส้นเท้า
(of shoe) sôn rorng táo
ส้นรองเท้า
could you heel these? bplèe-un sôn mài hâi nòy, dâi mái?
เปลี่ยนส้นใหม่ให้หน่อยได้ไหม
height kwahm sŏong
ความสูง
helicopter hay-li-korp-dter
เฮลิคอปเตอร์
hello sa-wùt dee
สวัสดี
(answer on phone) hun-loh
ฮัลโล
helmet (for motorbike) mòo-uk gun chon
หมวกกันชน
help (noun) kwahm chôo-ay lĕu-a
ความช่วยเหลือ
(verb) chôo-ay
ช่วย

help! chôo-ay dôo-ay!
ช่วยด้วย
can you help me? chôo-ay pǒm (chún) nòy, dâi mái?
ช่วยผม(ฉัน)หน่อยได้ไหม
thank you very much for your help kòrp-kOOn têe dâi chôo-ay lěu-a
ขอบคุณที่ได้ช่วยเหลือ
helpful bpen bpra-yòht mâhk
เป็นประโยชน์มาก
hepatitis dtùp ùk-sàyp
ตับอักเสบ
her*: I haven't seen her pǒm (chún) mâi dâi hěn káo
ผม(ฉัน)ไม่ได้เห็นเขา
to her gàir káo
แก่เขา
with her gùp káo
กับเขา
for her sǔm-rùp káo
สำหรับเขา
that's her nûn káo
นั่นเขา
that's her towel bpen pâh chét dtoo-a kǒrng káo
เป็นผ้าเช็ดตัวของเขา
herbs (for cooking) krêu-ung tâyt
เครื่องเทศ
(medicinal) sa-mOOn prai
สมุนไพร
here têe-nêe
ที่นี่
here is/are ... nêe ...
นี่ ...
here you are (offering) nêe ngai
นี่ไง
hers* kǒrng káo
ของเขา
that's hers nûn kǒrng káo
นั่นของเขา
hey! háy!
เฮ้
hi! (hello) bpai nǎi?
ไปไหน
hide (verb) sôrn
ซ่อน
high sǒong
สูง
highchair gâo êe sǒong
เก้าอี้สูง
highway tahng dòo-un
ทางด่วน
hill kǎo
เขา
him*: I haven't seen him pǒm (chún) mâi dâi hěn káo
ผม(ฉัน)ไม่ได้เห็นเขา
to him gàir káo
แก่เขา
with him gùp káo
กับเขา

for him sŭm-rùp káo
สำหรับเขา
that's him nûn káo
hip sa-pôhk
สะโพก
hire châo
เช่า
for hire hâi châo
ให้เช่า
where can I hire a bike?
(bicycle) châo jùk-ra-yahn dâi têe năi?
เช่าจักรยานได้ที่ไหน
his*: it's his car bpen rót kŏrng káo
เป็นรถของเขา
that's his nûn kŏrng káo
นั่นของเขา
hit (verb) dtee
ตี
hitch-hike bòhk rót
โบกรถ
hobby ngahn a-di-râyk
งานอดิเรก
hold (verb) tĕu
ถือ
hole roo
รู
holiday wun yÒOt
วันหยุด
on holiday yÒOt púk pòrn
หยุดพักผ่อน

Holland bpra-tâyt hor-lairn
ประเทศฮอลแลนด์
home bâhn
บ้าน
at home (in my house etc) têe bâhn
ที่บ้าน
(in my country) nai bpra-tâyt pŏm (chún)
ในประเทศผม(ฉัน)
we go home tomorrow (to country) rao glùp bâhn prÔOng née
เรากลับบ้านพรุ่งนี้
honest sêu dtrong
ซื่อตรง
honey núm pêung
น้ำผึ้ง
honeymoon hun-nee-moon
ฮันนีมูน
hood (US: car) gra-bprohng rót
กระโปรงรถ
hope wŭng
หวัง
I hope so wŭng wâh yung ngún
หวังว่าอย่างนั้น
I hope not wŭng wâh kông mâi
หวังว่าคงไม่
hopefully wŭng wâh ...
หวังว่า ...

horn (of car) dtrair
แตร
horrible nâh glèe-ut
น่าเกลียด
horse máh
ม้า
horse riding kèe máh
ขี่ม้า
hospital rohng pa-yah-bahn
โรงพยาบาล
hospitality gahn dtôrn rúp kùp sôo
การต้อนรับขับสู้
thank you for your hospitality kòrp-kOOn têe dtôrn rúp kùp sôo
ขอบคุณที่ตอนรับขับสู้
hostess (in bar) pôo-yǐng bah
ผู้หญิงบาร์
hot rórn
ร้อน
(spicy) pèt
เผ็ด
I'm hot pǒm (chún) rórn
ผม(ฉัน)ร้อน
it's hot today wun née ah-gàht rórn jung ler-ee
วันนี้อากาศร้อนจังเลย
hotel rohng rairm
โรงแรม
hotel room hôrng nai rohng rairm
ห้องในโรงแรม
hour chôo-a mohng
ชั่วโมง
house bâhn
บ้าน
how? yung-ngai?
อย่างไร
how many? gèe?
กี่
how do you do? sa-wùt dee krúp (kâ)
สวัสดีครับ(ค่ะ)

dialogues

how are you? bpen yung-ngai bâhng?
fine, thanks, and you?
sa-bai dee krúp (kâ) láir-o kOOn lâ?

how much is it?
tâo-rài?
50 baht hâh sìp baht
I'll take it ao

humid chéun
ชื้น
hungry hěw kâo
หิวข้าว
are you hungry? hěw kâo

mái?
หิวข้าวไหม

hurry (verb) rêep
รีบ

I'm in a hurry pŏm (chún) dtôrng rêep
ผม(ฉัน)ต้องรีบ

there's no hurry mâi dtôrng rêep
ไม่ต้องรีบ

hurry up! ray-o ray-o kâo!
เร็ว ๆ เข้า

hurt (verb) jèp
เจ็บ

it really hurts jèp jing jing
เจ็บจริง ๆ

husband săh-mee
สามี

I

I* (male) pŏm
ผม
(female) chún; dee-chún
ฉัน; ดิฉัน

ice núm kăirng
น้ำแข็ง

with ice sài núm kăirng
ใส่น้ำแข็ง

no ice, thanks mâi sài núm kăirng
ไม่ใส่น้ำแข็ง

ice cream ait-greem
ไอศกรีม

ice-cream cone groo-ay sài ait-greem
กรวยใส่ไอศกรีม

iced coffee gah-fair yen
กาแฟเย็น

ice lolly ait-greem tâirng
ไอศครีมแท่ง

idea kwahm kít
ความคิด

idiot kon bâh
คนบ้า

if tâh
ถ้า

ignition fai krêu-ung yon
ไฟเครื่องยนตร์

ill mâi sa-bai
ไม่สบาย

I feel ill pŏm (chún) mâi sa-bai
ผม(ฉัน)ไม่สบาย

illness kwahm jèp bpòo-ay
ความเจ็บป่วย

imitation (leather etc) tee-um
เทียม

immediately tun-tee
ทันที

important sŭm-kun
สำคัญ

it's very important sŭm-kun mâhk
สำคัญมาก
it's not important mâi sŭm-kun
ไม่สำคัญ
impossible bpen bpai mâi dâi
เป็นไปไม่ได้
impressive nâh têung
น่าทึ่ง
improve dee kêun
ดีขึ้น
I want to improve my Thai pŏm (chún) yàhk ja pôot pah-săh tai hâi dee kêun
ผม(ฉัน)อยากจะพูดภาษาไทยให้ดีขึ้น
in: it's in the centre nai jai glahng meu-ung
ในใจกลางเมือง
in my car nai rót pŏm (chún)
ในรถผม(ฉัน)
in Chiangmai têe chee-ung-mài
ที่เชียงใหม่
in two days from now èek sŏrng wun dtòr jàhk née
อีกสองวันต่อจากนี้
in five minutes èek hâh nah-tee
อีกห้านาที
in May deu-un préut-sa-pah-kom
เดือนพฤษภาคม
in English bpen pah-săh ung-grìt
เป็นภาษาอังกฤษ
in Thai bpen pah-săh tai
เป็นภาษาไทย
is he in? káo **yòo** mái?
เขาอยู่ไหม
inch* néw
นิ้ว
include roo-um
รวม
does that include meals? roo-um ah-hăhn dôo-ay rĕu bplào?
รวมอาหารด้วยหรือเปล่า
is that included? roo-um yòo dôo-ay rĕu bplào?
รวมอยู่ด้วยหรือเปล่า
inconvenient mâi sa-dòo-uk
ไม่สะดวก
incredible mâi nâh chêu-a
ไม่น่าเชื่อ
India bpra-tâyt in-dee-a
ประเทศอินเดีย
Indian (adj) kàirk
แขก
indicator (on car) fai lée-o
ไฟเลี้ยว
indigestion ah-hăhn mâi yôy
อาหารไม่ย่อย

Indonesia bpra-tâyt in-doh-nee-see-a
ประเทศอินโดนีเซีย
indoors kâhng nai
ข้างใน
inexpensive mâi pairng, tòok
ไม่แพง, ถูก
infection ah-gahn ùk-sàyp
อาการอักเสบ
infectious rôhk dtìt dtòr
โรคติดต่อ
inflammation ah-gahn bpòo-ut boo-um
อาการปวดบวม
informal bpen gun ayng
เป็นกันเอง
information kào-săhn
ข่าวสาร
do you have any information about ...? mee **rai la-èe-ut** gèe-o gùp ... mái?
มีรายละเอียดเกี่ยวกับ ... ไหม
information desk têe sòrp tăhm
ที่สอบถาม
injection chèet yah
ฉีดยา
injured bàht jèp
บาดเจ็บ
she's been injured káo bàht jèp
เขาบาดเจ็บ
inner tube (for tyre) yahng nai
ยางใน
innocent bor-ri-sòot
บริสุทธ์
insect ma-lairng
แมลง
insect bite ma-lairng gùt
แมลงกัด
do you have anything for insect bites? mee yah tah gâir ma-lairng gùt mái?
มียาทาแก้แมลงกัดไหม
insect repellent yah gun ma-lairng
ยากันแมลง
inside kâhng nai
ข้างใน
inside the hotel kâhng nai rohng rairm
ข้างในโรงแรม
let's sit inside bpai nûng kâhng nai tèr
ไปนั่งข้างในเถอะ
insist ka-yún ka-yor
คะยั้นคะยอ
I insist pŏm (chún) ka-yún ka-yor
ผม(ฉัน)คะยั้นคะยอ
insomnia norn mâi lùp
นอนไม่หลับ
instant coffee gah-fair pŏng
กาแฟผง

instead tairn
แทน
give me that one instead ao un nún tairn
เอาอันนั้นแทน
instead of ... tairn têe ja ...
แทนที่จะ ...
insulin in-soo-lin
อินซูลิน
insurance gahn bpra-gun pai
การประกันภัย
intelligent cha-làht
ฉลาด
interested: I'm interested in ... pŏm (chún) sŏn jai ...
ผม(ฉัน)สนใจ ...
interesting nâh sŏn jai
น่าสนใจ
that's very interesting nâh sŏn jai mâhk
น่าสนใจมาก
international săh-gon
สากล
interpret bplair
แปล
interpreter lâhm
ล่าม
intersection sèe yâirk
สี่แยก
interval (at theatre) púk krêung
พักครึ่ง
into nai
ใน
I'm not into ... pŏm (chún) mâi chôrp ...
ผม(ฉัน)ไม่ชอบ ...
introduce náir-num
แนะนำ
may I introduce ...? pŏm (chún) kŏr náir-num hâi róo-jùk gùp ...
ผม(ฉัน)ขอแนะนำให้รู้จักกับ ...
invitation kum chern
คำเชิญ
invite chern choo-un
เชิญชวน
Ireland ai-lairn
ไอร์แลนด์
iron (for ironing) dtao rêet
เตารีด
can you iron these for me? chôo-ay **rêet** hâi nòy dâi mái?
ช่วยรีดให้หน่อยได้ไหม
is* bpen
เป็น
island gòr
เกาะ
it mun
มัน
it is ... bpen ...
เป็น ...
is it ...? ... châi mái?
... ใช่ไหม

where is it? yòo têe năi?
อยู่ที่ไหน
it's him káo nûn lâir
เขานั่นแหละ
it was ... bpen ...
เป็น ...
Italy bpra-tâyt
ì-dtah-lee
ประเทศอิตาลี
itch: it itches kun
คัน

J

jack (for car) mâir rairng
แม่แรง
jacket sêu-a nôrk
เสื้อนอก
jam yairm
แยม
jammed: it's jammed mun dtìt
nâirn
มันติดแน่น
January mók-ga-rah-kom
มกราคม
Japan yêe-bpòOn
ญี่ปุ่น
Japanese yêe-bpòOn
ญี่ปุ่น
jar (noun) hăi
ไห
jaw kăh-gun-grai
ขากรรไกร
jazz jáirt
แจ๊ส
jealous hĕung
หึง
jeans yeen
ยีนส์
jellyfish mairng ga-prOOn
แมงกะพรุน
jersey sêu-a sa-wét-dtêr
เสื้อสเวตเตอร์
jetty tâh reu-a
ท่าเรือ
jeweller's ráhn kăi krêu-ung
pét ploy
ร้านขายเครื่องเพชรพลอย
jewellery pét ploy
เพชรพลอย
Jewish yew
ยิว
job ngahn
งาน
jogging jórk-gîng
จ๊อกกิ้ง
to go jogging bpai
jórk-gîng
ไปจ๊อกกิ้ง
joke dta-lòk
ตลก
journey gahn dern tahng
การเดินทาง

have a good journey! dern tahng dôo-ay dee ná!
เดินทางด้วยดีนะ

jug yèu-uk
เหยือก

a jug of water yèu-uk náhm
เหยือกน้ำ

juice náhm pŏn-la-mái
น้ำผลไม้

July ga-rúk-ga-dah-kom
กรกฎาคม

jump (verb) gra-dòht
กระโดด

jumper sêu-a sa-wét-dtêr
เสื้อสเวตเตอร์

junction tahng yâirk
ทางแยก

June mí-too-nah-yon
มิถุนายน

jungle bpàh
ป่า

just (only) tâo-nún
เท่านั้น

just two sŏrng un tâo-nún
สองอันเท่านั้น

just for me sŭm-rùp pŏm (chún) **kon dee-o**
สำหรับผม(ฉัน)คนเดียว

just here dtrong née
ตรงนี้

not just now mâi ao dĕe-o née
ไม่เอาเดี๋ยวนี้

we've just arrived rao **pêrng** mah mêu-a gêe née ayng
เราเพิ่งมาเมื่อกี้นี้เอง

K

keep gèp
เก็บ

keep the change mâi dtôrng torn
ไม่ต้องทอน

can I keep it? pŏm (chún) gèp wái dâi mái?
ผม(ฉัน)เก็บไว้ได้ไหม

please keep it ao wái ler-ee
เอาไว้เลย

ketchup sórt ma-kĕu-a tâyt
ซอสมะเขือเทศ

kettle gah náhm
กาน้ำ

key goon-jair
กุญแจ

the key for room 201, please kŏr goon-jair hôrng sŏrng sŏon sèe
ขอกุญแจห้องสองศูนย์สี่

keyring hòo-ung goon-jair
หวงกุญแจ

kidneys (in body) dtai
ไต

(food) krêu-ung nai
เครื่องใน

kill kâh
ฆ่า

kilo* gi-loh
กิโล

kilometre* gi-loh-mét
กิโลเมตร

how many kilometres is it to ...? bpai ... gèe gi-loh?
ไป ... กี่กิโล

kind (generous) jai dee
ใจดี

that's very kind koon jai dee mâhk
คุณใจดีมาก

dialogue

which kind do you want? ao bàirp năi?
I want this/that kind ao bàirp née/nún

king nai lŏo-ung
ในหลวง

kiosk dtôo
ตู้

kiss jòop
จูบ

kitchen hôrng kroo-a
ห้องครัว

knee hŏo-a kào
หัวเข่า

knickers gahng gayng nai sa-dtree
กางเกงในสตรี

knife mêet
มีด

knock (verb) kór
เคาะ

knock down (road accident) rót chon
รถชน

he's been knocked down káo tòok rót chon
เขาถูกรถชน

knock over (object, pedestrian) chon lóm
ชนล้ม

know (somebody) róo-jùk
รู้จัก

(something) róo; (formal) sâhp
รู้; ทราบ

(a place) róo-jùk
รู้จัก

I don't know pŏm (chún) mâi róo/sâhp
ผม(ฉัน)ไม่รู้/ทราบ

I didn't know that pŏm (chún) mâi róo/sâhp mah gòrn
ผม(ฉัน)ไม่รู้/ทราบมาก่อน

do you know where I can find ...? sâhp mái wâh ja hăh

... dâi têe năi?
ทราบไหมว่าจะหา ... ได้ที่ไหน

L

label bpâi
ป้าย
ladies' (room) sa-dtree
สตรี
ladies' wear krêu-ung dtàirng gai sa-dtree
เครื่องแต่งกายสตรี
lady pôo-yĭng
ผู้หญิง
lager lah-ger
ลาเกอร์
lake ta-lay sàhp
ทะเลสาบ
lamb (meat) néu-a gàir
เนื้อแกะ
lamp kohm fai fáh
โคมไฟฟ้า
lane (motorway) chôrng
ช่อง
(small road) soy
ซอย
language pah-săh
ภาษา
language course bàirp ree-un pah-săh
แบบเรียนภาษา
Laos bpra-tâyt lao
ประเทศลาว
large yài
ใหญ่
last sòot tái
สุดท้าย
last week mêu-a ah-tít **gòrn**
เมื่ออาทิตย์ก่อน
last Friday mêu-a wun sòok **gòrn**
เมื่อวันศุกร์ก่อน
last night mêu-a keun née
เมื่อคืนนี้
what time is the last train to Ubon? rót fai bpai oo-bon têe-o sòot tái òrk gèe mohng?
รถไฟไปอุบลเที่ยวสุดท้ายออกกี่โมง
late cháh
ช้า
sorry I'm late kŏr-tôht têe mah **cháh**
ขอโทษที่มาช้า
the train was late rót fai mah tĕung **cháh**
รถไฟมาถึงช้า
we must go – we'll be late rao dtôrng bpai dĕe-o ja **mâi tun**
เราต้องไป เดี๋ยวจะไม่ทัน
it's getting late dèuk láir-o
ดึกแล้ว

later tee lŭng
ทีหลัง
I'll come back later dĕe-o ja glùp mah
เดี๋ยวจะกลับมา
see you later dĕe-o jer gun èek
เดี๋ยวเจอกันอีก
later on tee lŭng
ทีหลัง

latest yàhng cháh têe sòot
อย่างช้าที่สุด
by Wednesday at the latest wun póot yàhng cháh têe sòot
วันพุธอย่างช้าที่สุด

laugh (verb) hŏo-a rór
หัวเราะ

laundry (clothes) sêu-a pâh
เสื้อผ้า
(place) ráhn súk pâh
ร้านซักผ้า

lavatory hôrng náhm
ห้องน้ำ

law gòt-măi
กฎหมาย

lawn sa-năhm yâh
สนามหญ้า

lawyer ta-nai kwahm
ทนายความ

laxative yah tài
ยาถ่าย

lazy kêe gèe-ut
ขี้เกียจ

lead (electrical) săi fai fáh
สายไฟฟ้า
(verb) num
นำ
where does this lead to? nêe bpai tĕung năi?
นี่ไปถึงไหน

leaf bai mái
ใบไม้

leaflet bai bplew
ใบปลิว

leak rôo-a
รั่ว
the roof leaks lŭng-kah rôo-a
หลังคารั่ว

learn ree-un
เรียน

least: not in the least mâi ler-ee
ไม่เลย
at least yàhng nóy têe sòot
อย่างน้อยที่สุด

leather nŭng
หนัง

leave (verb: behind) tíng wái
ทิ้งไว้
(go away) jàhk bpai
จากไป
I am leaving tomorrow pŏm

(chún) **bpai** prôong née
ผม(ฉัน)ไปพรุ่งนี้
he left yesterday káo **bpai** mêu-a wahn née
เขาไปเมื่อวานนี้
may I leave this here? kŏr **fàhk** wái têe nêe dâi mái?
ขอฝากไว้ที่นี่ได้ไหม
I left my coat in the bar pŏm (chún) **tíng** sêu-a wái têe bah
ผม(ฉัน)ทิ้งเสื้อไว้ที่บาร์
when does the bus for Bangsaen leave? rót bpai bahng-săirn **òrk** gèe mohng?
รถไปบางแสนออกกี่โมง

left sái
ซ้าย
on the left tahng sái
ทางซ้าย
to the left tahng sái
ทางซ้าย
turn left lée-o sái
เลี้ยวซ้าย
there's none left mâi mee **lĕu-a yòo**
ไม่มีเหลืออยู่

left-handed ta-nùt meu sái
ถนัดมือซ้าย

left luggage (office) têe fàhk gra-bpăo
ที่ฝากกระเป๋า

leg kăh
ขา

lemon ma-nao
มะนาว

lemonade núm ma-nao
น้ำมะนาว

lemon tea núm chah sài ma-nao
น้ำชาใส่มะนาว

lend: will you lend me your ... ? kŏr yeum ... nòy, dâi mái?
ขอยืม ... หน่อยได้ไหม

lens (of camera) layn
เลนซ์

lesbian 'lesbian'
เล็สเบียน

less nóy gwàh
น้อยกว่า
less than ... nóy gwàh ...
น้อยกว่า ...
less expensive tòok gwàh
ถูกกว่า

lesson bòt ree-un
บทเรียน

let (allow) hâi
ให้
will you let me know? chôo-ay bòrk hâi pŏm (chún) sâhp dôo-ay
ช่วยบอกให้ผม(ฉัน)ทราบด้วย
I'll let you know pŏm (chún)

ja bòrk hâi sâhp
ผม(ฉัน)จะบอกให้ทราบ
let's go for something to eat bpai tahn kâo mái?
ไปทานข้าวไหม
let off: will you let me off at ...? kŏr long têe ... dâi mái?
ขอลงที่ ... ได้ไหม
letter jòt-măi
จดหมาย
do you have any letters for me? mee jòt-măi mah tĕung pŏm (chún) mái?
มีจดหมายมาถึงผม(ฉัน)ไหม
letterbox dtôo jòt-măi
ตู้จดหมาย
lettuce pùk-gàht
ผักกาด
lever (noun) kun yók
คันยก
library hŏr sa-mòot
หอสมุด
licence bai un-nóo-yâht
ใบอนุญาต
lid făh
ฝา
lie (verb: tell untruth) goh-hòk
โกหก
lie down norn
นอน
life chee-wít
ชีวิต
lifebelt choo chêep
ชูชีพ
life jacket sêu-a choo chêep
เสื้อชูชีพ
lift (in building) líf
ลิฟท์
could you give me a lift? chôo-ay bpai sòng nòy, dâi mái?
ช่วยไปส่งหน่อยได้ไหม
would you like a lift? bpai sòng hâi ao mái?
ไปส่งให้เอาไหม
light (noun) fai
ไฟ
(not heavy) bao
เบา
do you have a light? (for cigarette) mee fai mái?
มีไฟไหม
light green sĕe kĕe-o òrn
สีเขียวอ่อน
light bulb lòrt fai fáh
หลอดไฟฟ้า
I need a new light bulb pŏm (chún) dtôrng-gahn lòrt fai fáh
ผม(ฉัน)ต้องการหลอดไฟฟ้า
lighter (cigarette) fai cháirk
ไฟแช็ก
lightning fáh lâirp
ฟ้าแลบ

like (verb) chôrp
ชอบ
I like it pŏm (chún) chôrp
ผม(ฉัน)ชอบ
I like going for walks pŏm (chún) chôrp bpai dern lên
ผม(ฉัน)ชอบไปเดินเล่น
I like you pŏm (chún) chôrp koon
ผม(ฉัน)ชอบคุณ
I don't like it pŏm (chún) mâi chôrp
ผม(ฉัน)ไม่ชอบ
do you like ...? koon chôrp ... mái?
คุณชอบ ...ไหม
I'd like a beer pŏm (chún) **ao** bee-a kòo-ut nèung
ผม(ฉัน)เอาเบียร์ขวดหนึ่ง
I'd like to go swimming pŏm (chún) **yàhk** bpai wâi náhm
ผม(ฉัน)อยากไปว่ายน้ำ
would you like a drink? koon dèum a-rai mái?
คุณดื่มอะไรไหม
would you like to go for a walk? koon **yàhk** bpai dern lên mái?
คุณอยากไปเดินเล่นไหม
what's it like? bpen **yung ngai**?
เป็นอย่างไร
I want one like this ao **bàirp née**
เอาแบบนี้
lime ma-nao
มะนาว
line (on paper) sên
เส้น
(phone) săi
สาย
could you give me an outside line? chôo-ay dtòr săi kâhng nôrk hâi nòy, dâi mái?
ช่วยต่อสายข้างนอกให้หน่อยได้ไหม
lips rim fĕe bpàhk
ริมฝีปาก
lip salve kêe pêung tah rim fĕe bpàhk
ขี้ผึ้งทาริมฝีปาก
lipstick líp sa-dtík
ลิปสติก
listen fung
ฟัง
litre* lít
ลิตร
little lék
เล็ก
just a little, thanks nít dee-o nít dee-o tâo-nún
นิดเดียวเท่านั้น
a little milk nom nít nòy
นมนิดหน่อย

a little bit more èek nít nèung
อีกนิดหนึ่ง

live (verb) mee chee-wít yòo
มีชีวิตอยู่

we live together rao yòo dôo-ay gun
เราอยู่ด้วยกัน

dialogue

where do you live? koon yòo têe năi?
I live in London pŏm (chún) yòo têe lorn-dorn

lively (person, town) mee chee-wít chee-wah
มีชีวิตชีวา

liver (in body, food) dtùp
ตับ

loaf bporn
ปอนด์

lobby (in hotel) pa-nàirk dtôrn rúp
แผนกต้อนรับ

lobster gôong yài
กุ้งใหญ่

local tăir-o née
แถวนี้

can you recommend a local restaurant? chôo-ay náir-num ráhn ah-hăhn tăir-o née hâi nòy dâi mái?
ช่วยแนะนำร้านอาหารแถวนี้ให้หน่อยได้ไหม

lock (noun) goon-jair
กุญแจ

(verb) sài goon-jair
ใส่กุญแจ

it's locked sài goon-jair láir-o
ใส่กุญแจแล้ว

lock out: I've locked myself out bpìt goon-jair láir-o kâo hôrng mâi dâi
ปิดกุญแจแล้วเข้าห้องไม่ได้

locker (for luggage etc) dtôo
ตู้

lollipop om-yím
อมยิ้ม

London lorn-dorn
ลอนดอน

long yao
ยาว

how long will it take to fix it? chái way-lah sôrm **nahn** tâo-rài?
ใช้เวลาซ่อมนานเท่าไร

how long does it take? chái way-lah **nahn** tâo-rài?
ใช้เวลานานเท่าไร

a long time nahn
นาน

one day/two days longer èek wun sŏrng wun
อีกวันสองวัน
long-distance call toh tahng glai
โทรทางไกล
long-tailed boat reu-a hăhng yao
เรือหางยาว
look: I'm just looking, thanks pŏm (chún) chom doo tâo-nún
ผม(ฉัน)ชมดูเท่านั้น
you don't look well koon tâh tahng mâi sa-bai
คุณท่าทางไม่สบาย
look out! ra-wung ná!
ระวังนะ
can I have a look? kŏr doo nòy, dâi mái?
ขอดูหน่อยได้ไหม
look after doo lair
ดูแล
look at doo
ดู
look for hăh
หา
I'm looking for ... pŏm (chún) gum-lung hăh ...
ผม(ฉัน)กำลังหา ...
loose (handle etc) lòot
หลุด
lorry rót bun-tóok
รถบรรทุก
lose hăi
หาย
I've lost my way pŏm (chún) lŏng tahng
ผม(ฉัน)หลงทาง
I'm lost, I want to get to ... pŏm (chún) lŏng tahng, dtôrng-gahn bpai ...
ผม(ฉัน)หลงทาง ต้องการไป ...
I've lost my bag gra-bpăo pŏm (chún) hăi
กระเป๋าผม(ฉัน)หาย
lost property (office) têe jâirng kŏrng hăi
ที่แจ้งของหาย
lot: a lot, lots mâhk
มาก
not a lot mâi mâhk
ไม่มาก
a lot of people kon mâhk
คนมาก
a lot bigger yài mâhk gwàh
ใหญ่มากกว่า
I like it a lot pŏm (chún) chôrp mâhk
ผม(ฉัน)ชอบมาก
lotion yah tah
ยาทา
loud dung
ดัง

lounge (in house, hotel) hôrng nûng lên
ห้องนั่งเล่น
(in airport) hôrng púk pôo doy-ee săhn
ห้องพักผู้โดยสาร
love (noun) kwahm rúk
ความรัก
(verb) rúk
รัก
I love Thailand pŏm (chún) rúk meu-ung tai
ผม(ฉัน)รักเมืองไทย
lovely sŏo-ay
สวย
low (prices, bridge) dtùm
ต่ำ
luck chôhk
โชค
good luck! chôhk dee!
โชคดี
luggage gra-bpăo
กระเป๋า
luggage trolley rót kĕn
รถเข็น
lump (on body) néu-a ngôrk
เนื้องอก
lunch ah-hăhn glahng wun
อาหารกลางวัน
lungs bpòrt
ปอด
luxurious (hotel, furnishings) rŏo-răh
หรูหรา
luxury kŏrng fôom feu-ay
ของฟุ่มเฟือย

M

machine krêu-ung
เครื่อง
mad (insane) bâh
บ้า
(angry) gròht
โกรธ
magazine nít-ta-ya-sàhn
นิตยสาร
maid (in hotel) yĭng rúp chái
หญิงรับใช้
maiden name nahm sa-goon derm
นามสกุลเดิม
mail (noun) jòt-măi
จดหมาย
(verb) sòng jòt-măi
ส่งจดหมาย
is there any mail for me? mee jòt-măi sŭm-rùp pŏm (chún) mái?
มีจดหมายสำหรับผม(ฉัน)ไหม
mailbox dtôo jòt-măi
ตู้จดหมาย

main sŭm-kun
สำคัญ
main post office bprai-sa-nee glahng
ไปรษณีย์กลาง
main road ta-nŏn yài
ถนนใหญ่
mains switch (for electricity) sa-wít săi fai yài
สวิชสายไฟใหญ่
make (brand name) yêe hôr
ยี่ห้อ
(verb) tum
ทำ
I make it 500 baht pŏm (chún) kít wâh hâh róy bàht
ผม(ฉัน)คิดว่าห้าร้อยบาท
what is it made of? tum dôo-ay a-rai?
ทำด้วยอะไร
make-up krêu-ung sŭm-ahng
เครื่องสำอาง
malaria kâi jùp sùn, mah-lay-ree-a
ไข้จับสั่น, มาเลเรีย
malaria tablets yah gâir mah-lay-ree-a
ยาแก้มาเลเรีย
Malay (adj) ma-lah-yoo
มลายู
Malaysia bpra-tâyt mah-lay-see-a
ประเทศมาเลเซีย
man pôo-chai
ผู้ชาย
manager pôo-jùt-gahn
ผู้จัดการ
can I see the manager? kŏr póp pôo-jùt-gahn nòy
ขอพบผู้จัดการหน่อย
mango ma-môo-ung
มะม่วง
many mâhk
มาก
not many mâi mâhk
ไม่มาก
map păirn-têe
แผนที่
March mee-nah-kom
มีนาคม
margarine ner-ee tee-um
เนยเทียม
market dta-làht
ตลาด
marmalade yairm
แยม
married: I'm married pŏm (chún) dtàirng ngahn láir-o
ผม(ฉัน)แต่งงานแล้ว
are you married? kOon dtàirng ngahn láir-o rĕu yung?
คุณแต่งงานแล้วหรือยัง

mascara mair-sa-kah-rah
แมสคารา
massage nôo-ut
นวด
match (football etc) gahn kàirng kǔn
การแข่งขัน
matches mái kèet
ไม้ขีด
material (fabric) pâh
ผ้า
matter: it doesn't matter mâi bpen rai
ไม่เป็นไร
what's the matter? bpen a-rai?
เป็นอะไร
mattress têe norn
ที่นอน
May préut-sa-pah-kom
พฤษภาคม
may: may I have another one? kŏr èek un nèung **dâi mái**?
ขออีกอันหนึ่งได้ไหม
may I come in? kâo mah **dâi mái**?
เข้ามาได้ไหม
may I see it? kŏr doo nòy **dâi mái**?
ขอดูหน่อยได้ไหม
may I sit here? nûng têe nêe **dâi mái**?
นั่งที่นี่ได้ไหม
maybe bahng tee
บางที
mayonnaise núm sa-lùt
น้ำสลัด
me* (male) pŏm
ผม
(female) dee-chún, chún
ดิฉัน, ฉัน
that's for me nûn sŭm-rùp pŏm (chún)
นั่นสำหรับผม(ฉัน)
send it to me sòng mah hâi pŏm (chún)
ส่งมาให้ผม(ฉัน)
me too pŏm (chún) gôr mĕu-un gun
ผม(ฉัน)ก็เหมือนกัน
meal ah-hăhn
อาหาร

dialogue

did you enjoy your meal?
ah-hăhn a-ròy mái?
it was excellent, thank you
a-ròy mâhk

mean (verb) măi kwahm
หมายความ
what do you mean? kOOn

măi kwahm wâh a-rai?
คุณหมายความว่าอะไร

dialogue

what does this word mean? kum née **bplàir wâh** a-rai?
it means ... in English pah-săh ung-grìt **bplair wâh** ...

measles rôhk hùt
โรคหัด

meat néu-a
เนื้อ

mechanic châhng krêu-ung
ช่างเครื่อง

medicine yah
ยา

medium (adj: size) glahng
กลาง

medium-rare (steak) sòok sòok dìp dìp
สุกๆดิบๆ

medium-sized ka-nàht glahng
ขนาดกลาง

meet (verb) póp
พบ

nice to meet you yin dee têe dâi róo-jùk gun
ยินดีที่ได้รู้จักกัน

where shall I meet you? póp gun têe năi?
พบกันที่ไหน

meeting bpra-chOOm
ประชุม

meeting place têe nút póp
ที่นัดพบ

melon dtairng tai
แตงไทย

men pôo-chai
ผู้ชาย

mend sôrm
ซ่อม

could you mend this for me?
kOOn sôrm hâi dâi mái?
คุณซ่อมให้ได้ไหม

men's room boo-ròot
บุรุษ

menswear krêu-ung dtàirng gai boo-ròot
เครื่องแต่งกายบุรุษ

mention (verb) glào tĕung
กล่าวถึง

don't mention it mâi bpen rai
ไม่เป็นไร

menu may-noo
เมนู

may I see the menu, please?
kŏr doo may-noo nòy krúp (kâ)
ขอดูเมนูหน่อยครับ(คะ)

see Menu Reader page 246

message kào
ข่าว
are there any messages for me? mee krai sùng a-rai wái rěu bplào?
มีใครสั่งอะไรไว้หรือเปล่า
I want to leave a message for ... pǒm (chún) yàhk ja fàhk bòrk a-rai hâi ...
ผม(ฉัน)อยากจะฝากบอกอะไรให้ ...
metal (noun) lŏh-hà
โลหะ
metre* mét
เมตร
midday têe-ung wun
เที่ยงวัน
at midday têe-ung wun
เที่ยงวัน
middle: in the middle yòo dtrong glahng
อยู่ตรงกลาง
in the middle of the night dtorn glahng keun
ตอนกลางคืน
the middle one un glahng
อันกลาง
midnight têe-ung keun
เที่ยงคืน
at midnight têe-ung keun
เที่ยงคืน

might: I might ... bahng tee pǒm (chún) àht ja ...
บางทีผม(ฉัน)อาจจะ ...
I might not ... bahng tee pǒm (chún) àht ja mâi ...
บางทีผม(ฉัน)อาจจะไม่ ...
I might want to stay another day bahng tee pǒm (chún) àht ja yòo èek wun nèung
บางทีผม(ฉัน)อาจจะอยู่อีกวันหนึ่ง
migraine bpòo-ut hŏo-a kâhng dee-o
ปวดหัวข้างเดียว
mild (taste) mâi pèt
ไม่เผ็ด
mile* mai
ไมล์
milk nom
นม
millimetre* min-li-mét
มิลลิเมตร
minced meat néu-a sùp
เนื้อสับ
mind: never mind mâi bpen rai
ไม่เป็นไร
I've changed my mind pǒm (chún) bplèe-un jai láir-o
ผม(ฉัน)เปลี่ยนใจแล้ว

dialogue

do you mind if I open the window? kŏr bpèrt nâh-dtàhng nòy, dâi mái?
no, I don't mind dâi

mine*: it's mine kŏrng pŏm (chún)
ของผม(ฉัน)

mineral water núm râir
น้ำแร่

minute nah-tee
นาที

in a minute èek bpra-dĕe-o
อีกประเดี๋ยว

just a minute dĕe-o, dĕe-o
เดี๋ยว ๆ

mirror gra-jòk ngao
กระจกเงา

Miss nahng-săo
นางสาว

miss: I missed the bus pŏm (chún) dtòk rót may
ผม(ฉัน)ตกรถเมล์

missing hăi bpai
หายไป

one of my ... is missing kŏng pŏm (chún) hăi bpai ...
ของผม(ฉัน)หายไป ...

there's a suitcase missing mee gra-bpăo hăi bpai
มีกระเป๋าหายไป

mist mòrk
หมอก

mistake (noun) kwahm pìt
ความผิด

I think there's a mistake pŏm (chún) kít wâh mee kôr pìt lék nóy
ผม(ฉัน)คิดว่ามีข้อผิดเล็กน้อย

sorry, I've made a mistake kŏr-tôht, pŏm (chún) tum pìt
ขอโทษผม(ฉัน)ทำผิด

misunderstanding kwahm kâo jai pìt
ความเข้าใจผิด

mix-up: sorry, there's been a mix-up kŏr-tôht, mee kwahm kâo jai pìt
ขอโทษ มีความเข้าใจผิด

mobile phone toh-ra-sùp rái săi
โทรศัพท์ไร้สาย

modern tun sa-măi
ทันสมัย

moisturizer kreem bum-roong pĕw
ครีมบำรุงผิว

moment: I won't be a moment ror dĕe-o
รอเดี๋ยว

monastery wút
วัด
Monday wun jun
วันจันทร์
money ngern
เงิน
monk prá
พระ
monsoon mor-ra-sŏom
มรสุม
month deu-un
เดือน
monument a-noo-sàh-wa-ree
อนุสาวรีย์
moon prá-jun
พระจันทร์
moped rót mor-dter-sai
รถมอร์เตอร์ไซค์
more* èek
อีก
can I have some more water, please? kŏr náhm èek nòy krúp (kâ)
ขอน้ำอีกหน่อยครับ(ค่ะ)
more expensive/interesting pairng/nâh sŏn jai gwàh
แพง/น่าสนใจกว่า
more than 50 hâh sìp gwàh
ห้าสิบกว่า
more than that mâhk gwàh nún
มากกว่านั้น
a lot more èek mâhk
อีกมาก

dialogue

would you like some more? ao èek mái?
no, no more for me, thanks por láir-o, kòrp-koon krúp (kâ)
how about you? láir-o koon lâ?
I don't want any more, thanks por láir-o krúp (kâ)

morning dtorn cháo
ตอนเช้า
this morning cháo née
เช้านี้
in the morning dtorn cháo
ตอนเช้า
mosquito yoong
ยุง
mosquito net móong
มุ้ง
mosquito repellent yah gun yoong
ยากันยุง
most: I like this one most of all pŏm (chún) chôrp un née **mâhk têe sòot**
ผม(ฉัน)ชอบอันนี้มากที่สุด

most of the time sòo-un mâhk
ส่วนมาก
most tourists núk tôrng têe-o **sòo-un mâhk**
นักท่องเที่ยวส่วนมาก
mostly sòo-un mâhk
ส่วนมาก
mother mâir
แม่
mother-in-law (of a man) mâir yai
แม่ยาย
(of a woman) mâir pŏo-a
แม่ผัว
motorbike rót mor-dter-sai
รถมอร์เตอร์ไซค์
motorboat reu-a yon
เรือยนตร์
motorway tahng dòo-un
ทางด่วน
mountain poo-kăo
ภูเขา
in the mountains nai poo-kăo
ในภูเขา
mouse nŏo
หนู
moustache nòo-ut
หนวด
mouth bpàhk
ปาก
mouth ulcer plăir nai bpàhk
แผลในปาก
move: he's moved to another room káo **yái** bpai yòo èek hôrng nèung
เขาย้ายไปอยู่อีกห้องหนึ่ง
could you move your car? chôo-ay **lêu-un** rót kŏrng kOOn, dâi mái?
ช่วยเลื่อนรถของคุณได้ไหม
could you move up a little? **chít nai** nòy dâi mái?
ชิดในหน่อยได้ไหม
where has it moved to? (shop, restaurant etc) **yái** bpai yòo têe năi?
ย้ายไปอยู่ที่ไหน
movie nŭng
หนัง
movie theater rohng nŭng
โรงหนัง
Mr nai
นาย
Mrs nahng
นาง
much mâhk
มาก
much better/worse dee/yâir mâhk gwàh
ดี/แย่มากกว่า
much hotter rórn mâhk gwàh
ร้อนมากกว่า

not much mâi mâhk
ไม่มาก
not very much mâi kôy mâhk
ไม่ค่อยมาก
I don't want very much pŏm (chún) mâi ao mâhk
ผม(ฉัน)ไม่เอามาก
mud klohn
โคลน
mug: I've been mugged pŏm (chún) tòok jêe
ผม(ฉัน)ถูกจี้
mum mâir
แม่
mumps kahng toom
คางทูม
museum pí-pít-ta-pun
พิพิธภัณฑ์
mushrooms hèt
เห็ด
music don-dtree
ดนตรี
musician núk don-dtree
นักดนตรี
Muslim (adj) ì-sa-lahm
อิสลาม
mussels hŏy mairng pôo
หอยแมงภู่
must*: I must pŏm (chún) dtôrng
ผม(ฉัน)ต้อง
I mustn't drink alcohol pŏm (chún) dtôrng mâi gin lâo
ผม(ฉัน)ต้องไม่กินเหล้า
mustard núm jîm mut-sa-dtàht
น้ำจิ้มมัสตาด
my* kŏrng pŏm (chún)
ของผม(ฉัน)
myself: I'll do it myself pŏm (chún) ja tum ayng
ผม(ฉัน)จะทำเอง
by myself dôo-ay dton ayng
ด้วยตนเอง

N

nail (finger) lép meu
เล็บมือ
(metal) dta-bpoo
ตะปู
nailbrush bprairng kùt lép
แปรงขัดเล็บ
nail varnish yah tah lép
ยาทาเล็บ
name chêu
ชื่อ
my name's ... pŏm chêu ...
ผมชื่อจอห์น ...
what's your name? koon chêu a-rai?
คุณชื่ออะไร

what is the name of this street? nêe ta-nŏn a-rai?
นี่ถนนอะไร

napkin pâh chét bpàhk
ผ้าเช็ดปาก

nappy pâh ôrm
ผ้าอ้อม

narrow (street) kâirp
แคบ

nasty nâh too-râyt
น่าทุเรศ

national hàirng châht
แห่งชาติ

nationality sŭn-châht
สัญชาติ

natural tum-ma-châht
ธรรมชาติ

nausea ah-gahn klêun hĕe-un
อาการคลื่นเหียน

navy (blue) sĕe fáh gàir
สีฟ้าแก่

near glâi
ใกล้

is it near the city centre? yòo glâi meu-ung mái?
อยู่ใกล้เมืองไหม

do you go near the museum? koon pàhn bpai glâi glâi pí-pít-ta-pun mái?
คุณผ่านไปใกล้ๆ พิพิธภัณฑ์ไหม

where is the nearest ...? ... glâi têe sòot yòo têe năi?
... ใกล้ที่สุดอยู่ที่ไหน

nearby yòo glâi
อยู่ใกล้

nearly gèu-up
เกือบ

necessary jum-bpen
จำเป็น

neck kor
คอ

necklace sôy kor
สร้อยคอ

necktie nék-tai
เน็คไท

need: I need ... pŏm (chún) dtôrng-gahn ...
ผม(ฉัน)ต้องการ ...

do I need to pay? dtôrng jài rĕu bplào?
ต้องจ่ายหรือเปล่า

needle kĕm
เข็ม

negative (film) feem nay-gah-dteef
ฟิล์มเนกาตีฟ

nephew lăhn chai
หลานชาย

net (in sport) dtah-kài
ตาข่าย

never mâi ker-ee
ไม่เคย

dialogue

have you ever been to Hua Hin? kOOn ker-ee bpai hŏo-a hĭn mái?
no, never, I've never been there mâi ker-ee, pŏm (chún) mâi ker-ee bpai

new mài
ใหม่

news (radio, TV etc) kào
ข่าว

newsagent's ráhn kăi núng-sĕu pim
ร้านขายหนังสือพิมพ์

newspaper núng-sĕu pim
หนังสือพิมพ์

newspaper kiosk dtôo núng-sĕu pim
ตู้หนังสือพิมพ์

New Year bpee mài
ปีใหม่

Happy New Year! sa-wùt dee bpee mài!
สวัสดีปีใหม่

New Year's Eve wun sîn bpee
วันสิ้นปี

New Zealand bpra-tâyt new see-láirn
ประเทศนิวซีแลนด์

New Zealander: I'm a New Zealander pŏm (chún) bpen kon new see-láirn
ผม(ฉัน)เป็นคนนิวซีแลนด์

next nâh
หน้า

the next turning on the left lée-o sái têe tahng yâirk kâhng nâh
เลี้ยวซ้ายที่ทางแยกข้างหน้า

at the next stop bpâi nâh
ป้ายหน้า

next week ah-tít nâh
อาทิตย์หน้า

next to dtìt gùp
ติดกับ

nice (food) a-ròy
อร่อย

(looks, view etc) sŏo-ay
สวย

(person) dee
ดี

niece lăhn săo
หลานสาว

night glahng keun
กลางคืน

at night dtorn glahng keun
ตอนกลางคืน

good night sa-wùt dee
สวัสดี

dialogue

do you have a single room for one night? mee hôrng sǔm-rùp keun dee-o mái?
yes, madam mee krúp
how much is it per night? keun la tâo-rài?
it's 1,000 baht for one night keun la pun bàht
thank you, I'll take it kòrp-kOOn ao hôrng née

nightclub náit klúp
ไนทคลับ

nightdress chóOt norn
ชุดนอน

no* mâi
ไม่

I've no change mâi mee sàyt sa-dtahng
ไม่มีเศษสตางค์

there's no ... left mâi mee ... lěu-a yòo
ไม่มี ... เหลืออยู่

no way! mâi mee tahng!
ไม่มีทาง

oh no! (upset) dtai jing!
ตายจริง

nobody mâi mee krai
ไม่มีใคร

there's nobody there mâi mee krai yòo
ไม่มีใครอยู่

noise sěe-ung
เสียง

noisy: it's too noisy nòo-uk hǒo
หนวกหู

non-alcoholic mâi mee un-gor-horl
ไม่มีอัลกอฮอล

nonsmoking hâhm sòop bOO-rèe
ห้ามสูบบุหรี่

noodles gǒo-ay dtěe-o
ก๋วยเตี๋ยว

noodle shop ráhn gǒo-ay dtěe-o
ร้านก๋วยเตี๋ยว

noon têe-ung wun
เที่ยงวัน

at noon têe-ung wun
เที่ยงวัน

no-one mâi mee krai
ไม่มีใคร

nor: nor do I pǒm (chún) gôr mâi měu-un gun
ผม(ฉัน)ก็ไม่เหมือนกัน

normal tum-ma-dah
ธรรมดา

north něu-a
เหนือ

in the north nai pâhk nĕu-a
ในภาคเหนือ
to the north tahng nĕu-a
ทางเหนือ
north of Bangkok tahng nĕu-a kŏrng grOOng-tâyp
ทางเหนือของกรุงเทพฯ
northeast dta-wun òrk chĕe-ung nĕu-a
ตะวันออกเฉียงเหนือ
Northern Ireland ai-lairn nĕu-a
ไอร์แลนด์เหนือ
northwest dta-wun dtòk chĕe-ung nĕu-a
ตะวันตกเฉียงเหนือ
Norway bpra-tâyt nor-way
ประเทศนอรเว
nose ja-mòok
จมูก
nosebleed lêu-ut gum-dao ŏrk
เลือดกำเดาออก
not* mâi
ไม่
no thanks, I'm not hungry mâi krúp (kâ) pŏm (chún) mâi hĕw
ไม่ครับ (ค่ะ) ผม(ฉัน)ไม่หิว
I don't want any, thank you pŏm (chún) mâi ao kòrp-kOOn
ผม(ฉัน)ไม่เอาขอบคุณ
it's not necessary mâi jum-bpen
ไม่จำเป็น
I didn't know that pŏm (chún) mâi sâhp rêu-ung nún
ผม(ฉัน)ไม่ทราบเรื่องนั้น
not that one – this one mâi châi un nún – un nêe
ไม่ใช่อันนั้นอันนี่
note (banknote) bai báirng
ใบแบ๊งค์
notebook sa-mòOt
สมุด
notepaper (for letters) gra-dàht kĕe-un jòt-măi
กระดาษเขียนจดหมาย
nothing mâi mee a-rai
ไม่มีอะไร
nothing for me, thanks mâi ao a-rai krúp (kâ) kòrp-kOOn
ไม่เอาอะไรครับ(ค่ะ)ขอบคุณ
nothing else mâi mee a-rai èek
ไม่มีอะไรอีก
novel na-wa-ni-yai
นวนิยาย
November préut-sa-ji-gah-yon
พฤศจิกายน
now dĕe-o née
เดี๋ยวนี้
number măi-lâyk
หมายเลข

I've got the wrong number toh pìt **ber**
โทรผิดเบอร์
what is your phone number? **ber** toh-ra-sùp kŏrng koon lâyk a-rai?
เบอร์โทรศัพท์ของคุณเลขอะไร
number plate bpâi ta-bee-un rót
ป้ายทะเบียนรถ
nurse (woman) nahng pa-yah-bahn
นางพยาบาล
nut (for bolt) glee-o
เกลียว
nuts tòo-a
ถั่ว

occupied (line etc) mâi wâhng
ไม่ว่าง
o'clock* mohng
โมง
October dtoo-lah-kom
ตุลาคม
odd (strange) bplàirk
แปลก
of* kŏrng
ของ
off (lights) bpìt
ปิด
it's just off Sukhumwit Road yòo tăir-o ta-nŏn soo-kŏom-wít
อยู่แถวถนนสุขุมวิท
we're off tomorrow (leaving) rao bpai prôong née
เราไปพรุ่งนี้
offensive nâh rung-gèe-ut
น่ารังเกียจ
office (place of work) sŭm-núk ngahn
สำนักงาน
officer (said to policeman) nai dtum-ròo-ut
นายตำรวจ
often bòy bòy
บ่อย ๆ
not often mâi bòy
ไม่บ่อย
how often are the buses? rót mah bòy kâir năi?
รถมาบ่อยแค่ไหน
oil núm mun
น้ำมัน
(motor) núm mun krêu-ung
น้ำมันเครื่อง
ointment yah tah
ยาทา
OK oh-kay
โอเค

are you OK? koon oh-kay mái?
คุณโอเคไหม
is that OK with you? koon oh-kay mái?
คุณโอเคไหม
is it OK to ...? ... dâi mái?
... ได้ไหม
that's OK thanks (it doesn't matter) mâi bpen rai
ไม่เป็นไร
I'm OK (nothing for me, I've got enough) pŏm (chún) por láir-o
ผม(ฉัน)พอแล้ว
(I feel OK) pŏm (chún) oh kay
ผม(ฉัน)โอเค
is this train OK for ...? rót fai née bpai ... châi mái?
รถไฟนี้ไป ... ใช่ไหม

old (person) gàir
แก่
(thing) gào
เก่า

dialogue

how old are you? koon ah-yóo tâo-rài?
I'm 25 pŏm (chún) ah-yóo yêe-sìp hâh bpee
and you? láir-o koon lâ?

old-fashioned láh sa-măi
ล้าสมัย
old town (old part of town) meu-ung gào
เมืองเก่า
olive oil núm mun ma-gòrk
น้ำมันมะกอก
olives ma-gòrk
มะกอก
omelette kài jee-o
ไข่เจียว
on* bon
บน
on the beach têe chai hàht
ที่ชายหาด
on the street bon ta-nŏn
บนถนน
is it on this road? yòo ta-nŏn née rĕu bplào?
อยู่ถนนนี้หรือเปล่า
on the plane bon krêu-ung bin
บนเครื่องบิน
on Saturday wun sâo
วันเสาร์
on television nai tee wee
ในทีวี
I haven't got it on me pŏm (chún) mâi dâi ao mah dôo-ay
ผม(ฉัน)ไม่ได้เอามาด้วย
this one's on me (drink) pŏm

(chún) lée-ung
ผม(ฉัน)เลี้ยง
the light wasn't on fai mâi bpèrt yòo
ไฟไม่เปิดอยู่
what's on tonight? keun née mee a-rai?
คืนนี้มีอะไร

once (one time) krúng nèung
ครั้งหนึ่ง
at once (immediately) tun-tee
ทันที

one* nèung
หนึ่ง
the white one un sěe kǎo
อันสีขาว

one-way ticket dtǒo-a bpai
ตั๋วไป

onion hǒo-a hǒrm
หัวหอม

only tâo-nún
เท่านั้น
only one un dee-o tâo-nún
อันเดียวเท่านั้น
it's only 6 o'clock pee-ung hòk mohng tâo-nún
เพียงหกโมงเท่านั้น
I've only just got here pǒm (chún) **pêung** mah děe-o née ayng
ผม(ฉัน)เพิ่งมาเดี๋ยวนี้เอง

on/off switch sa-wít bpèrt/bpìt
สวิชเปิด/ปิด

open (adj, verb) bpèrt
เปิด
when do you open? bpèrt gèe mohng?
เปิดกี่โมง
I can't get it open bpèrt mâi dâi
เปิดไม่ได้
in the open air glahng jâirng
กลางแจ้ง

opening times way-lah bpìt-bpèrt
เวลาปิดเปิด

open ticket dtǒo-a mâi jum-gùt way-lah
ตั๋วไม่จำกัดเวลา

operation (medical) gahn pàh dtùt
การผ่าตัด

operator (telephone) pa-núk ngahn toh-ra-sùp
พนักงานโทรศัพท์

opposite: the opposite direction tahng dtrong kâhm
ทางตรงข้าม
the bar opposite bah dtrong kâhm
บาร์ตรงข้าม
opposite my hotel dtrong

kâhm rohng rairm
ตรงข้ามโรงแรม
optician jùk-sòo pâirt
จักษุแพทย์
or rĕu
หรือ
orange (fruit) sôm
ส้ม
(colour) sĕe sôm
สีส้ม
orange juice núm sôm
น้ำส้ม
orchestra wong don-dtree
วงดนตรี
order: can we order now? (in restaurant) kŏr sùng dĕe-o née dâi mái?
ขอสั่งเดี๋ยวนี้ได้ไหม
I've already ordered, thanks pŏm (chún) sùng láir-o
ผม(ฉัน)สั่งแล้ว
I didn't order this pŏm (chún) mâi dâi sùng
ผม(ฉัน)ไม่ได้สั่ง
out of order sĕe-a
เสีย
ordinary tum-ma-dah
ธรรมดา
other èun
อื่น
the other one (person) **èek** kon nèung
อีกคนหนึ่ง
(thing) **èek** un nèung
อีกอันหนึ่ง
the other day (recently) mêu-a mâi gèe wun
เมื่อไม่กี่วัน
I'm waiting for the others (other people) pŏm (chún) ror **kon èun**
ผม(ฉัน)รอคนอื่น
do you have any others? mee **yàhng èun** mái?
มีอย่างอื่นไหม
otherwise mí-cha-nún
มิฉะนั้น
our* kŏrng rao
ของเรา
ours* kŏrng rao
ของเรา
out: he's out (not at home) káo mâi yòo
เขาไม่อยู่
three kilometres out of town nôrk meu-ung bpai săhm gi-loh
นอกเมืองไปสามกิโล
outdoors glahng jâirng
กลางแจ้ง
outside kâhng nôrk
ข้างนอก
can we sit outside? nûng

kâhng nôrk dâi mái?
นั่งข้างนอกได้ไหม

oven dtao
เตา

over: over here têe nêe
ที่นี่

over there têe nôhn
ที่โน่น

over 500 hâh róy gwàh
ห้าร้อยกว่า

it's over (finished) jòp láir-o
จบแล้ว

overcharge: you've overcharged me koon kít ngern mâhk bpai
คุณคิดเงินมากไป

overcoat sêu-a nôrk
เสื้อนอก

overnight (travel) dern tahng glahng keun
เดินทางกลางคืน

overtake sairng
แซง

owe: how much do I owe you? pŏm (chún) bpen nêe koon tâo-rài?
ผม(ฉัน)เป็นหนี้คุณเท่าไร

own: my own ... kŏrng pŏm (chún) **ayng ...**
ของผม(ฉัน)เอง ...

are you on your own? koon mah **kon dee-o** rĕu bplào?
คุณมาคนเดียวหรือเปล่า

I'm on my own pŏm (chún) mah **kon dee-o**
ผม(ฉัน)มาคนเดียว

owner jâo-kŏrng
เจ้าของ

oyster hŏy nahng rom
หอยนางรม

P

pack (verb) jùt gra-bpăo
จัดกระเป๋า

a pack of ... hòr ...
ห่อ ...

package (parcel) hòr
ห่อ

packed lunch ah-hăhn glahng wun glòrng
อาหารกลางวันกล่อง

packet: a packet of cigarettes sorng boo-rèe
ซองบุหรี่

paddy field nah
นา

page (of book) nâh
หน้า

could you page Mr ...? chôo-ay hăh ber toh-ra-sùp koon

... hâi dôo-ay
ช่วยหาเบอร์โทรศัพท์คุณ ... ให้ด้วย

pagoda jay-dee
เจดีย์

pain kwahm jèp bpòo-ut
ความเจ็บปวด

I have a pain here jèp dtrong née
เจ็บตรงนี้

painful jèp bpòo-ut
เจ็บปวด

painkillers yah ra-ngúp bpòo-ut
ยาระงับปวด

paint (noun) sěe
สี

painting (picture) pâhp kěe-un
ภาพเขียน

pair: a pair of ... ... kôo nèung
... คู่หนึ่ง

Pakistani (adj) kon bpah-gee-sa-tăhn
คนปากีสถาน

palace wung
วัง

pale sěe òrn
สีอ่อน

pale blue sěe fáh òrn
สีฟ้าอ่อน

pan (frying pan) gra-tá
กระทะ

panties gahng gayng nai sa-dtree
กางเกงในสตรี

pants (underwear: men's) gahng gayng nai
กางเกงใน

(women's) gahng gayng nai sa-dtree
กางเกงในสตรี

(US: trousers) gahng-gayng
กางเกง

pantyhose tŏong yai boo-a
ถุงใยบัว

paper gra-dàht
กระดาษ

(newspaper) núng-sěu-pim
หนังสือพิมพ์

a piece of paper gra-dàht pàirn nèung
กระดาษแผ่นหนึ่ง

paper handkerchiefs gra-dàht chét nâh
กระดาษเช็ดหน้า

parcel hòr
ห่อ

pardon (me)? (didn't understand, hear) a-rai ná krúp (ká)?
อะไรนะครับ(คะ)

parents pôr mâir
พ่อแม่

parents-in-law (wife's parents)

pôr dtah mâir yai
พ่อตาแม่ยาย
(husband's parents) pôr pŏo-a mâir pŏo-a
พ่อผัวแม่ผัว
park (noun) sŏo-un săh-tah-ra-ná
สวนสาธารณะ
(verb) jòrt
จอด
can I park here? jòrt têe nêe dâi mái?
จอดที่นี่ได้ไหม
parking lot têe jòrt rót
ที่จอดรถ
part (noun) sòo-un
ส่วน
partner (boyfriend, girlfriend etc) fairn
แฟน
party (group) glòom kon
กลุ่มคน
(celebration) ngahn lée-ung
งานเลี้ยง
pass (in mountains) chôrng kăo
ช่องเขา
passenger pôo doy-ee săhn
ผู้โดยสาร
passport núng-sĕu dern tahng
หนังสือเดินทาง
past*: in the past mêu-a gòrn
เมื่อก่อน
just past the post office ler-ee bprai-sa-nee bpai èek nít nèung
เลยไปรษณีย์ไปอีกนิดหนึ่ง
path tahng
ทาง
pattern bàirp
แบบ
pavement bàht wít-tĕe
บาทวิถี
on the pavement bon bàht wít-tĕe
บนบาทวิถี
pay (verb) jài
จ่าย
can I pay, please? kŏr bin nòy
ขอบิลหน่อย
it's already paid for jài láir-o
จ่ายแล้ว

dialogue

who's paying? krai bpen kon jài ngern?
I'll pay pŏm (chún) ayng
no, you paid last time, I'll pay kOOn jài dtorn krúng gòrn láir-o ná pŏm (chún) jài ayng

pay phone toh-ra-sùp săh-tah-ra-ná
โทรศัพท์สาธารณะ
peaceful (quiet) ngêe-up
เงียบ
peach lôok pêech
ลูกพีช
peanuts tòo-a
ถั่ว
pear lôok pair
ลูกแพร์
peculiar (taste, custom) bplàirk
แปลก
pedestrian crossing tahng máh-lai
ทางม้าลาย
pedestrian precinct têe hâhm rót kâo
ที่ห้ามรถเข้า
peg (for washing) mái nèep pâh
ไม้หนีบผ้า
pen bpàhk-gah
ปากกา
pencil din-sŏr
ดินสอ
penfriend pêu-un tahng jòt-măi
เพื่อนทางจดหมาย
penicillin yah pen-ni-seen-lin
ยาเพนนิซีลลิน
penknife mêet púp
มีดพับ

people kon
คน
the other people in the hotel kon èun nai rohng rairm
คนอื่นในโรงแรม
too many people kon mâhk bpai
คนมากไป
pepper (spice) prík tai
พริกไทย
(vegetable) prík yòo-uk
พริกหยวก
per: per night keun la ...
คืนละ ...
how much per day? wun la tâo-rài?
วันละเท่าไร
per cent bper-sen
เปอร์เซ็นต์
perfect yôrt yêe-um
ยอดเยี่ยม
perfume núm hŏrm
น้ำหอม
perhaps bahng tee
บางที
perhaps not bahng tee mâi
บางทีไม่
period (of time) chôo-a rá-yá
ชั่วระยะ
(menstruation) bpra-jum deu-un
ประจำเดือน

perm dùt pŏm
ดัดผม

permit (noun) bai un-nóo-yâht
ใบอนุญาต

person kon
คน

personal stereo work-mairn
วอล์กแมน

petrol núm mun
น้ำมัน

petrol can gra-bpŏrng núm mun
กระป๋องน้ำมัน

petrol station bpúm núm mun
ปั๊มน้ำมัน

pharmacy hâhng kăi yah
ห้างขายยา

phone toh-ra-sùp
โทรศัพท์

phone book sa-mòot măi-lâyk toh-ra-sùp
สมุดหมายเลขโทรศัพท์

phone box dtôo toh-ra-sùp
ตู้โทรศัพท์

phonecard bùt toh-ra-sùp
บัตรโทรศัพท์

phone number ber toh-ra-sùp
เบอร์โทรศัพท์

photo rôop tài
รูปถ่าย

excuse me, could you take a photo of us? kŏr-tôht krúp (kâ), chôo-ay tài rôop rao hâi nòy dâi mái? ขอโทษครับ(ค่ะ)ช่วยถ่ายรูปเราให้หน่อยได้ไหม

phrasebook kôo meu sŏn-ta-nah
คู่มือสนทนา

Phuket poo-gèt
ภูเก็ต

piano bpee-a-noh
เปียโน

pickpocket ka-moy-ee lóo-ung gra-bpăo
ขโมยล้วงกระเป๋า

pick up: will you be there to pick me up? ja bpai rúp pŏm (chún) mái?
จะไปรับผม(ฉัน)ไหม

picnic (noun) bpìk-ník
ปิคนิค

picture (painting, photo) rôop
รูป

pie pai
ไพ

piece chín
ชิ้น

a piece of ... ... chín nèung
... ชิ้นหนึ่ง

pill (contraceptive pill) yah koom gum-nèrt
ยาคุมกำเนิด

I'm on the pill chún chái yah

kOOm gum-nèrt
ฉันใช้ยาคุมกำเนิด

pillow mŏrn
หมอน

pillow case bplòrk mŏrn
ปลอกหมอน

pin (noun) kĕm mòOt
เข็มหมุด

pineapple sùp-bpa-rót
สับปะรด

pineapple juice núm sùp-bpa-rót
น้ำสับปะรด

pink sĕe chom-poo
สีชมพู

pipe (for smoking) glôrng yah sên
กล้องยาเส้น

(for water) tôr
ท่อ

pipe cleaners mái tum kwahm sà-aht glôrng yah sên
ไม้ทำความสะอาดกล้องยาเส้น

pity: it's a pity nâh sŏng-săhn
น่าสงสาร

pizza pee-sâh
พิซซ่า

place (noun) sa-tăhn-têe
สถานที่

at your place têe bâhn kOOn
ที่บ้านคุณ

at his place têe bâhn káo
ที่บ้านเขา

plain (not patterned) mâi mee lôo-ut lai
ไม่มีลวดลาย

plane krêu-ung bin
เครื่องบิน

by plane doy-ee krêu-ung bin
โดยเครื่องบิน

plant dtôn mái
ต้นไม้

plaster cast fèu-uk
เฝือก

plasters plah-sa-dter
พลาสเตอร์

plastic bplah-sa-dtìk
ปลาสติค

(credit cards) bùt kray-dìt
บัตรเครดิต

plastic bag tŏong bplah-sa-dtìk
ถุงปลาสติค

plate jahn
จาน

platform chahn chah-lah
ชานชาลา

which platform is it for Chiangmai? bpai chee-ung-mài chahn chah-lah a-rai?
ไปเชียงใหม่ชานชาลาอะไร

play (verb) lên
เล่น

(noun: in theatre) la-korn
ละคร
playground (for children)
sa-năhm dèk lên
สนามเด็กเล่น
pleasant sa-nòok
สนุก
please (requesting something)
kŏr ...
ขอ ...
(offering) chern krúp (kâ)
เชิญครับ(ค่ะ)
yes please ao krúp (kâ)
เอาครับ(ค่ะ)
could you please ...? chôo-ay ... nòy dâi mái?
ช่วยหน่อย ... ได้ไหม
please don't yàh ler-ee krúp (kâ)
อย่าเลยครับ(ค่ะ)
pleased: pleased to meet you
yin dee têe dâi róo-jùk gun
ยินดีที่ได้รู้จักกัน
pleasure: my pleasure (response to thanks) mâi bpen rai
ไม่เป็นไร
plenty: plenty of ... ... mâhk
... มาก
there's plenty of time mee way-lah mâhk
มีเวลามาก
that's plenty, thanks por láir-o kòrp-koon
พอแล้วขอบคุณ
pliers keem bpàhk kêep
คีมปากคีบ
plug (electrical) bplúk
ปลั๊ก
(for car) hŏo-a tee-un
หัวเทียน
(in sink) jòok òot
จุกอุด
plumber châhng bpra-bpah
ช่างประปา
p.m.*
pocket gra-bpăo
กระเป๋า
point: two point five sŏrng jòot hâh
สองจุดห้า
there's no point mâi mee bpra-yòht
ไม่มีประโยชน์
points (in car) torng kăo
ทองขาว
poisonous bpen pít
เป็นพิษ
police dtum-ròo-ut
ตำรวจ
call the police! rêe-uk dtum-ròo-ut mah!
เรียกตำรวจมา
policeman dtum-ròo-ut
ตำรวจ

police station sa-tăh-nee dtum-ròo-ut
สถานีตำรวจ
policewoman dtum-ròo-ut yĭng
ตำรวจหญิง
polish (noun) yah kùt
ยาขัด
polite sOO-pâhp
สุภาพ
polluted bpen pít
เป็นพิษ
pony máh glàirp
ม้าแกลบ
pool (for swimming) sà wâi náhm
สระว่ายน้ำ
poor (not rich) jon
จน
(quality) mâi ao năi
ไม่เอาไหน
pop music don-dtree pórp
ดนตรีพ๊อพ
pop singer núk rórng
นักร้อง
popular bpen têe nee-yom
เป็นที่นิยม
population bpra-chah-gorn
ประชากร
pork néu-a mŏo
เนื้อหมู
port (for boats) tâh reu-a
ท่าเรือ
porter (in hotel) kon fâo bpra-dtoo
คนเฝ้าประตู
portrait pâhp kĕe-un dtoo-a jing
ภาพเขียนตัวจริง
posh (restaurant, people) rŏo-răh
หรูหรา
possible bpen bpai dâi
เป็นไปได้
is it possible to ...? ... bpen bpai dâi mái?
... เป็นไปได้ไหม
as ... as possible yahng ... têe sOOt tee ja ... dâi
อย่าง ... ที่สุดที่จะ ... ได้
post (noun: mail) jòt-măi
จดหมาย
(verb) sòng jòt-măi
ส่งจดหมาย
could you post this for me? chôo-ay sòng jòt-măi née hâi nòy dâi mái?
ช่วยส่งจดหมายนี้ให้หน่อยได้ไหม
postbox dtôo bprai-sa-nee
ตู้ไปรษณีย์
postcard bpóht-gáht
โปสการ์ด
postcode ra-hùt bprai-sa-nee
รหัสไปรษณีย์

poster bpoh-sa-dter
โปสเตอร์

poste restante 'poste restante'

post office bprai-sa-nee
ไปรษณีย์

potato mun fa-rùng
มันฝรั่ง

potato chips (US) mun fa-rùng tôrt
มันฝรั่งทอด

pots and pans môr kâo môr gairng
หม้อข้าวหม้อแกง

pottery krêu-ung bpûn din pǎo
เครื่องปั้นดินเผา

pound* (money) bporn
ปอนด์

power cut dtùt fai
ตัดไฟ

power point bplúk fai
ปลั๊กไฟ

practise: I want to practise my Thai pǒrm (chún) yàhk ja fèuk pôot pah-sǎh tai
ผม(ฉัน)อยากจะฝึกพูดภาษาไทย

prawns gôong
กุ้ง

prefer: I prefer ... pǒrm (chún) chôrp ... mâhk gwàh
ผม(ฉัน)ชอบ ... มากกว่า

pregnant mee tórng
มีท้อง

prescription (for medicine) bai sùng yah
ใบสั่งยา

present (gift) kǒrng kwǔn
ของขวัญ

president (of country) bpra-tah-nah-tí-bor-dee
ประธานาธิบดี

pretty sǒo-ay
สวย

it's pretty expensive pairng **měu-un gun** ná
แพงเหมือนกันนะ

price rah-kah
ราคา

priest prá
พระ

prime minister nah-yók rút-ta-mon-dtree
นายกรัฐมนตรี

printed matter sìng dtee pim
สิ่งตีพิมพ์

priority (in driving) sìt pàhn bpai gòrn
สิทธผ่านไปก่อน

prison kóok
คุก

private sòo-un dtoo-a
ส่วนตัว

private bathroom hôrng náhm sòo-un dtoo-a
ห้องน้ำส่วนตัว
probably kong-ja
คงจะ
problem bpun-hăh
ปัญหา
no problem! mâi mee bpun-hăh!
ไม่มีปัญหา
program(me) (noun) bproh-grairm
โปรแกรม
promise: I promise pŏm (chún) sŭn-yah
ผม(ฉัน)สัญญา
pronounce: how is this pronounced? nêe òrk sĕe-ung yung-ngai?
นี่ออกเสียงอย่างไร
properly (repaired, locked etc) tòok dtôrng
ถูกต้อง
Protestant krít
คริสต์
public convenience sôo-um săh-tah-ra-ná
ส้วมสาธารณะ
public holiday wun yòot râht-cha-gahn
วันหยุดราชการ
pudding (dessert) kŏrng wăhn
ของหวาน
pull deung
ดึง
pullover sêu-a sa-wét-dtêr
เสื้อสเวตเตอร์
puncture (noun) yahng dtàirk
ยางแตก
purple sĕe môo-ung
สีม่วง
purse (for money) gra-bpăo sa-dtahng
กระเป๋าสตางค์
(US) gra-bpăo tĕu
กระเป๋าถือ
push plùk
ผลัก
pushchair rót kĕn
รถเข็น
put sài
ใส่
where can I put ...? ... sài dâi têe năi?
... ใส่ได้ที่ไหน
could you put us up for the night? kŏr káhng keun têe nêe nòy dâi mái?
ขอค้างคืนที่นี่หน่อยได้ไหม
pyjamas sêu-a gahng-gayng norn
เสื้อกางเกงนอน

Q

quality koon-na-pâhp
คุณภาพ

quarantine (place) dâhn gùk rôhk
ด่านกักโรค
(period) ra-yá way-lah têe gùk rôhk wái
ระยะเวลาที่กักโรคไว้

quarter nèung nai sèe
หนึ่งในสี่

quayside: on the quayside têe tâh reu-a
ที่ท่าเรือ

question kum tăhm
คำถาม

queue (noun) kew
คิว

quick ray-o
เร็ว

that was quick ray-o jing
เร็วจริง

what's the quickest way there? bpai tahng năi ray-o têe sòot?
ไปทางไหนเร็วที่สุด

fancy a quick drink? yàhk bpai dèum a-rai mái?
อยากไปดื่มอะไรไหม

quickly ray-o
เร็ว

quiet (place, hotel) ngêe-up
เงียบ

quiet! ngêe-up ngêe-up nòy!
เงียบ ๆ หน่อย

quite (fairly) por sŏm-koo-un
พอสมควร
(very) tee dee-o
ทีเดียว

that's quite right tòok láir-o
ถูกแล้ว

quite a lot mâhk por sŏm-koo-un
มากพอสมควร

R

rabbit (meat) gra-dtài
กระต่าย

race (for runners, cars) gahn kàirng kŭn
การแข่งขัน

racket (tennis, squash) mái dtee
ไม้ตี

radiator môr náhm
หม้อน้ำ

radio wít-ta-yóo
วิทยุ

on the radio tahng wít-ta-

yóo
ทางวิทยุ
rail: by rail doy-ee rót fai
โดยรถไฟ
railway tahng rót fai
ทางรถไฟ
rain (noun) fŏn
ฝน
in the rain dtàhk fŏn
ตากฝน
it's raining fŏn dtòk
ฝนตก
raincoat sêu-a fŏn
เสื้อฝน
rape (noun) kòm kĕun
ข่มขืน
rare (uncommon) hăh yâhk
หายาก
(steak) sòok sòok dìp dìp
สุก ๆ ดิบ ๆ
rash (on skin) pèun
ผื่น
rat nŏo
หนู
rate (for changing money) ùt-dtrah
อัตรา
rather: it's rather good kôrn kâhng dee
ค่อนข้างดี
I'd rather ... pŏm (chún) yàhk ja ... dee gwàh
ผม(ฉัน)อยากจะ ... ดีกว่า
razor (dry, electric) mêet gohn
มีดโกน
razor blades bai mêet gohn
ใบมีดโกน
read àhn
อ่าน
ready prórm, sèt
พร้อม, เสร็จ
are you ready? sèt láir-o rĕu yung?
เสร็จแล้วหรือยัง
I'm not ready yet pŏm (chún) yung mâi sèt
ผม(ฉัน)ยังไม่เสร็จ

dialogue

when will it be ready? sèt mêu-a rài?
it should be ready in a couple of days èek sŏrng săhm wun koo-un ja sèt

real jing
จริง
really jing jing
จริง ๆ
I'm really sorry pŏm (chún) sĕe-a jai jing jing
ผม(ฉัน)เสียใจจริง ๆ
that's really great dee jung

ler-ee
ดีจังเลย
really? (doubt) jing lĕr?
จริงหรือ
(polite interest) lĕr?
หรือ
rear lights fai lŭng rót
ไฟหลังรถ
rearview mirror gra-jòk lŭng
กระจกหลัง
reasonable (price) rah-kah yao
ราคาเยา
receipt bai sèt rúp ngern
ใบเสร็จรับเงิน
recently mêu-a ray-o ray-o née
เมื่อเร็ว ๆ นี้
reception (in hotel) pa-nàirk dtôrn rúp
แผนกต้อนรับ
(for guests) ngahn lée-ung dtôrn rúp
งานเลี้ยงต้อนรับ
at reception têe pa-nàirk dtôrn rúp
ที่แผนกต้อนรับ
reception desk pa-nàirk dtôrn rúp
แผนกต้อนรับ
receptionist pa-núk ngahn dtôrn rúp
พนักงานต้อนรับ
recognize jum dâi
จำได้
recommend: could you recommend ...? kOOn náir-num ... dâi mái?
คุณแนะนำ ... ได้ไหม
record (music) pàirn sĕe-ung
แผ่นเสียง
red sĕe dairng
สีแดง
red wine lâo wai dairng
เหล้าไวน์แดง
refund (noun) keun ngern
คืนเงิน
can I have a refund? keun ngern hâi dâi mái?
คืนเงินให้ได้ไหม
region pâhk
ภาค
registered: by registered mail jòt-măi long ta-bee-un
จดหมายลงทะเบียน
registration number ta-bee-un rót
ทะเบียนรถ
relative (noun) yâht
ญาติ
religion sàh-sa-năh
ศาสนา
remember: I don't remember pŏm (chún) jum

mâi dâi
ผม(ฉัน)จำไม่ได้
I remember pŏm (chún) jum dâi
ผม(ฉัน)จำได้
do you remember? jum dâi mái?
จำได้ไหม
rent (noun: for apartment etc) kâh châo
ค่าเช่า
(verb: car etc) châo
เช่า
rented car rót châo
รถเช่า
repair (verb) sôrm
ซ่อม
can you repair it? sôrm dâi mái?
ซ่อมได้ไหม
repeat pôot èek tee
พูดอีกที
could you repeat that? pôot èek tee dâi mái?
พูดอีกทีได้ไหม
reservation jorng
จอง
I'd like to make a reservation kŏr jorng
ขอจอง

dialogue

I have a reservation pŏm (chún) dâi jorng wái láir-o
yes sir, what name please? krúp kOOn chêu a-rai?

reserve (verb) jorng
จอง

dialogue

can I reserve a table for tonight? chún kŏr jorng dtór sŭm-rùp keun née dâi mái?
yes madam, for how many people? dâi krúp mee gèe kon?
for two sŏrng kon
and for what time? láir-o gèe mohng?
for eight o'clock sŏrng tôOm
and could I have your name, please? láir-o kOOn chêu a-rai krúp?

rest: I need a rest pŏm (chún) dtôrng púk pòrn
ผม(ฉัน)ต้องพักผ่อน
the rest of the group pôo-uk

kon èun
พวกคนอื่น

restaurant ráhn ah-hăhn
ร้านอาหาร

restaurant car rót sa-bee-ung
รถเสบียง

rest room hôrng náhm
ห้องน้ำ

retired: I'm retired pŏm (chún) ga-see-un
ผม(ฉัน)เกษียน

return: a return to ... dtŏo-a bpai glùp ...
ตั๋วไปกลับ ...

return ticket dtŏo-a bpai glùp
ตั๋วไปกลับ

reverse charge call toh-ra-sùp gèp ngern bplai tahng
โทรศัพท์เก็บเงินปลายทาง

reverse gear gee-a tŏy lŭng
เกียร์ถอยหลัง

revolting nâh rung-gèe-ut
น่ารังเกียจ

rib sêe krohng
ซี่โครง

rice kâo
ข้าว

rich (person) roo-ay
รวย

(food) mun
มัน

ridiculous nâh hŏo-a rór
น่าหัวเราะ

right (correct) tòok
ถูก

(not left) kwăh
ขวา

you were right koon **tòok** láir-o
คุณถูกแล้ว

that's right tòok láir-o
ถูกแล้ว

this can't be right mâi **tòok** nâir nâir
ไม่ถูกแน่ๆ

right! ao lá!
เอาละ

is this the right road for ...? bpai ... tahng ta-nŏn née **tòok** mái?
ไป ... ทางถนนนี้ถูกไหม

on the right tahng **kwăh**
ทางขวา

turn right lée-o **kwăh**
เลี้ยวขวา

right-hand drive poo-ung ma-lai kwăh
พวงมาลัยขวา

ring (on finger) wăirn
แหวน

I'll ring you pŏm (chún) ja toh bpai tĕung
ผม(ฉัน)จะโทรไปถึง

ring back toh glùp mah
โทรกลับมา
ripe (fruit) sòok
สุก
rip-off: it's a rip-off lòrk dtôm
หลอกต้ม
rip-off prices rah-kah lòrk dtôm
ราคาหลอกต้ม
risky sèe-ung
เสี่ยง
river mâir náhm
แม่น้ำ
road (in town, country) ta-nŏn
ถนน
is this the road for ...? nêe ta-nŏn bpai ... châi mái?
นี่ถนนไป ... ใช่ไหม
down the road yòo glâi glâi kâir née
อยู่ใกล้ๆแค่นี้
road accident rót chon gun
รถชนกัน
road map păirn-têe ta-nŏn
แผนที่ถนน
roadsign krêu-ung măi ja-rah jorn
เครื่องหมายจราจร
rob: I've been robbed pŏm (chún) tòok ka-moy-ee
ผม(ฉัน)ถูกขโมย
rock hĭn
หิน
(music) rórk
ร็อค
on the rocks (with ice) sài núm kăirng
ใส่น้ำแข็ง
roll (bread) ka-nŏm-bpung
ขนมปัง
roof lŭng-kah
หลังคา
roof rack gròrp dtìt lŭng-kah rót
กรอบติดหลังคารถ
room hôrng
ห้อง
in my room nai hôrng pŏm (chún)
ในห้องผม(ฉัน)
room service bor-ri-gahn rúp chái nai hôrng púk
บริการรับใช้ในห้องพัก
rope chêu-uk
เชือก
roughly (approximately) bpra-mahn
ประมาณ
round: it's my round bpen tee kŏrng pŏm
เป็นทีของผม
roundabout (for traffic) wong

wee-un
วงเวียน

round trip ticket dtŏo-a bpai glùp
ตั๋วไปกลับ

route tahng
ทาง

what's the best route? bpai tahng năi dee têe sòot?
ไปทางไหนดีที่สุด

rubber (material) yahng
ยาง

(eraser) yahng lóp
ยางลบ

rubber band yahng rút
ยางรัด

rubbish (waste) ka-yà
ขยะ

(poor quality goods) mâi ao năi
ไม่เอาไหน

rubbish! (nonsense) mâi bpen rêu-ung!
ไม่เป็นเรื่อง

rucksack bpây lŭng
เป้หลัง

rude mâi sOO-pâhp
ไม่สุภาพ

ruins sâhk sa-lùk hùk pung
ซากสลักหักพัง

rum lâo rum
เหล้ารัม

rum and Coke® rum airn kóhk
รัมแอนด์โค้ก

run (verb: person) wîng
วิ่ง

how often do the buses run? rót may wîng tèe mái?
รถเมล์วิ่งถี่ไหม

I've run out of money pŏm (chún) mót ngern
ผม(ฉัน)หมดเงิน

S

sad sâo
เศร้า

saddle (for bike) ahn jùk-gra-yahn
อานจักรยาน

(for horse) ahn máh
อานม้า

safe (not in danger) bplòrt-pai
ปลอดภัย

(not dangerous) mâi un-dta-rai
ไม่อันตราย

safety pin kĕm glùt
เข็มกลัด

sail (noun) bai reu-a
ใบเรือ

sailboard (noun) gra-dahn dtôh lom
กระดานโต้ลม

sailboarding gahn lên gra-dahn dtôh lom
การเล่นกระดานโต้ลม
salad sa-lùt
สลัด
salad dressing náhm sa-lùt
น้ำสลัด
sale: for sale kăi
ขาย
salt gleu-a
เกลือ
same: the same mĕu-un gun
เหมือนกัน
the same as this mĕu-un yàhng née
เหมือนอย่างนี้
the same again, please kŏr yàhng derm
ขออย่างเดิม
it's all the same to me a-rai gôr dâi
อะไรก็ได้
sand sai
ทราย
sandals rorng táo dtàir
รองเท้าแตะ
sandwich sairn-wít
แซนด์วิช
sanitary napkins, sanitary towels pâh un-nah-mai
ผ้าอนามัย

Saturday wun săo
วันเสาร์
sauce núm jîm
น้ำจิ้ม
saucepan môr
หม้อ
saucer jahn rorng tôo-ay
จานรองถ้วย
sauna sao-nah
เซานา
sausage sâi gròrk
ไส้กรอก
say (verb) bòrk, pôot
บอก, พูด
how do you say ... in Thai? pah-săh tai ... **pôot** wâh yung-ngai?
ภาษาไทย ... พูดว่าอย่างไร
what did he say? káo **pôot** wâh yung-ngai?
เขาพูดว่าอย่างไร
she said ... káo **bòrk** wâh ...
เขาบอกว่า ...
could you say that again? **pôot** èek tee dâi mái?
พูดอีกทีได้ไหม
scarf (for neck) pâh pun kor
ผ้าพันคอ
(for head) pâh pôhk sěe-sà
ผ้าโพกศีรษะ
scenery poo-mi-bpra-tâyt
ภูมิประเทศ

schedule (US) dtah-rahng way-lah
ตารางเวลา
scheduled flight dtah-rahng têe-o bin
school rohng ree-un
โรงเรียน
scissors: a pair of scissors dta-grai
ตะไกร
scooter rót sa-góot-dter
รถสกู๊ตเตอร์
scotch lâo wít-sa-gêe
เหล้าวิสกี้
Scotch tape® sa-górt táyp
สก๊อตเทป
Scotland sa-górt-lairn
สกอตแลนด์
Scottish kon sa-górt
คนสกอต
I'm Scottish pŏm (chún) bpen kon sa-górt
ผม(ฉัน)เป็นคนสกอต
scrambled eggs kài kon
ไข่ขน
scratch (noun) roy kòo-un
รอยข่วน
screw (noun) dta-bpoo koo-ung
ตะปูควง
screwdriver kăi koo-ung
ไขควง

sea ta-lay
ทะเล
by the sea chai ta-lay
ชายทะเล
seafood ah-hăhn ta-lay
อาหารทะเล
seafood restaurant pút-ta-kahn ah-hăhn ta-lay
ภัตตาคารอาหารทะเล
seafront chai ta-lay
ชายทะเล
seagull nók nahng noo-un
นกนางนวล
search (verb) hăh
หา
seashell bplèu-uk hŏy
เปลือกหอย
seasick: I feel seasick pŏm (chún) róo-sèuk mao klêun
ผม(ฉัน)รู้สึกเมาคลื่น
I get seasick pŏm (chún) mao klêun ngâi
ผม(ฉัน)เมาคลื่นง่าย
seaside: by the seaside chai ta-lay
ชายทะเล
seat têe nûng
ที่นั่ง
is this seat taken? têe nêe wâhng mái?
ที่นี่ว่างไหม

seat belt kĕm kùt ni-ra-pai
เข็มขัดนิรภัย

sea urchin bpling ta-lay
ปลิงทะเล

seaweed săh-rài-ta-lay
สาหร่ายทะเล

secluded dòht dèe-o
โดดเดี่ยว

second (adj) têe sŏrng
ที่สอง

(of time) wí-nah-tee
วินาที

just a second! dĕe-o gòrn!
เดี๋ยวก่อน

second class (travel etc) chún sŏrng
ชั้นสอง

second floor (UK) chún nèung
ชั้นหนึ่ง

(US) chún sŏrng
ชั้นสอง

see hĕn
เห็น

can I see? kŏr doo nòy, dâi mái?
ขอดูหน่อยได้ไหม

have you seen ...? hĕn ... rĕu bplào?
เห็น ... หรือเปล่า

I saw him this morning hĕn mêu-a cháo née
เห็นเมื่อเช้านี้

see you! jer gun mài ná!
เจอกันใหม่นะ

I see (I understand) kâo jai láir-o
เข้าใจแล้ว

self-service bor-ri-gahn chôo-ay dtoo-a ayng
บริการช่วยตัวเอง

sell kăi
ขาย

do you sell ...? mee ... kăi mái?
มี ... ขายไหม

Sellotape® sa-górt táyp
สก๊อตเทป

send sòng
ส่ง

I want to send this to England pŏm (chún) yàhk ja sòng nêe bpai ung-grìt
ผม(ฉัน)อยากจะส่งนี่ไปอังกฤษ

senior citizen kon cha-rah
คนชรา

separate dtàhng hàhk
ต่างหาก

separated: I'm separated (man) pŏm yâirk gun gùp pun-ra-yah
ผมแยกกันกับภรรยา

(woman) chún yâirk gun gùp săh-mee
ฉันแยกกันกับสามี

separately (pay, travel) yâirk

gun
แยกกัน

September gun-yah-yon
กันยายน

septic mee chéu-a
มีเชื้อ

serious (person) ao jing ao jung
เอาจริงเอาจัง
(situation) dtreung krêe-ut
ตรึงเครียด
(problem, illness) nùk
หนัก

service charge (in restaurant) kâh bor-ri-gahn
ค่าบริการ

service station bpúm núm mun
ปั๊มน้ำมัน

serviette pâh chét bpàhk
ผ้าเช็ดปาก

set menu ah-hăhn chóot
อาหารชุด

several lăi
หลาย

sew yép
เย็บ

could you sew this back on?
chôo-ay yép hâi nòy dâi mái?
ช่วยเย็บให้หน่อยได้ไหม

sex gahn rôo-um bpra-way-nee
การร่วมประเวณี

sexy sek-sêe
เซ็กซี่

shade: in the shade nai rôm
ในร่ม

shake: let's shake hands jùp meu gun
จับมือกัน

shallow (water) dtêun
ตื้น

shame: what a shame! nâh sĕe-a dai!
น่าเสียดาย

shampoo (noun) chairm-poo
แชมภู

shampoo and set sà sét
สระเซ็ท

share (verb: room, table etc) bàirng
แบ่ง

sharp (knife) kom
คม
(taste) bprêe-o
เปรี้ยว
(pain) sĕe-o
เสียว

shattered (very tired) nèu-ay mâhk
เหนื่อยมาก

shaver krêu-ung gohn nòo-ut
เครื่องโกนหนวด

shaving foam kreem gohn

nòo-ut
ครีมโกนหนวด
shaving point bplúk krêu-ung gohn nòo-ut
ปลั๊กเครื่องโกนหนวด
she* káo
เขา
is she here? káo yòo têe nêe mái?
เขาอยู่ที่นี่ไหม
sheet (for bed) pâh bpoo têe norn
ผ้าปูที่นอน
shelf hîng
หิ้ง
shellfish hŏy
หอย
ship reu-a
เรือ
by ship tahng reu-a
ทางเรือ
shirt sêu-a chért
เสื้อเชิ้ต
shit! âi hàh!
ไอ้ห่า
shock: I got an electric shock from the ... pŏm (chún) tòok fai chórk têe ...
ผม(ฉัน)ถูกไฟช๊อคที่ ...
shock-absorber chórk
ช๊อค
shocked dtòk jai
ตกใจ
shocking lĕu-a gern jing jing
เหลือเกินจริงๆ
shoe rorng táo
รองเท้า
a pair of shoes rorng táo kôo nèung
รองเท้าคู่หนึ่ง
shoelaces chêu-uk pòok rorng táo
เชือกผูกรองเท้า
shoe polish yah kùt rorng táo
ยาขัดรองเท้า
shoe repairer kon sôrm rorng táo
คนซ่อมรองเท้า
shop ráhn
ร้าน
shopping: I'm going shopping pŏm (chún) bpai séu kŏrng
ผม(ฉัน)ไปซื้อของ
shopping centre sŏon gahn káh
ศูนย์การค้า
shop window nâh gra-jòk ráhn
หน้ากระจกร้าน
shore chai fùng
ชายฝั่ง
short (person) dtêe-a
เตี้ย
(time) sûn
สั้น

shortcut tahng lút
ทางลัด
shorts gahng-gayng kăh sûn
กางเกงขาสั้น
(US: underwear) gahng gayng nai
กางเกงใน
should: what should I do? pŏm (chún) koo-un ja tum yung-ngai?
ผม(ฉัน)ควรจะทำอย่างไร
you should ... koon koo-un ja ...
คุณควรจะ ...
you shouldn't ... koon mâi koo-un ja ...
คุณไม่ควรจะ ...
he should be back soon dĕe-o káo kong glùp mah
เดี๋ยวเขาคงกลับมา
shoulder lài
ไหล่
shout (verb) dta-gohn
ตะโกน
show (in theatre) gahn sa-dairng
การแสดง
could you show me? kŏr doo nòy
ขอดูหน่อย
shower (rain) fŏn bproy bproy
ฝนปรอยๆ
(in bathroom) fùk boo-a
ฝักบัว
with shower mee fùk boo-a
มีฝักบัว
shower gel kreem àhp náhm
ครีมอาบน้ำ
shut (verb) bpìt
ปิด
when do you shut? koon bpìt gèe mohng?
คุณปิดกี่โมง
when does it shut? bpìt gèe mohng?
ปิดกี่โมง
they're shut káo bpìt láir-o
เขาปิดแล้ว
I've shut myself out leum ao goon-jair òrk mah
ลืมเอากุญแจออกมา
shut up! yòot pôot ná!
หยุดพูดนะ
shutter (on camera) chút-dter
ชัตเตอร์
(on window) bahn glèt nâh-dtàhng
บานเกล็ดหน้าต่าง
shy ai
อาย
sick (ill) mâi sa-bai
ไม่สบาย
I'm going to be sick (vomit)

róo-sèuk wâh klêun sâi
รู้สึกว่าคลื่นไส้

side kâhng
ข้าง

the other side of the street
èek fâhk nèung kŏrng ta-nŏn
อีกฟากหนึ่งของถนน

sidelights fai kâhng
ไฟข้าง

side salad sa-lùt
สลัด

side street soy
ซอย

sidewalk bàht wít-tĕe
บาทวิถี

sight: the sights of ... sa-tăhn-têe nâh têe-o nai ...
สถานที่น่าเที่ยวใน ...

sightseeing: we're going sightseeing rao ja bpai têe-o
เราจะไปเที่ยว

sightseeing tour rai gahn num têe-o
รายการนำเที่ยว

sign (roadsign etc) bpâi sŭn-yahn ja-rah-jorn
ป้ายสัญญาณจราจร

signal: he didn't give a signal (driver, cyclist) káo mâi dâi hâi sŭn-yahn
เขาไม่ได้ให้สัญญาณ

signature lai sen
ลายเซ็น

signpost dtìt bpâi ja-rah-jorn
ติดป้ายจราจร

silence kwahm ngêe-up
ความเงียบ

silk măi
ไหม

silly ngôh
โง่

silver (noun) ngern
เงิน

silver foil gra-dàht dta-gòo-a
กระดาษตะกั่ว

similar mĕu-un
เหมือน

simple (easy) ngâi
ง่าย

since: since last week dtûng dtàir ah-tít gòrn
ตั้งแต่อาทิตย์ก่อน

since I got here dtûng dtàir pŏm (chún) mah tĕung
ตั้งแต่ผม(ฉัน)มาถึง

sing rórng playng
ร้องเพลง

singer núk rórng
นักร้อง

single: a single to ... dtŏo-a bpai ...
ตั๋วไป ...

I'm single pŏm (chún) bpen sòht
ผม(ฉัน)เป็นโสด

single bed dtee-ung dèe-o
เตียงเดี่ยว

single room hôrng dèe-o
ห้องเดี่ยว

single ticket dtŏo-a bpai
ตั๋วไป

sink (in kitchen) àhng
อ่าง

sister (older) pêe săo
พี่สาว

(younger) nórng săo
น้องสาว

sister-in-law (older) pêe sa-pái kŏrng
พี่สะใภ้ของ

(younger) nórng sa-pái kŏrng
น้องสะใภ้ของ

sit: can I sit here? kŏr nûng têe nêe, dâi mái?
ขอนั่งที่นี่ได้ไหม

is anyone sitting here? mee kon nûng têe nêe rĕu bplào?
มีคนนั่งที่นี่หรือเปล่า

sit down nûng
นั่ง

do sit down chern nûng see
เชิญนั่งซิ

size ka-nàht
ขนาด

skin pĕw
ผิว

skin-diving gahn dum náhm léuk
การดำน้ำลึก

skinny pŏrm
ผอม

skirt gra-bprohng
กระโปรง

sky fáh
ฟ้า

sleep (verb) norn lùp
นอนหลับ

did you sleep well? lùp dee mái?
หลับดีไหม

sleeper (on train) rót norn
รถนอน

sleeping bag tŏong norn
ถุงนอน

sleeping car rót norn
รถนอน

sleeping pill yah norn lùp
ยานอนหลับ

sleepy: I'm feeling sleepy pŏm (chún) ngôo-ung norn
ผม(ฉัน)ง่วงนอน

sleeve kăirn sêu-a
แขนเสื้อ

slide (photographic) sa-lai
สไลด์

slip (garment) gra-bprohng

chún nai
กระโปรงชั้นใน

slippery lêun
ลื่น

slow cháh
ช้า

slow down! (driving) kùp cháh cháh nòy!
ขับช้า ๆ หน่อย
(speaking) pôot cháh cháh nòy!
พูดช้า ๆ หน่อย

slowly cháh
ช้า

very slowly cháh mâhk
ช้ามาก

small lék
เล็ก

smell: it smells (smells bad) měn
เหม็น

smile (verb) yím
ยิ้ม

smoke (noun) kwun
ควัน

do you mind if I smoke? kŏr sòop boo-rèe dâi mái?
ขอสูบบุหรี่ได้ไหม

I don't smoke pŏm (chún) mâi sòop boo-rèe
ผม(ฉัน)ไม่สูบบุหรี่

do you smoke? koon sòop boo-rèe mái?
คุณสูบบุหรี่ไหม

snake ngoo
งู

sneeze (verb) jahm
จาม

snorkel tôr hăi jai
ท่อหายใจ

snow (noun) hí-má
หิมะ

so: it's so good dee jung ler-ee
ดีจังเลย

it's so expensive pairng jung ler-ee
แพงจังเลย

not so much mâi kôy mâhk
ไม่ค่อยมาก

not so bad mâi kôy lay-o
ไม่ค่อยเลว

so am I pŏm (chún) gôr mĕu-un gun
ผม(ฉัน)ก็เหมือนกัน

so do I pŏm (chún) gôr mĕu-un gun
ผม(ฉัน)ก็เหมือนกัน

so-so rêu-ay rêu-ay
เรื่อย ๆ

soap sa-bòo
สบู่

soap powder pŏng súk fôrk
ผงซักฟอก

sober mâi mao
ไม่เมา

sock tǒong táo
ถุงเท้า
socket (electrical) bplúk fai
ปลั๊กไฟ
soda (water) núm soh-dah
น้ำโซดา
sofa têe nûng rúp kàirk
ที่นั่งรับแขก
soft (material etc) nîm
นิ่ม
soft drink náhm kòo-ut
น้ำขวด
sole (of shoe, of foot) péun rorng táo
พื้นรองเท้า
could you put new soles on these? sài péun rórng táo mài hâi nòy, dâi mái?
ใส่พื้นรองเท้าใหม่ให้หน่อยได้ไหม
some bahng
บาง
some people bahng kon
บางคน
can I have some? kǒr nòy, dâi mái?
ขอหน่อยได้ไหม
somebody, someone krai
ใคร
something a-rai
อะไร
something to eat kǒrng gin
ของกิน
sometimes bahng tee
บางที
somewhere têe nǎi
ที่ไหน
son lôok chai
ลูกชาย
song playng
เพลง
son-in-law lôok kěr-ee
ลูกเขย
soon děe-o
เดี๋ยว
I'll be back soon děe-o glùp ná
เดี๋ยวกลับนะ
as soon as possible yàhng ray-o têe sòot têe ja ray-o dâi
อย่างเร็วที่สุดที่จะเร็วได้
sore: it's sore jèp
เจ็บ
sore throat jèp kor
เจ็บคอ
sorry: (I'm) sorry pǒm (chún) sěe-a jai
ผม(ฉัน)เสียใจ
sorry? (didn't understand) a-rai na?
อะไรนะ
sort: what sort of ...? ... bàirp

năi?
... แบบไหน

soup sóop
ซุป

sour (taste) bprêe-o
เปรี้ยว

south dtâi
ใต้

in the south nai pâhk dtâi
ในภาคใต้

South Africa ah-fri-gah dtâi
อาฟริกาใต้

South China Sea ta-lay jeen dtâi
ทะเลจีนใต้

southeast dta-wun òrk chĕe-ung dtâi
ตะวันออกเฉียงใต้

southwest dta-wun dtòk chĕe-ung dtâi
ตะวันตกเฉียงใต้

souvenir kŏrng têe ra-léuk
ของที่ระลึก

soy sauce núm see éw
น้ำซีอิ๊ว

Spain bpra-tâyt sa-bpayn
ประเทศสเปน

spanner gOOn-jair bpàhk dtai
กุญแจปากตาย

spare part a-lài
อะไหล่

spare tyre yahng a-lài
ยางอะไหล่

spark plug hŏo-a tee-un
หัวเทียน

speak: do you speak English?
kOOn pôot pah-săh ung-grìt bpen mái?
คุณพูดภาษาอังกฤษเป็นไหม

I don't speak ... pŏm (chún) pôot ... mâi bpen
ผม(ฉัน)พูด ... ไม่เป็น

can I speak to ...? kŏr pôot gùp ... nòy, dâi mái?
ขอพูดกับ ... หน่อยได้ไหม

dialogue

can I speak to Tongchai?
kŏr pôot gùp kOOn Tong-chai nòy, dâi mái ká?
who's calling? krai pôot krúp?
it's Patricia chún Patricia pôot kâ
I'm sorry, he's not in, can I take a message? káo mâi yòo krúp mee a-rai ja fàhk bòrk mái?
no thanks, I'll call back later mâi mee kâ ja toh glùp mah dtorn lŭng
please tell him I called

Sp

chôo-ay bòrk káo wâh chún toh mah

spectacles wâirn dtah
แว่นตา

speed (noun) kwahm ray-o
ความเร็ว

speed limit ùt-dtrah kwahm ray-o
อัตราความเร็ว

speedometer krêu-ung wút kwahm ray-o
เครื่องวัดความเร็ว

spell: how do you spell it?
sa-gòt yung-ngai?
สะกดอย่างไร

spend chái ngern
ใช้เงิน

spider mairng moom
แมงมุม

spin-dryer krêu-ung bpùn pâh hâi hâirng
เครื่องปั่นผ้าให้แห้ง

splinter sa-gèt mái
สะเก็ดไม้

spoke (in wheel) sêe lór rót
ซี่ล้อรถ

spoon chórn
ช้อน

sport gee-lah
กีฬา

sprain: I've sprained my ...
pŏm (chún) tum ... klét
ผม(ฉัน)ทำเคล็ด ...

spring (season) réu-doo bai mái plì
ฤดูใบไม้ผลิ

in the spring dtorn réu-doo bai mái plì
ตอนฤดูใบไม้ผลิ

squid bplah-mèuk
ปลาหมึก

stairs bun-dai
บันได

stale mâi sòt
ไม่สด

stall: the engine keeps stalling krêu-ung dùp bòy
เครื่องดับบ่อย

stamp (noun) sa-dtairm
แสตมป์

dialogue

a stamp for England, please kŏr sa-dtairm sòng bpai ung-grìt
what are you sending?
koon ja sòng a-rai bpai?
this postcard bpóht-káht nêe

standby 'standby'
star dao
ดาว
(in film) dah-rah nŭng
ดาราหนัง
start (verb) rêrm
เริ่ม
when does it start? rêrm mêu-rai?
เริ่มเมื่อไร
the car won't start rót sa-dtàht mâi dtìt
รถสตาร์ทไม่ติด
starter (of car) bpÒOm sa-dtàht
ปุ่มสตาร์ท
starving: I'm starving pŏm (chún) hĕw jung ler-ee
ผม(ฉัน)หิวจังเลย
state (country) rút
รัฐ
the States (USA) sa-hăh-rút
สหรัฐ
station sa-tăh-nee rót fai
สถานีรถไฟ
statue rôop bpûn
รูปปั้น
stay: where are you staying? kOOn púk yòo têe năi?
คุณพักอยู่ที่ไหน
I'm staying at ... pŏm (chún) púk yòo têe ...
ผม(ฉัน)พักอยู่ที่ ...
I'd like to stay another two nights pŏm (chún) yàhk ja púk yòo èek sŏrng keun
ผม(ฉัน)อยากจะพักอยู่อีกสองคืน
steak néu-a sa-dték
เนื้อสเต๊ก
steal ka-moy-ee
ขโมย
my bag has been stolen gra-bpăo tòok ka-moy-ee
กระเป๋าถูกขโมย
steep (hill) chun
ชัน
steering mŏOn poo-ung mah-lai
หมุนพวงมาลัย
step: on the steps têe kûn bun-dai
ที่ขั้นบันได
stereo sa-dtay-ri-oh
สเตริโอ
sterling ngern bporn
เงินปอนด์
steward (on plane) pa-núk ngahn krêu-ung bin
พนักงานเครื่องบิน
stewardess pa-núk ngahn dtôrn rúp bon krêu-ung bin
พนักงานต้อนรับบนเครื่องบิน

sticking plaster plah-sa-dter
พลาสเตอร์
sticky rice kâo nĕe-o
ข้าวเหนียว
still: I'm still here pŏm (chún) yung yòo têe nêe
ผม(ฉัน)ยังอยู่ที่นี่
is he still there? káo yung yòo têe nûn mái?
เขายังอยู่ที่นั่นไหม
keep still! yòo nîng nîng!
อยู่นิ่ง ๆ
sting: I've been stung pŏm (chún) tòok ma-laırng dtòy
ผม(ฉัน)ถูกแมลงต่อย
stockings tŏong nôrng
ถุงน่อง
stomach tórng
ท้อง
stomach ache bpòo-ut tórng
ปวดท้อง
stone (rock) hĭn
หิน
stop (verb) yòot
หยุด
please stop here (to taxi driver etc) yòot dtrong née krúp (kâ)
หยุดตรงนี้ครับ(ค่ะ)
do you stop near ...? koon yòot glâi glâi ... mái?
คุณหยุดใกล้ ๆ ... ไหม
stop it! yòot na!
หยุดนะ
stopover wáir
แวะ
storm pah-yóo
พายุ
straight: it's straight ahead yòo dtrong nâh
อยู่ตรงหน้า
a straight whisky wít-sa-gêe pee-o
วิสกี้เพียว
straightaway tun-tee
ทันที
strange (odd) bplàirk
แปลก
stranger kon bplàirk nâh
คนแปลกหน้า
I'm a stranger here pŏm (chún) mâi châi kon têe nêe
ผม(ฉัน)ไม่ใช่คนที่นี่
strap săi
สาย
strawberry sa-dtor-ber-rêe
สตรอเบอร์รี่
stream lum-tahn
ลำธาร
street ta-nŏn
ถนน
on the street bon ta-nŏn
บนถนน

streetmap păirn-têe ta-nŏn
แผนที่ถนน

string chêu-uk
เชือก

strong kăirng rairng
แข็งแรง

stuck dtìt
ติด

it's stuck mun dtìt
มันติด

student núk-sèuk-săh
นักศึกษา

stupid ngôh
โง่

suburb bor-ri-wayn chahn meu-ung
บริเวณชานเมือง

suddenly tun-tee
ทันที

suede nŭng glùp
หนังกลับ

sugar núm dtahn
น้ำตาล

suit (noun) chóot
ชุด

it doesn't suit me (jacket etc) mâi **mòr gùp** pŏm (chún)
ไม่เหมาะกับผม(ฉัน)

it suits you mòr gùp koon dâi dee
เหมาะกับคุณได้ดี

suitcase gra-bpăo dern tahng
กระเป๋าเดินทาง

summer nâh rórn
หน้าร้อน

in the summer dtorn nâh rórn
ตอนหน้าร้อน

sun prá-ah-tít
พระอาทิตย์

in the sun dtàhk dàirt
ตากแดด

out of the sun nai rôm
ในร่ม

sunbathe àhp dàirt
อาบแดด

sunblock (cream) yah tah gun dàirt
ยาทากันแดด

sunburn tòok dàirt
ถูกแดด

sunburnt tòok dàirt mâi
ถูกแดดไหม้

Sunday wun ah-tít
วันอาทิตย์

sunglasses wâirn gun dàirt
แว่นกันแดด

sun lounger máh nûng àhp dàirt
ม้านั่งอาบแดด

sunny: it's sunny dàirt òrk
แดดออก

sunroof (in car) lŭng-kah

gra-jòk
หลังคากระจก
sunset ah-tít dtòk
อาทิตย์ตก
sunshade ngao dàirt
เงาแดด
sunshine dàirt òrk
แดดออก
sunstroke rôhk páir dàirt
โรคแพ้แดด
suntan pěw klúm dàirt
ผิวคล้ำแดด
suntan lotion kreem tah àhp dàirt
ครีมทาอาบแดด
suntanned mee pěw klúm dàirt
มีผิวคล้ำแดด
suntan oil núm mun tah àhp dàirt
น้ำมันทาอาบแดด
super yôrt yêe-um
ยอดเยี่ยม
supermarket sOO-bper-mah-get
ซุเปอร์มาร์เก็ต
supper ah-hăhn yen
อาหารเย็น
supplement (extra charge) kâh bor-ri-gahn pi-sàyt
ค่าบริการพิเศษ
sure: are you sure? kOOn nâir-jai rěu?
คุณแน่ใจหรือ
sure! nâir-norn!
แน่นอน
surname nahm sa-gOOn
นามสกุล
swearword kum sa-bòt
คำสบถ
sweater sêu-a sa-wet-dter
สเวตเตอร์
Sweden bpra-tâyt sa-wee-den
ประเทศสวีเดน
sweet (taste) wăhn
หวาน
(noun: dessert) kŏrng wăhn
ของหวาน
sweets tórp-fêe
ท๊อฟฟี่
swelling boo-um
บวม
swim (verb) wâi náhm
ว่ายน้ำ
I'm going for a swim pŏm (chún) bpai wâi náhm
ผม(ฉัน)ไปว่ายน้ำ
let's go for a swim bpai wâi náhm mái?
ไปว่ายน้ำไหม
swimming costume chóOt àhp náhm
ชุดอาบน้ำ

swimming pool sà wâi náhm
สระว่ายน้ำ
swimming trunks gahng-gayng wâi náhm
กางเกงว่ายน้ำ
switch (noun) sa-wít
สวิช
switch off bpìt
ปิด
switch on bpèrt
เปิด
Switzerland bpra-tâyt sa-wìt
ประเทศสวิส
swollen boo-um
บวม

T

table dtó
โต๊ะ
a table for two dtó sǔm-rùp sŏrng kon
โต๊ะสำหรับสองคน
tablecloth pâh bpoo dtó
ผ้าปูโต๊ะ
table tennis bping bporng
ปิงปอง
tailback (of traffic) rót dtìt
รถติด
tailor châhng dtùt sêu-a pâh
ช่างตัดเสื้อผ้า

take (lead: something somewhere) ao ... bpai
เอา ... ไป
(someone somewhere) pah ... bpai
พา ... ไป
take (accept) rúp
รับ
can you take me to the ...? pah bpai ... dâi mái?
พาไป ... ได้ไหม
do you take credit cards? rúp bùt kray-dìt rěu bplào?
รับบัตรเครดิตหรือเปล่า
fine, I'll take it oh kay, pŏm (chún) ao
โอเค ผม(ฉัน)เอา
can I take this? (leaflet etc) kŏr un née dâi mái?
ขออันนี้ได้ไหม
how long does it take? chái way-lah nahn tâo-rài?
ใช้เวลานานเท่าไร
it takes three hours chái way-lah săhm chôo-a mohng
ใช้เวลาสามชั่วโมง
is this seat taken? têe nêe wâhng mái?
ที่นี่ว่างไหม
can you take a little off here? (to hairdresser) dtùt dtrong née

òrk nít-nòy dâi mái?
ตัดตรงนี้ออกนิดหน่อยได้ไหม

talcum powder bpâirng
แป้ง

talk (verb) pôot
พูด

tall sŏong
สูง

tampons tairm-porn
แทมพอน

tan (noun) klúm
คล้ำ

to get a tan hâi pĕw klúm
ให้ผิวคล้ำ

tank (of car) tŭng núm mun
ถังน้ำมัน

tap górk náhm
ก๊อกน้ำ

tape (for cassette) táyp
เทป

tape measure săi wút
สายวัด

tape recorder krêu-ung bun-téuk sĕe-ung
เครื่องบันทึกเสียง

taste (noun) rót
รส

can I taste it? kŏr **lorng chim** nòy, dâi mái?
ขอลองชิมหน่อยได้ไหม

taxi táirk-sêe
แท๊กซี่

will you get me a taxi? chôo-ay rêe-uk táirk-sêe hâi nòy, dâi mái?
ช่วยเรียกแท๊กซี่ให้หน่อย ได้ไหม

dialogue

to the airport/to the Regent Hotel, please bpai sa-năhm bin/rohng rairm ree-yen
how much will it be? tâo-rài?
300 baht săhm róy bàht
that's fine right here, thanks jòrt dtrong née na

taxi-driver kon kùp táirk-sêe
คนขับแท๊กซี่

taxi rank têe jòrt rót táirk-sêe
ที่จอดรถแท๊กซี่

tea (drink) núm chah
น้ำชา

tea for one/two, please kŏr núm chah têe nèung/sŏrng têe
ขอน้ำชาที่หนึ่ง/สองที่

teabags chah tŏong
ชาถุง

teach: could you teach me? sŏrn hâi dâi mái?
สอนให้ได้ไหม

teacher kroo
ครู
team teem
ทีม
teaspoon chórn chah
ช้อนชา
tea towel pâh chét jahn
ผ้าเช็ดจาน
teenager dèk wai rôOn
เด็กวัยรุ่น
telephone toh-ra-sùp
โทรศัพท์
television toh-ra-tút
โทรทัศน์
tell: could you tell him ...?
chôo-ay bòrk káo wâh ...
nòy, dâi mái?
ช่วยบอกเขาว่า ...
หน่อยได้ไหม
temperature (weather) OOn-na-ha-poom
อุณหภูมิ
(fever) kâi
ไข้
temple wút
วัด
tennis tay-nit
เทนนิส
tennis ball lôok ten-nít
ลูกเทนนิส
tennis court sa-năhm ten-nít
สนามเทนนิส
tennis racket mái dtee ten-nít
ไม้ตีเทนนิส
tent dten
เต็นท์
term term
เทอร์ม
terminus (rail) sa-tăh-nee
สถานี
terrible yâir
แย่
terrific yôrt yêe-um
ยอดเยี่ยม
text (message) ték
เท็คซ์
Thai (adj) tai
ไทย
(language) pah-săh tai
ภาษาไทย
a Thai, the Thais kon tai
คนไทย
Thailand (formal) bpra-tâyt tai
ประเทศไทย
(informal) meu-ung tai
เมืองไทย
than* gwàh
กว่า
smaller than lék gwàh
เล็กกว่า
thanks, thank you kòrp-koon
ขอบคุณ
thank you very much kòrp-

kOOn mâhk
ขอบคุณมาก
thanks for the lift korp-kOOn tee mah song
ขอบคุณที่มาส่ง
no thanks mâi ao kòrp-kOOn
ไม่เอาขอบคุณ

dialogue

thanks kòrp-kOOn
that's OK, don't mention it mâi bpen rai

that: that boy pôo-chai kon nún
ผู้ชายคนนั้น
that girl pôo-yĭng kon nún
ผู้หญิงคนนั้น
that one un nún
อันนั้น
I hope that ... pŏm (chún) wŭng wâh ...
ผม(ฉัน)หวังว่า ...
that's nice sŏo-ay
สวย
is that ...? ... châi mái?
... ใช่ไหม
that's it (that's right) châi láir-o
ใช่แล้ว
the*

theatre rohng la-korn
โรงละคร
their kŏrng káo
ของเขา
theirs kŏrng káo
ของเขา
them káo
เขา
for them sŭm-rùp káo
สำหรับเขา
with them gùp káo
กับเขา
to them gàir káo
แก่เขา
who? – them krai? – pôo-uk káo
ใคร – พวกเขา
then (at that time) dtorn nún
ตอนนั้น
(after that) lŭng jàhk nún
หลังจากนั้น
there têe nûn
ที่นั่น
over there têe-nôhn
ที่โน่น
up there kâhng bon nún
ข้างบนนั้น
is/are there ...? mee ... mái?
มี ... ไหม
there is/are ... mee ...
มี ...
there you are (giving something)

nêe krúp (kâ)
นี่ครับ(ค่ะ)

thermometer bpròrt
ปรอท

Thermos flask® gra-dtìk náhm
กระติกน้ำ

these*: these men pôo-chai pôo-uk lào née
ผู้ชายพวกเหล่านี้

these women pôo-yĭng pôo-uk lào née
ผู้หญิงพวกเหล่านี้

I'd like these ao pôo-uk lào née
เอาพวกเหล่านี้

they káo
เขา

thick năh
หนา

(stupid) ngôh
โง่

thief ka-moy-ee
ขโมย

thigh nôrng
น่อง

thin pŏrm
ผอม

thing kŏrng
ของ

my things kŏrng pŏm (chún)
ของผม(ฉัน)

think kít
คิด

I think so pŏm (chún) kít wâh yung-ngún
ผม(ฉัน)คิดว่าอย่างนั้น

I don't think so pŏm (chún) kít wâh kong mâi
ผม(ฉัน)คิดว่าคงไม่

I'll think about it pŏm (chún) ja lorng kít doo gòrn
ผม(ฉัน)จะลองคิดดูก่อน

thirsty: I'm thirsty pŏm (chún) hĕw náhm
ผม(ฉัน)หิวน้ำ

this: this boy pôo-chai kon née
ผู้ชายคนนี้

this girl pôo-yĭng kon née
ผู้หญิงคนนี้

this one un née
อันนี้

this is my wife nêe pun-ra-yah kŏrng pŏm
นี่ภรรยาของผม

is this ...? ... châi mái?
... ใช่ไหม

those: those men pôo chai pôo-uk lào nún
ผู้ชายพวกเหล่านั้น

those women pôo yĭng pôo-uk lào nún
ผู้หญิงพวกเหล่านั้น

which ones? – those un nâi? – un nún
อันไหน – อันนั้น

thread (noun) sên dâi
เส้นด้าย

throat kor hŏy
คอหอย

throat pastilles yah om gâir kor jèp
ยาอมแก้คอเจ็บ

through pàhn
ผ่าน

does it go through ...? (train, bus) pàhn ... rĕu bplào?
ผ่าน ... หรือเปล่า

throw (verb) kwâhng
ขว้าง

throw away (verb) tíng
ทิ้ง

thumb néw hŏo-a mâir meu
นิ้วหัวแม่มือ

thunderstorm pah-yóo fŏn
พายุฝน

Thursday wun pá-réu-hùt
วันพฤหัส

ticket dtŏo-a
ตั๋ว

dialogue

a return to Chiangmai
dtŏo-a bpai glùp chee-ung-mài
coming back when? glùp mêu-rai?
today/next Tuesday wun née/wun ung-kahn nâh
that will be 200 baht sŏrng róy bàht

ticket office (bus, rail) têe jum-nài dtŏo-a
ที่จำหน่ายตั๋ว

tie (necktie) nék-tai
เน็คไท

tight (clothes etc) kúp
คับ

it's too tight kúp gern bpai
คับเกินไป

tights tŏong yai boo-a
ถุงใยบัว

till (cash desk) têe gèp ngern
ที่เก็บเงิน

time* way-lah
เวลา

what's the time? gèe mohng láir-o?
กี่โมงแล้ว

this time krúng née
ครั้งนี้

last time krúng têe láir-o
ครั้งที่แล้ว

next time krúng nâh
ครั้งหน้า
three times săhm krúng
สามครั้ง
timetable dtah-rahng way-lah
ตารางเวลา
tin (can) gra-bpŏrng
กระป๋อง
tinfoil gra-dàht a-loo-mi-nee-um
กระดาษอลูมิเนียม
tin-opener têe bpèrt gra-bpŏrng
ที่เปิดกระป๋อง
tiny lék
เล็ก
tip (to waiter etc) ngern típ
เงินทิป
tired nèu-ay
เหนื่อย
I'm tired pŏm (chún) nèu-ay
ผม(ฉัน)เหนื่อย
tissues pâh chét meu
ผ้าเช็ดมือ
to: to Bangkok bpai groong-tâyp
ไปกรุงเทพฯ
to Thailand bpai meu-ung tai
ไปเมืองไทย
to the post office bpai bprai-sa-nee
ไปไปรษณีย์
toast (bread) ka-nŏm bpung bpîng
ขนมปังปิ้ง
today wun née
วันนี้
toe néw táo
นิ้วเท้า
together dôo-ay gun
ด้วยกัน
we're together (in shop etc) rao mah dôo-ay gun
เรามาด้วยกัน
toilet hôrng náhm
ห้องน้ำ
where is the toilet? hôrng náhm yòo têe năi?
ห้องน้ำอยู่ที่ไหน
I have to go to the toilet pŏm (chún) dtôrng bpai hôrng náhm
ผม(ฉัน)ต้องไปห้องน้ำ
toilet paper gra-dàht chum-rá
กระดาษชำระ
tomato ma-kĕu-a tâyt
มะเขือเทศ
tomato juice núm ma-kĕu-a tâyt
น้ำมะเขือเทศ
tomato ketchup sórt ma-kĕu-a tâyt
ซอสมะเขือเทศ

tomorrow prôOng née
พรุ่งนี้
tomorrow morning cháo prôOng née
เช้าพรุ่งนี้
the day after tomorrow wun ma-reun née
วันมะรืนนี้
toner (cosmetic) toner
tongue lín
ลิ้น
tonic (water) núm toh-ník
น้ำโทนิค
tonight keun née
คืนนี้
tonsillitis dtòrm torn-sin ùk-sàyp
ต่อมทอนซิลอักเสป
too (excessively) ... gern bpai
... เกินไป
(also) dôo-ay
ด้วย
too hot rórn gern bpai
ร้อนเกินไป
too much mâhk gern bpai
มากเกินไป
me too pŏm (chún) gôr mĕu-un gun
ผม(ฉัน)ก็เหมือนกัน
tooth fun
ฟัน
toothache bpòo-ut fun
ปวดฟัน
toothbrush bprairng sĕe fun
แปรงสีฟัน
toothpaste yah sĕe fun
ยาสีฟัน
top: on top of ... yòo bon ...
อยู่บน ...
at the top yòo kâhng bon
อยู่ข้างบน
top floor chún bon
ชั้นบน
topless bpleu-ay òk
เปลือยอก
torch fai chăi
ไฟฉาย
total (noun) roo-um yôrt
รวมยอด
tour (noun) rai-gahn num têe-o
รายการนำเที่ยว
is there a tour of ...? mee rai-gahn num têe-o bpai ... mái?
มีรายการนำเที่ยวไป ... ไหม
tour guide múk-kOO-tâyt
มัคคุเทศก์
tourist núk tôrng têe-o
นักท่องเที่ยว
tourist information office sŭm-núk kào săhn núk tôrng têe-o
สำนักงานข่าวสารนักท่องเที่ยว

tour operator pôo-jùt bor-ri-gahn num têe-o
ผู้จัดการบริการนำเที่ยว

towards sòo
สู่

towel pâh chét dtoo-a
ผ้าเช็ดตัว

town meu-ung
เมือง

in town nai meu-ung
ในเมือง

just out of town nork meu-ung bpai noy
นอกเมืองไปหนอย

town centre jai glahng meu-ung
ใจกลางเมือง

town hall tâyt-sa-bahn
เทศบาล

toy kŏrng lên
ของเล่น

track chahn chah-lah
ชานชาลา

which track is it for Chiangmai? bpai chee-ung-mài chahn chah-lah a-rai?
ไปเชียงใหม่ชานชาลาอะไร

tracksuit chóot gee-lah
ชุดกีฬา

traditional bpen ka-nòp-tum nee-um
เป็นขนบธรรมเนียม

traffic ja-rah-jorn
จราจร

traffic jam rót dtìt
รถติด

traffic lights fai sŭn-yahn ja-rah-jorn
ไฟสัญญาณจราจร

trailer (for carrying tent etc) rót pôo-ung
รถพ่วง

train rót fai
รถไฟ

by train doy-ee rót fai
โดยรถไฟ

dialogue

is this the train for Korat?
rót fai née bpai koh-râht mái?
sure nâir-norn
no, you want that platform there mâi bpai koon dtôrng bpai chahn chah-lah un nún

trainers (shoes) rorng táo gee-lah
รองเท้ากีฬา

train station sa-tăhn-nee rót fai
สถานีรถไฟ

translate bplair
แปล
could you translate that? chôo-ay bplair hâi nòy, dâi mái?
ช่วยแปลให้หน่อยได้ไหม
translation gahn bplair
การแปล
translator pôo bplair
ผู้แปล
trash can tŭng ka-yà
ถังขยะ
travel gahn dern tahng
การเดินทาง
we're travelling around rao dern tahng bpai rêu-ay rêu-ay
เราเดินทางไปเรื่อย ๆ
travel agent's trah-wern ay-yen
ทราเวิลเอเยนต์
traveller's cheque chék dern tahng
เช็คเดินทาง
tray tàht
ถาด
tree dtôn mái
ต้นไม้
tremendous wí-sàyt
วิเศษ
trendy tun sa-măi
ทันสมัย
trim: just a trim, please (to hairdresser) chôo-ay dtùt òrk nít-nòy tâo-nún krúp (ká)
ช่วยตัดออกนิดหน่อยเท่านั้นครับ(คะ)
trip (excursion) têe-o
เที่ยว
I'd like to go on a trip to ... pŏm (chún) yàhk ja bpai têe-o ...
ผม(ฉัน)อยากจะไปเที่ยว ...
trolley rót kĕn
รถเข็น
trouble (noun) bpun-hăh
ปัญหา
I'm having trouble with ... pŏm (chún) mee bpun-hăh gùp ...
ผม(ฉัน)มีปัญหากับ ...
trousers gahng-gayng
กางเกง
true jing
จริง
that's not true mâi jing
ไม่จริง
trunk (US: car) gra-bprohng tái rót
กระโปรงท้ายรถ
trunks (swimming) gahng-gayng wâi náhm
กางเกงว่ายน้ำ
try (verb) pa-yah-yahm
พยายาม

can I try it? kŏr lorng nòy, dâi mái?
ขอลองหน่อยได้ไหม

try on lorng sài doo
ลองใส่ดู

can I try it on? kŏr lorng sài doo nòy, dâi mái?
ขอลองใส่ดูหน่อยได้ไหม

T-shirt sêu-a yêut
เสื้อยืด

Tuesday wun ung-kahn
วันอังคาร

tuna bplah too-nah
ปลาทูน่า

tunnel oo-mohng
อุโมงค์

turn: turn left/right lée-o sái/kwăh
เลี้ยวซ้าย/ขวา

turn off: where do I turn off? ja **lée-o** têe năi?
จะเลี้ยวที่ไหน

can you turn the air-conditioning off? chôo-ay **bpìt** krêu-ung bprùp ah-gàht nòy, dâi mái?
ช่วยปิดเครื่องปรับอากาศหน่อยได้ไหม

turn on: can you turn the air-conditioning on? chôo-ay **bpèrt** krêu-ung bprùp ah-gàht nòy, dâi mái?
ช่วยเปิดเครื่องปรับอากาศหน่อยได้ไหม

turning (in road) tahng lée-o
ทางเลี้ยว

TV tee-wee
ทีวี

tweezers bpàhk kêep
ปากคีบ

twice sŏrng krúng
สองครั้ง

twice as much mâhk sŏrng tâo
มากสองเท่า

twin beds dtee-ung kôo
เตียงคู่

twin room hôrng kôo
ห้องคู่

twist: I've twisted my ankle kôr táo pŏm (chún) plík
ข้อเท้าผม(ฉัน)พลิก

type (noun) bàirp
แบบ

another type of ... ... èek bàirp nèung
... อีกแบบหนึ่ง

typical bàirp cha-bùp
แบบฉบับ

tyre yahng rót
ยางรถ

U

ugly nâh glèe-ut
น่าเกลียด

UK bpra-tâyt ung-grìt
ประเทศอังกฤษ

ulcer plăir gra-pór
แผลกระเพาะ

umbrella rôm
ร่ม

uncle (older brother of mother/father) loong
ลุง

(younger brother of father) ah
อา

(younger brother of mother) náh
น้า

unconscious mòt sa-dtì
หมดสติ

under (in position) dtâi
ใต้

(less than) dtùm gwàh
ต่ำกว่า

underdone (meat) sòok-sòok dìp-dìp
สุก ๆ ดิบ ๆ

underpants gahng-gayng nai
กางเกงใน

understand: I understand pŏm (chún) kâo jai
ผม(ฉัน)เข้าใจ

I don't understand pŏm (chún) mâi kâo jai
ผม(ฉัน)ไม่เข้าใจ

do you understand? kâo jai mái?
เข้าใจไหม

United States sa-hà-rút a-may-ri-gah
สหรัฐอเมริกา

university ma-hăh-wít-ta-yah-lai
มหาวิทยาลัย

unleaded petrol núm mun rái săhn dta-gòo-a
น้ำมันไร้สารตะกั่ว

unlimited mileage mâi jum-gùt ra-ya tahng
ไม่จำกัดระยะทาง

unlock kăi goon-jair
ไขกุญแจ

unpack gâir hòr
แก้ห่อ

until jon
จน

unusual pìt tum-ma-dah
ผิดธรรมดา

up kêun
ขึ้น

up there yòo bon nún
อยู่บนนั้น

he's not up yet (not out of bed)

káo yung mâi dtèun
เขายังไม่ตื่น
what's up? (what's wrong?)
bpen a-rai?
เป็นอะไร
upmarket rŏo-răh
หรูหรา
upset stomach tórng sĕe-a
ท้องเสีย
upside down kwûm
คว่ำ
upstairs kâhng bon
ข้างบน
urgent dòo-un
ด่วน
us* rao
เรา
with us gùp rao
กับเรา
for us sŭm-rùp rao
สำหรับเรา
USA sa-hà-rút a-may-ri-gah
สหรัฐอเมริกา
use (verb) chái
ใช้
may I use ...? kŏr chái ... dâi mái?
ขอใช้ ... ได้ไหม
useful mee bpra-yòht
มีประโยชน์
usual tum-ma-dah
ธรรมดา

V

vacancy: do you have any vacancies? (hotel) mee hôrng wâhng mái?
มีห้องว่างไหม
vacation wun yÒOt
วันหยุด
on vacation yÒOt púk pòrn
หยุดพักผ่อน
vaccination chèet wúk-seen
ฉีดวัคซีน
vacuum cleaner krêu-ung dòot fÒOn
เครื่องดูดฝุ่น
valid (ticket etc) chái dâi
ใช้ได้
how long is it valid for? chái dâi tĕung mêu-a rài?
ใช้ได้ถึงเมื่อไร
valley hòOp kăo
หุบเขา
valuable (adj) mee kâh
มีค่า
can I leave my valuables here? ao kâo kŏrng tíng wái têe nêe, dâi mái?
เอาข้าวของทิ้งไว้ที่นี่ได้ไหม
value (noun) kâh
ค่า

van rót dtôo
รถตู้

vanilla wá-ní-lah
วานิลา

a vanilla ice cream ait kreem wá-née-lah

vary: it varies láir-o dtàir
แล้วแต่

vase jair-gun
แจกัน

vegetables pùk
ผัก

vegetarian (noun) kon mâi gin néu-a
คนไม่กินเนื้อ

vending machine dtôo
ตู้

very mâhk
มาก

very little for me kŏr nít dee-o tâo-nún
ขอนิดเดียวเท่านั้น

I like it very much pŏm (chún) chôrp mâhk
ผม(ฉัน)ชอบมาก

vest (under shirt) sêu-a glâhm
เสื้อกล้าม

via pàhn
ผ่าน

video (noun: film) wee-dee-o
วีดีโอ

(recorder) krêu-ung wee-dee-oh
เครื่องวีดีโอ

Vietnam bpra-tâyt wêe-ut-nahm
ประเทศเวียดนาม

Vietnamese (adj) wêe-ut-nahm
เวียดนาม

view wew
วิว

village mòo bâhn
หมู่บ้าน

vinegar núm sôm
น้ำส้ม

visa wee-sâh
วีซ่า

visit (verb: place) têe-o
เที่ยว

(person) yêe-um
เยี่ยม

I'd like to visit ... pŏm (chún) yàhk ja bpai têe-o/yêe-um ...
ผม(ฉัน)อยากจะไปเที่ยว/เยี่ยม ...

vital: it's vital that ... sŭm-kun mâhk têe ja dtôrng ...
สำคัญมากที่จะต้อง ...

vodka word-kâh
วอร์ดก้า

voice sěe-ung
เสียง

voltage rairng fai fáh
แรงไฟฟ้า

vomit ah-jee-un
อาเจียน

W

waist ay-o
เอว

waistcoat sêu-a gúk
เสื้อกั๊ก

wait ror
รอ

wait for me ror pŏm (chún) noy ná
รอผม(ฉัน)หน่อยนะ

don't wait for me mâi dtôrng ror pŏm (chún) ná
ไม่ต้องรอผม(ฉัน)นะ

can I wait until my wife/partner gets here? ror jon pun-ra-yah/fairn mah dâi mái?
รอจนภรรยา/แฟนมาได้ไหม

can you do it while I wait? pŏm (chún) ror ao dâi mái?
ผม(ฉัน)รอเอาได้ไหม

could you wait here for me? ror pŏm (chún) têe nêe dâi mái?
รอผม(ฉัน)ที่นี่ได้ไหม

waiter kon sérp
คนเสริฟ

waiter! kOOn krúp (kâ)!
คุณครับ(ค่ะ)

waitress kon sérp
คนเสริฟ

waitress! kOOn krúp (kâ)!
คุณครับ(ค่ะ)

wake: can you wake me up at 5.30? chôo-ay **bplòok** pŏm (chún) way-lah dtee hâh krêung dâi mái?
ช่วยปลุกผม(ฉัน)เวลาตีห้าครึ่งได้ไหม

Wales Wales
เวลส์

walk: is it a long walk? dern glai mái?
เดินไกลไหม

it's only a short walk dern mâi glai
เดินไม่ไกล

I'll walk pŏm (chún) dern bpai
ผม(ฉัน)เดินไป

I'm going for a walk pŏm (chún) bpai dern lên
ผม(ฉัน)ไปเดินเล่น

Walkman® walkman®
วอล์กแมน

wall (inside) făh
ฝา

(outside) gum-pairng
กำแพง
wallet gra-bpăo sa-dtahng
กระเป๋าสตางค์
wander: I like just wandering around pŏm (chún) chôrp dern lên rêu-ay bpèu-ay bpai
ผม(ฉัน)ชอบเดินเล่นเรื่อยเปื่อยไป
want: I want a ... pŏm (chún) ao ...
ผม(ฉัน)เอา ...
I don't want any ... pŏm (chún) mâi yàhk dâi ...
ผม(ฉัน)ไม่อยากได้ ...
I want to go home pŏm (chún) yàhk ja glùp bâhn
ผม(ฉัน)อยากจะกลับบ้าน
I don't want to ... pŏm (chún) mâi yàhk ...
ผม(ฉัน)ไม่อยาก ...
he wants to ... káo yàhk ja ...
เขาอยากจะ ...
what do you want? kOon dtôrng-gahn a-rai?
คุณต้องการอะไร
ward (in hospital) hŏr pôo bpòo-ay
หอผู้ป่วย
warm rórn
ร้อน
I'm so warm pŏm (chún) rórn jung
ผม(ฉัน)ร้อนจัง
was*: he was káo bpen
เขาเป็น
she was káo bpen
เขาเป็น
it was (mun) bpen
มันเป็น
wash (verb) súk
ซัก
(oneself) láhng
ล้าง
can you wash these? súk un née hâi nòy dâi mái?
ซักอันนี้ให้หน่อยได้ไหม
washer (for bolt etc) wong-wăirn
วงแหวน
washhand basin àhng láhng nâh
อ่างล้างหน้า
washing machine krêu-ung súk pâh
เครื่องซักผ้า
washing powder pŏng súk fôrk
ผงซักฟอก
washing-up liquid núm yah láhng
น้ำยาล้าง

wasp dtairn
แตน
watch (wristwatch) nah-li-gah
นาฬิกา
will you watch my things for me? chôo-ay fâo kŏrng hâi nòy dâi mái?
ช่วยเฝ้าของให้หน่อยได้ไหม
watch out! ra-wung!
ระวัง
watch strap săi nah-li-gah
สายนาฬิกา
water náhm
น้ำ
may I have some water? kŏr náhm nòy dâi mái?
ขอน้ำหน่อยได้ไหม
waterproof (adj) gun náhm
กันน้ำ
waterskiing sa-gee náhm
สกีน้ำ
wave (in sea) klêun
คลื่น
way: it's this way bpai tahng née
ไปทางนี้
it's that way bpai tahng nóhn
ไปทางโน้น
is it a long way to ...? bpai ... glai mái?
ไป ... ไกลไหม
no way! mâi mee tahng!
ไม่มีทาง

dialogue

could you tell me the way to ...? chôo-ay bòrk tahng bpai ... hâi nòy, dâi mái?
go straight on until you reach the traffic lights dern dtrong bpai jon tĕung fai sŭn-yahn
turn left lée-o sái
take the first on the right lée-o kwăh têe tahng yâirk un râirk
see where

we* rao
เรา
weak (person, drink) òrn-air
อ่อนแอ
weather ah-gàht
อากาศ
wedding pi-tee dtàirng ngahn
พิธีแต่งงาน
wedding ring wăirn dtàirng ngahn
แหวนแต่งงาน
Wednesday wun pÓOt
วันพุธ

week ah-tít
อาทิตย์
a week (from) today èek ah-tít nèung jàhk wun née bpai
อีกอาทิตย์หนึ่งจากวันนี้ไป
a week (from) tomorrow èek ah-tít nèung jàhk prOong née bpai
อีกอาทิตย์หนึ่งจากพรุ่งนี้ไป
weekend wun săo wun ah-tít
วันเสาร์วันอาทิตย์
at the weekend wun săo ah-tít
วันเสาร์อาทิตย์
weight núm-nùk
น้ำหนัก
weird bplàirk
แปลก
weirdo kon bplàirk
คนแปลก
welcome: welcome to ... kŏr dtôrn rúp ...
ขอต้อนรับ ...
you're welcome (don't mention it) mâi bpen rai
ไม่เป็นไร
well: I don't feel well pŏm (chún) róo-sèuk mâi kôy sa-bai
ผม(ฉัน)รู้สึกไม่ค่อยสบาย
she's not well káo mâi sa-bai
เขาไม่สบาย
you speak English very well kOon pôot pah-săh ung-grìt dâi dee mâhk
คุณพูดภาษาอังกฤษได้ดีมาก
well done! dee mâhk!
ดีมาก
this one as well un née dôo-ay
อันนี้ด้วย
well well! (surprise) măir!
แหม

dialogue

how are you? bpen yung-ngai bâhng?
very well, thanks, and you? sa-bai dee kòrp-kOon, láir-o kOon lâ?

well-done (meat) sòok sòok
สุก ๆ
Welsh: I'm Welsh pŏm (chún) bpen kon Wales
ผม(ฉัน)เป็นคนเวลส์
were*: we were rao bpen
เราเป็น
you were kOon bpen
คุณเป็น
they were káo bpen
เขาเป็น
west dta-wun dtòk
ตะวันตก

in the west dta-wun dtòk
ตะวันตก

West Indian (adj) mah jahk mòo gòr in-dee-a dta-wun dtòk
มาจากหมู่เกาะอินเดียตะวันตก

wet bpèe-uk
เปียก

what? a-rai?
อะไร

what's that? nûn a-rai?
นั่นอะไร

what should I do? ja tum yung ngai dee?
จะทำอย่างไรดี

what a view! wew sŏo-ay jung ler-ee!
วิวสวยจังเลย

what bus do I take? kêun rót may săi năi?
ขึ้นรถเมล์สายไหน

wheel lór
ล้อ

wheelchair rót kĕn sŭm-rùp kon bpòo-ay
รถเข็นสำหรับคนป่วย

when? mêu-rai?
เมื่อไร

when we get back mêu-a rao glùp mah/bpai
เมื่อเรากลับมา/ไป

when's the train/ferry? rót fai/reu-a òrk gèe mohng?
รถไฟ/เรือออกกี่โมง

where? têe-năi?
ที่ไหน

I don't know where it is pŏm (chún) mâi sâhp wâh yòo têe-năi
ผม(ฉัน)ไม่ทราบว่าอยู่ที่ไหน

dialogue

where is the temple? wút yòo têe năi?
it's over there yòo têe nôhn
could you show me where it is on the map? chôo-ay chée hâi hĕn wâh yòo têe năi nai păirn-têe
it's just here yòo dtrong née
see way

which: which bus? rót may săi năi?
รถเมล์สายไหน

dialogue

which one? un năi?
that one un nún

this one? un née, châi mái?
no, that one mâi châi un nún

while: while I'm here ka-nà têe pŏm (chún) yòo têe nêe
ขนะที่ผม(ฉัน)อยู่ที่นี่

whisky lâo wít-sa-gêe
เหล้าวิสกี้

white sĕe kăo
สีขาว

white wine lâo wai kăo
เหล้าไวน์ขาว

who? krai?
ใคร

who is it? nûn krai lâ?
นั่นใครล่ะ

the man who ... kon têe ...
คนที่ ...

whole: the whole week dta-lòrt ah-tít
ตลอดอาทิตย์

the whole lot túng mòt
ทั้งหมด

whose: whose is this? nêe kŏrng krai?
นี่ของใคร

why? tum-mai?
ทำไม

wide gwâhng
กว้าง

wife: my wife pun-ra-yah kŏrng pŏm
ภรรยาของผม

will*: will you do it for me? chôo-ay tum hâi nòy dâi mái?
ช่วยทำให้หน่อยได้ไหม

wind (noun) lom
ลม

window nâh-dtàhng
หน้าต่าง

near the window glâi nâh-dtàhng
ใกล้หน้าต่าง

in the window (of shop) têe nâh-dtàhng
ที่หน้าต่าง

window seat têe nûng dtìt nâh-dtàhng
ที่นั่งติดหน้าต่าง

windscreen gra-jòk nâh rót yon
กระจกหน้ารถยนต์

windscreen wiper têe bpùt núm fŏn
ที่ปัดน้ำฝน

windsurfing gahn lên gra-dahn dtôh lom
การเล่นกระดานโต้ลม

windy: it's so windy lom rairng jung
ลมแรงจัง

wine wai
ไวน์

can we have some more wine? kŏr wai èek dâi mái?
ขอไวน์อีกได้ไหม

wine list rai-gahn wai
รายการไวน์

winter nâh năo
หน้าหนาว

in the winter nai nâh năo
ในหน้าหนาว

wire lôo-ut
ลวด

(electric) săi fai fáh
สายไฟฟ้า

wish: best wishes dôo-ay kwahm bprah-ta-năh dee
ด้วยความปรารถนาดี

with gùp
กับ

I'm staying with ... pŏm (chún) púk yòo gùp ...
ผม(ฉัน)พักอยู่กับ ...

without doy-ee mâi
โดยไม่

witness pa-yahn
พยาน

will you be a witness for me? chôo-ay bpen pa-yahn hâi pŏm (chún) dâi mái?
ช่วยเป็นพยานให้ผม(ฉัน)ได้ไหม

woman pôo-yĭng
ผู้หญิง

wonderful yôrt yêe-um
ยอดเยี่ยม

won't*: it won't start mâi yorm dtìt
ไม่ยอมติด

wood (material) mái
ไม้

woods (forest) bpàh
ป่า

wool kŏn sùt
ขนสัตว์

word kum
คำ

work (noun) ngahn
งาน

it's not working mun sĕe-a
มันเสีย

I work in ... pŏm (chún) tum ngahn têe ...
ผม(ฉัน)ทำงานที่ ...

world lôhk
โลก

worry: I'm worried pŏm (chún) bpen hòo-ung
ผม(ฉัน)เป็นห่วง

worse: it's worse yâir gwàh
แย่กว่า

worst yâir têe sòot
แย่ที่สุด

worth: is it worth a visit? nâh têe-o mái?
น่าเที่ยวไหม

would: would you give this to ...? chôo-ay ao nêe bpai hâi ... dâi mái?
ช่วยเอานี่ไปให้ ... ได้ไหม
wrap: could you wrap it up? chôo-ay hòr hâi nòy, dâi mái?
ช่วยห่อให้หน่อยได้ไหม
wrapping paper gra-dàht hòr kŏrng kwŭn
กระดาษห่อของขวัญ
wrist kôr meu
ข้อมือ
write kĕe-un
เขียน
could you write it down? chôo-ay kĕe-un long hâi nòy, dâi mái?
ช่วยเขียนลงให้หน่อยได้ไหม
how do you write it? kĕe-un yung-ngai?
เขียนอย่างไร
writing paper gra-dàht kĕe-un jòt-măi
กระดาษเขียนจดหมาย
wrong: it's the wrong key gOOn-jair **pìt**
กุญแจผิด
this is the wrong train rót fai **pìt** ka-boo-un
รถไฟผิดขบวน
the bill's wrong kít bin **pìt**
คิดบิลผิด
sorry, wrong number kŏr-tôht dtòr ber **pìt**
ขอโทษ ต่อเบอร์ผิด
sorry, wrong room kŏr-tôht, **pìt** hôrng
ขอโทษ ผิดห้อง
there's something wrong with ... ... mee a-rai **pìt**
... มีอะไรผิด
what's wrong? bpen a-rai?
เป็นอะไร

X-ray 'X-ray'
เอ็กซ์เรย์

yacht reu-a yórt
เรือยอชท์
yard*
year bpee
ปี
yellow sĕe lĕu-ung
สีเหลือง
yes* krúp (kâ); châi
ครับ(ค่ะ); ใช่
yesterday mêu-a wahn née
เมื่อวานนี้

yesterday morning cháo wahn née
เช้าวานนี้

the day before yesterday wun seun née
วันซืนนี้

yet yung
ยัง

dialogues

is it here yet? mah láir-o rĕu yung?
no, not yet yung
you'll have to wait a little longer yet koon dtôrng koy èek sùk nòy

yoghurt yoh-gut
โยกัด

you* koon
คุณ

this is for you nêe sŭm-rùp koon
นี่สำหรับคุณ

with you gùp koon
กับคุณ

young (man) nòom
หนุ่ม

(woman) săo
สาว

young (child) dèk lék
เด็กเล็ก

your* kŏrng koon
ของคุณ

your camera glôrng tài rôop kŏrng koon
กล้องถ่ายรูปของคุณ

yours kŏrng koon
ของคุณ

Z

zero sŏon
ศูนย์

zip sìp
ซิบ

could you put a new zip on? chôo-ay sài sìp mài dâi mái?
ช่วยใส่ซิบใหม่ได้ไหม

zip code ra-hùt bprai-sa-nee
รหัสไปรษณีย์

zoo sŏo-un sùt
สวนสัตว์

Thai

→

English

Colloquialisms

You might well hear the following expressions but you shouldn't be tempted to use any of the stronger ones – local people will not be amused or impressed by your efforts.

âi hàh! shit!
bpai (hâi pón)! go away!
bpai năi! hi!
chìp-hăi! damn!
dtai hàh! oh hell!
dtai jing! oh no!
mâi chêu-a! come on!, I don't believe you!
mâi mee tahng! no chance!, no way!
măir! goodness!
òrk bpai hâi pón! get out!
tôh! good heavens!
yòot pôot ná! shut up!
yôrt! great!

Entries are listed alphabetically according to the first complete word, for example, entries beginning with **bâhn** precede those beginning with **bahng.**

A

ah uncle (younger brother of father); aunt (younger sister of father)
ah-fri-gah Africa; African
ah-gahn klêun hěe-un nausea
ah-gahn ùk-sàyp infection
ah-gàht air; weather
ah hăhn meal; food; cuisine; cooking
ah-hăhn bpen pít food poisoning
ah-hăhn cháo breakfast
ah-hăhn glahng wun lunch
ah-hăhn kao savoury
ah-hăhn mâi yôy indigestion
ah-hăhn pí-sàyt speciality
ah-hăhn yen evening meal; supper; dinner
ah-jahn teacher
ah-kahn building
àhn read
àhng sink, basin
àhng àhp náhm bath
àhng láhng nâh washbasin
àhp dàirt sunbathe
ah-tít week
ah-tít dtòk sunset
ah-tít kêun sunrise
ah-yóo age
koon ah-yóo tâo-rài? how old are you?
ai cough; shy
âi hàh! shit!
ai-lairn Ireland
ai-lairn něu-a Northern Ireland
air hóht-tet air stewardess
ai-rít Irish
airm amp
airt-pai-rin aspirin
a-lài spare part(s)
a-may-ri-gah America; American (person)
a-may-ri-gun American (adj)
a-nah-kót future
a-nóo săh-wa-ree monument; statue
ao like; want
ào bay
ao ... bpai take; remove
ao jing ao jung serious
ao krúp (kâ) yes please
ao lá! right!, OK!
ao ... mah fetch; bring
ao ... mái? do you want ...?
ào tai Gulf of Siam
a-páht-mén flat, apartment
a-rai something
a-rai? what?
a-rai èek something else
a-rai èek? what else?
a-rai gôr dâi anything
a-rai ná? pardon (me)?, sorry?; excuse me?
a-ròy nice, delicious
àyk-ga-săhn document; leaflet
ay-o waist
ay-see-a Asia

ay-see-a ah-ka-nay South East Asia

B

bâh mad, crazy
bâhn house; home
 têe bâhn at home
bâhn tùt bpai nextdoor
bahng thin; some
bâhng a few; some
bahng krúng bahng krao occasionally
bahng tee sometimes; maybe; perhaps
bàht baht (unit of currency)
bàht jèp injured
bàht plăir wound
bàht wít-tĕe pavement, sidewalk
bài afternoon
 bài ... mohng ... p.m. (in the afternoon)
 bài née this afternoon
 bài prôong née tomorrow afternoon
 bài wahn née yesterday afternoon
bai bai ná cheerio, bye
bai báirng banknote, (US) bill
bai bplew leaflet
bai bpra-gàht kôht-sa-nah poster
bai kùp kèe driving licence
bai kùp kèe săh-gon international driving licence
bai mái leaf
bai mêet gohn razor blade(s)
bai reu-a sail
bai rúp bpra-gun guarantee
bai rúp-rorng guarantee; certificate
bai sèt rúp ngern receipt
bai sùng yah prescription
bai ùn-nóo-yâht licence, permit
bair-dta-rêe battery
bàirk carry
bairn flat (adj)
bàirng share; divide
bàirp sort, kind, type; pattern
bàirp cha-bùp typical
bàirp fa-rùng European-style
bàirp form form
bàirp ree-un pah-săh language course
bàirp yàhng pattern
bao light (not heavy)
ber toh-ra-sùp phone number
bèu-a bored
bin bill, (US) check; fly (verb)
bòhk rót hitchhike, hitch
boh-rahn ancient
boh-rahn wút-thóo antique
bon on; on top of
 bon péun din on the ground
bòn complain
bóop-fay buffet
boo-rèe cigarette(s)
boo-rèe gôn grorng tipped cigarettes
boo-ròot gents' toilet, men's room
bòo-uk plus
boo-um swollen
bòrk say; tell
bòrk wâh say

bor-ri-gahn service
bor-ri-gahn ngern dòo-un cashpoint, ATM
bor-ri-gahn num têe-o excursion
bor-ri-gahn rót châo car rental
bor-ri-gahn rúp chái nai hôrng púk room service
bor-ri-gahn sòrp tăhm ber toh-ra-sùp directory enquiries
bor-ri-sÒOt innocent
bor-ri-sùt company, firm
bor-ri-wayn bâhn backyard
bor-ri-wayn chahn meu-ung suburb
bòt ree-un lesson
bòy bòy often
bpà-dti-tin calendar
bpâh aunt (elder sister of mother/father)
bpàh jungle; forest
bpàh cháh cemetery
bpàh dong dìp forest, jungle
bpàh mái sùk teak forest
bpah-gee-sa-tăhn Pakistan
bpàhk mouth
bpàhk-gah pen
bpàhk-gah lôok lêun ballpoint pen
bpai to; go; go away
 bpai (hâi pón)! go away!
 bpai tèr let's go
bpâi label
bpai glùp wun dee-o day trip
bpai gùp pŏm (chún) come with me
bpai năi! hi!
bpâi rót may bus stop
bpai séu kŏrng go shopping
bpâi ta-bee-un rót licence plates
bpâirng powder; face powder; talcum powder
bpàirt eight
bpa-rin-yah degree
bpây lŭng rucksack
bpee year
 bpee têe láir-o last year; a year ago
bpee mài New Year
bpèek wing
bpèe-uk wet
bpen be; is; in; can; be capable of
 bpen ... it is ...; it was ...
 bpen a-rai? what's up?, what's wrong?
bpen bâi dumb (can't speak)
bpen bpai dâi possible
bpen bpai mâi dâi impossible
bpen bpra-yòht beneficial
bpen gun ayng informal
bpen hòo-ung worry
bpen ìt-sa-rá independent
bpen ka-nòp-tum nee-um traditional
bpen lom faint (verb); stroke; attack
bpen mun greasy
bpen nêe bOOn-kOOn grateful
bpen nern hilly
bpen pèun heat rash
bpen pêu-un friendly
bpen pít poisonous; polluted
bpen sai sandy
bpen sòht single, unmarried
bpen tahng gahn formal
bpen têe nâh por jai

satisfactory
bpen têe nee-yom popular
bpen yung-ngai bâhng? how are you?
bper-sen per cent
bpèrt open (adj); on
bpèt duck
bpeun gun
bpeun pók pistol
bpeun yao rifle
bpìt close, shut; closed
bplah fish
bplah cha-lăhm shark
bplah-sa-dter Elastoplast®, Bandaid®
bplah-sa-dtìk plastic
bplair interpret; translate
bplàirk strange, odd, funny, weird
bplàirk bpra-làht strange
bplay cot
bplèe-un change
bplèe-un rót fai change trains
bpleu-ay naked
bplòrk condom
bplòrk mŏrn pillow case
bplòrt-pai safe
bplúk plug; adaptor
bplúk fai power point
bplúk krêu-ung gohn nòo-ut shaving point
bpoh-sa-dter poster
bpóht-gáht postcard
bpoo crab
bpòo grandfather (paternal)
bpÒOm dtìt krêu-ung ignition
bpÒOm sa-dtàht starter (of car)
bpòo-ut it aches
bpòo-ut fun toothache
bpòo-ut hŏo-a headache; hangover
bpòo-ut lŭng backache
bpòo-ut tórng stomach ache
bpòrt lungs; nervous
bpra-chah-chon public; population
bpra-chOOm meeting
bpra-chót sarcastic
bpra-dtoo door; gate; goal
bpra-gun insurance
bprah-sàht castle
bprairng brush
bprairng pŏm hairbrush
bprairng sěe fun toothbrush
bprairng tah kreem gohn nòo-ut shaving brush
bprairng tŏo lép nailbrush
bprai-sa-nee post office; mail
bprai-sa-nee dòo-un express mail
bprai-sa-nee glahng central post office
bpra-jum deu-un period (menstruation)
bpra-làht jai suprised
bpra-mahn roughly, about, approximately
bpra-pay-nee custom
bpra-tahn director, president (of company)
bpra-tah-nah-tí-bor-dee president (of country)
bpra-tâyt country
bpra-tâyt bayl-yee-um Belgium
bpra-tâyt fa-rùng-sàyt France
bpra-tâyt fi-líp-bpin Philippines

bpra-tâyt gao-lĕe Korea
bpra-tâyt gum-poo-chah Cambodia
bpra-tâyt hor-lairn Holland
bpra-tâyt ì-dtah-lee Italy
bpra-tâyt in-dee-a India
bpra-tâyt in-don-nee-see-a Indonesia
bpra-tâyt jeen China
bpra-tâyt kairn-nah-dah Canada
bpra-tâyt lao Laos
bpra-tâyt mah-lay-see-a Malaysia
bpra-tâyt new see-láirn New Zealand
bpra-tâyt pa-mâh Burma
bpra-tâyt sa-bpayn Spain
bpra-tâyt sa góht-lairn Scotland
bpra-tâyt tai Thailand (formal)
bpra-tâyt ung-grìt England; Britain
bpra-tâyt wêe-ut-nahm Vietnam
bpra-tâyt yêe-bpÒOn Japan
bpra-tâyt yer-ra-mun Germany
bpra-wùt-sàht history
bprêe-o sour; sharp (taste)
bprèe-up têe-up compare
bpròht favourite
bpròrt thermometer
bpúm núm mun petrol station, gas station
bpun-hăh problem; trouble
bpùt-jOO-bun-née nowadays
brayk meu handbrake
bum-nahn pension
bun-dai ladder; stairs
bun-dai lêu-un escalator
bun-dai sŭm-rùp nĕe fai fire escape
bung-ern quite by chance
bun-yai describe
bùt bpra-jum dtoo-a identity card
bùt chern invitation
bùt kray-dìt credit card
bùt têe-nûng boarding pass

Ch

cháh late; slow; slowly
cháh cháh slowly
chahm dish, bowl
chahn chah-lah platform, (US) track
chahn meu-ung outskirts
cháhng elephant
châhng bpra-bpah plumber
châhng dtùt pŏm hairdresser; barber
châhng dtùt sêu-a pâh tailor
châhng fai fáh electrician
châhng ngern silversmith
châhng tài rôop photographer
châhng torng goldsmith
chai man; male
chái use
chái dâi valid
chai dairn border
chai hàht beach
châi láir-o that's it, that's right
châi láir-o! exactly!
châi mái? isn't it?
chái ngern spend

chái ... rôo-um gun share
chai ta-lay seaside; coast
châir kăirng deep-freeze; frozen
cha-làht clever, intelligent
cha-ná win
châo rent, hire
cháo morning
 cháo née this morning
 cháo prôong née tomorrow morning
 cháo wahn née yesterday morning
chao bâhn villager
chao dtàhng bpra-tâyt foreigner
chao kăo hill tribe
chao nah rice farmer
chao yóo-rôhp European
chèet yah injection
chee-wít life
chék cheque, (US) check
chék dern tahng traveller's cheque
chék doo check (verb)
chên for example
chern choo-un invite
chern gòrn after you
chern kâo mah! come in!
chern krúp (kâ) ... please ...
cherng kăo hillside
chêu first name
 koon chêu a-rai? what's your name?
chêu lên nickname
chêu-a believe
chéu-a châht race (ethnic)
chéun humid; damp
chêu-uk rope; string
chêu-uk rorng táo shoelaces
chim taste
chín piece
 chín yài a big bit
chìp-hăi! damn!
chôhk luck
chôhk dee fortunately; good luck!
chôhk rái unfortunately; hard luck!
chon glòom nói ethnic minority
chon-na-bòt countryside
choo chêep lifebelt
chôo-a krao temporary
chôo-a mohng hour
chôo-a rá-yá period (of time)
chôo-ay help
 chôo-ay ...? please ...?, would you please ...?
 chôo-ay dôo-ay! help!
chòok chĕrn emergency
chòok-la-hòok hectic
chóot suit
chóot ah-hăhn course (of meal)
chóot àhp náhm swimming costume
chóot bpa-thŏm pa-yah-bahn first-aid kit
chóot fun tee-um false teeth
chóot norn nightdress
chórk shock-absorber
chórn spoon
chórn sôrm cutlery
chôrng lane (on motorway)
chôrng kâo gate
chôrng kăo mountain pass
chôrp like
chôrp ... mâhk gwàh prefer

chun steep
chún I; me; myself (said by a woman); floor, storey
chún nèung first class; ground floor, (US) first floor
chún săhm third class; second floor, (US) third floor
chún sŏrng second class; first floor, (US) second floor

D

dâhm handle
dâi get, obtain; may; might; be able
dâi glìn smell
... dâi mái? can I/you ... ?
dâi yìn hear
dàirt òrk sunny, sunshine
dao star
dee good; fine; nice
dee! good!
dee gwàh better
dee jai happy; pleased
dee kêun mâhk much better
dee láir-o! good!; that'll do nicely!
dee mâhk! well done!; magnificent!
dee têe sòot (the) best
dee-chún I; me (said by a woman)
dee-o just, only
dĕe-o soon
dĕe-o, dĕe-o just a minute
dĕe-o gòrn! just a second!
dĕe-o née now; at present
dèk child; children
dèk chai boy
dèk òrn baby; young child
dèk wai rôon teenager
dèk yĭng girl
dern walk
dern bpai on foot
dern tahng travel
dern tahng bpai tóo-rá gìt business trip
dèuk late
dèum drink (verb)
deung pull
deu-un in; month
din earth; land
din-sŏr pencil
dip raw
dòht dèe-o secluded
don-dtree music
don dtree pêun meu-ung folk music
don-dtree pórp pop music
don-dtree tai derm Thai classical music
doo look (at); watch
doo lair take care of
doo mĕu-un look, seem; look like
dôo-ay too, also
dôo-ay gun together
dôo-ay kwahm bprah-ta-nah dee with best wishes
dòo-un urgent
dòrk goo-làhp rose
dòrk-mái flower
doy-ee by
doy-ee rót yon by car
doy-ee cha-pòr especially
doy-ee jay-dta-nah deliberately

doy-ee mâi without
dta-bai (fŏn) lép nailfile
dta-gèe-up chopsticks
dta-gla greedy
dta-gohn shout
dta-grâh basket
dta-grâh ka-yà wastepaper basket
dta-grai scissors
dtah eye; grandfather (maternal)
dtah bòrt blind
dtahm follow
dtahm tum-ma-dah as usual
dtàhng different
dtàhng bpra-tâyt abroad; foreign
dtàhng dtàhng various
dtàhng hàhk separate
dtàhng jung-wùt up-country (outside Bangkok)
dtah-rahng têe-o bin scheduled flight
dtah-rahng way-lah timetable, (US) schedule
dtai die; dead; kidneys (in body)
dtâi south; under, below
dtai hàh! oh hell!
dtai jing! oh no!
dtàir but
dtàir la kon each of them (people)
dtàir la krúng each time
dtàir la un each of them (things)
dtàirk break
dtàirk láir-o broken
dtàirk ngâi fragile
dtâirm score
dtàirng ngahn láir-o married
dta-làht market
dta-làht náhm floating market
dta-làht yen night market
dta-lòk funny, amusing; joke
dta-lòrt throughout; whole
dtao cooker
dtào turtle; tortoise
dtao òp oven
dtao rêet iron
dta-wun dtòk west
dta-wun dtòk chĕe-ung dtâi southwest
dta-wun dtòk chĕe-ung nĕu-a northwest
dta-wun òrk east
dta-wun òrk chĕe-ung dtâi southeast
dta-wun òrk chĕe-ung nĕu-a northeast
dtee hit
dtêe-a short
dteen bottom (of hill)
dtee-ung bed
dtee-ung dèe-o single bed
dtee-ung kôo twin beds
dtem, dtem láir-o full
dten tent
dtên rum dance
dterm fill
dtèuk block of flats, apartment block
dtêun shallow
dtèun awake; wake up; get up
dtèun-dtên excited; nervous
dtìt stuck
dtìt dtòr contact
dtìt gùp next to
dtó table
dtó jài ngern cash desk, cashier

dtòk miss (bus etc)
dtòk jai shock
dtôn bpahm palm tree
dtôn mái plant; tree
dtôo cupboard, closet; compartment; kiosk
dtôo bprai-sa-nee letterbox, mailbox
dtôo châir kăirng freezer
dtôo gèp gra-bpăo locker
dtôo jòt-măi letterbox, mailbox
dtôo norn sleeper, sleeping car
dtôo núng-sĕu pim newsstand
dtôo toh-ra-sùp phone box, phone booth
dtôo yen fridge; refrigerator
dtŏo-a ticket
dtŏo-a bpai single ticket, one-way ticket
dtŏo-a bpai glùp return ticket, round trip ticket
dtoo-a yàhng example
dtóok-ga-dtah doll
dtoo-lah-kom October
dtôom hŏo earring(s)
dtòr connection
dtòr rah-kah bargain (verb)
dtòr wâh complain
dtorn bài afternoon
dtorn cháo morning
dtorn glahng keun evening; night
dtorn yen late afternoon
dtôrng must; have to
dtôrng-gahn need
dtòy sting (verb)
dtrah brand
dtreung krêe-ut serious
dtrong direct
dtrong dtrong straight
dtrong kâhm opposite
dtrong nâh straight ahead
dtrong née right here, just here
dtrong way-lah on time
dtròot jeen Chinese New Year
dtròo-ut examine
dtròo-ut chûng núm-nùk check-in
dtròrk lane (off a soi)
dtúk-dtúk tuk-tuk (motorized three-wheeled taxi)
dtùm low
dtùm gwàh under, less than
dtum-ròo-ut police; policeman
dtun blocked
dtûng-dtàir since (time)
dtùp liver
dtùp ùk-sàyp hepatitis
dtùt cut
dtùt fai power cut
dtùt pŏm haircut
dum dark (adj)
dum náhm dive
dung loud

E

èek more; again
èek bpra-dĕe-o in a minute
èek kon nèung the other one (person)
èek mâhk a lot more

èek ... nèung another ... ; the other ...
èek un nèung the other one (thing)
èun other; others; another

F

fáh sky
făh wall; lid
fáh lâirp lightning
fáh rórng thunder
fai fire; light
fâi cotton
fai chăi torch, flashlight
fai cháirk cigarette lighter
fai fáh electric; electricity
fai kâhng sidelights
fai krêu-ung yon ignition
fai lée-o indicator
fai lŭng rót rear lights
fai mâi fire (blaze)
  fai mâi! fire!, it's on fire!
fai mòrk fog lights
fai nâh rót headlights
fairn boyfriend; girlfriend; partner
fàirt twins
fa-rùng European; Caucasian; Westerner; foreigner
fa-rùng-sàyt France; French
feem film (for camera); negative
feem sěe colour film
fláirt flat, apartment; flash
fók-chúm bruise
fŏn rain
  fŏn dtòk it's raining
fŏong kon crowd
fóot-born football
fùk boo-a shower
fun tooth
fung listen (to)
  fung si! listen!
fùng shore; bank
... fùng dtrong kâhm across the ...

G

gah núm chah teapot
gahn bpa-tŏm pa-yah-bahn first aid
gahn bplair translation
gahn bpra-gun pai insurance
gahn chók dtòy fight
gahn dern tahng journey; travel
gahn dtai death
gahn dtôrn rúp kùp sôo hospitality
gahn dum náhm léuk skin-diving
gahn fórn rum péun meu-ung folk dancing
gahn jùp bplah fishing
gahn kàirng kŭn match; race
gahn lót rah-kah reduction
gahn meu-ung politics
gahn pàh dtùt operation
gahn rôo-um bpra-way-nee sex
gahn sa-dairng don-dtree concert
gahn sòrp exam
gahn sùng ngót cancellation
gahn ta-hăhn military

gahn wâi náhm swimming
gahng-gayng trousers, (US) pants
gahng-gayng kăh sûn shorts
gahng-gayng nai underpants, underwear
gahng-gayng nai sa-dtree pants, panties
gahng-gayng wâi náhm swimming trunks
gahng-gayng yeen jeans
gàir strong; dark; old
gâir hòr unpack
gâirm cheek (on face)
gâir-o glass
gáirt gas
gao glue; scratch
gào old
gâo nine
găo êe chair
gâo êe pâh bai deckchair
gâo êe rúp kàirk sofa
gâo êe sŏong highchair
ga-rúk-ga-dah-kom July
ga-see-un retired
găy găi smart
gáyt háot guesthouse
gèe? how many?
gèe mohng láir-o? what time is it?
gee-a tŏy lŭng reverse gear
gee-lah sport
gee-lah náhm water sports
gèng well
... gern bpai too ...
gèrt kêun happen
gèrt a-rai kêun? what's happening?
gèu-up nearly, almost
gin dâi edible
gin (kâo) eat
gin yòo prórm full board
glâh hăhn brave
glahng medium; middle
glahng jâirng outdoors
glahng keun night; overnight
glahng meu-ung central
glai far (away)
glai gwàh farther (than)
glâi near; near here
... têe glâi têe sòot the nearest ...
glèe-ut hate
gler pal, mate
glom round
gloo-a afraid; fear
glòom group
glôom jai depressed
glòom kon party, group
glòrng carton
glòrng gee-a gearbox
glôrng tài nŭng movie camera
glôrng tài pâhp-pa-yon camcorder
glôrng tài rôop camera
glôrng yah sên, glôrng yah sòop pipe (for smoking)
glùp get back
glùp bâhn go home
glùp bpai go back
glùp mah come back
glùp mah nêe! come back!
goh-hòk lie (tell untruth)
gohn shave
goh-roh-goh-sŏh junk, rubbish
gôn bottom (of body)
gôn grorng filter-tipped

gOOm-pah-pun February
gOOn-jair key; lock
gôr then
gòr island
gòr ai-lairn Ireland
gôr mĕu-un gun too, also
gôr yàhng nún làir so-so
górk náhm tap, faucet
gòrn ago; before
săhm wun gòrn three days ago
gorng dtum-ròo-ut dùp plerng fire brigade
górp golf
gòt-măi law
gra-bpăo bag; briefcase; luggage, baggage; pocket
gra-bpăo dern tahng suitcase; baggage
gra-bpăo kwâi lŭng backpack
gra-bpăo sa-dtahng purse; wallet, billfold
gra-bpăo tĕu handbag, (US) purse; hand luggage, hand baggage
gra-bpŏrng can, tin
gra-bprohng skirt
gra-bprohng rót bonnet (of car), (US) hood
gra-bprohng tái (rót) boot (of car), (US) trunk
gra-dàht paper
gra-dàht chét meu, gra-dàht chét nâh paper handkerchiefs, Kleenex®
gra-dàht chum-rá toilet paper
gra-dàht hòr kŏrng kwŭn wrapping paper
gra-dàht kĕe-un jòt-măi writing paper
gra-dìng bell
gra-dòok bone
gra-dòok hùk fracture
gra-dOOm button
gra-dtìk náhm vacuum flask
gra-jòk nâh rót yon windscreen
gra-jòk ngao mirror
gra-ter-ee gay, homosexual
grìng bell
gròht angry
grom dtròo-ut kon kâo meu-ung Immigration Department
grOOng-tâyp Bangkok
grum gramme
gum-lai meu bracelet
... gum-lung pôot speaking
gum-pairng wall
gun chon bumper, (US) fender
gun-chah marijuana
gun-grai scissors
gun-yah-yon September
gùp with
gùp kâo dish; meal
gùt insect bite
gwàh than; more; over, more than
gwâhng wide

H

hâh five
hăh look for
hăh yâhk rare
hâhm prohibited, forbidden; prohibit

hâhm sòop bOO-rèe non-smoking
hâhng department store
hàhng glai remote
hâhng kăi yah pharmacy
hàht beach
hâi give; for
hăi lose
hăi bpai disappear
hâi châo for hire, to rent
hâir fishing net
hâirng dry
hàirng châht national
hăi-ya-ná disaster
hàyt cause
hèep box
hĕn see
hĕn dôo-ay agree
hĕw hungry
hĕw carry
hĕw kâo hungry
hĕw náhm thirsty
hi-má snow
hĭn stone, rock
hîng shelf
hòk six
hŏo ear
hŏo nòo-uk deaf
hŏo-a head; corner
hŏo-a jai heart
hŏo-a jai wai heart attack
hŏo-a kào knee
hŏo-a láhn bald
hŏo-a mOOm corner
hŏo-a nom lòrk dummy
hŏo-a rór laugh
hŏo-a tee-un spark plug
hòop kăo valley
hòr package, parcel
hŏr sa-mòot library
hôrng room
hôrng ah-hăhn dining room
hôrng air air-conditioned room
hôrng bprùp ah-gàht air-conditioned room
hôrng dèe-o single room
hôrng kôo twin-bedded room
hôrng kórk-tayn cocktail bar
hôrng kroo-a kitchen
hôrng náhm bathroom; toilet, rest room
hôrng náhm pôo-chai gents' toilet, men's room
hôrng náhm pôo-yĭng ladies' toilet, ladies' room
hôrng náhm sòo-un dtoo-a private bathroom
hôrng norn bedroom
hôrng pôo doy-ee săhn kăh òrk departure lounge
hôrng púk waiting room
hôrng rúp kàirk living room
hôrng rúp-bpra-tahn ah-hăhn dining room
hôrng sa-mòot library
hôrng tŏhng lounge
hŏy shell
hùk break; deduct
hŭn bpai tahng ... facing the ...
hun-loh hello

I

ì-sa-rá free

J

jàhk from
jàhk .... bpai ... from ... to ...
jàhk bpai leave, go away
jàhk meu-ung 'Wales' Welsh
jahn dish; plate
jahn rorng tôo-ay saucer
jahn sĕe-ung record
jài pay
jai dee kind, generous
jai glahng meu-ung city centre
jair-gun vase
jàirm săi pleasant
ja-mòok nose
jâo-bào bridegroom
jâo-fáh chai prince
jâo-fáh yĭng princess
jâo-kŏrng owner
jâo kŏrng bâhn landlord
jâo nai boss
jâo-săo bride
ja-rah-jorn traffic
jay-dee pagoda
jeen China; Chinese
jèp sore; hurt
jèp bpòo-ut painful
jer find
jèt seven
jing true; real
jing jai sincere
jing jing lĕr? honestly?
jîng-jòk lizard
jìt-dta-gum făh pa-nŭng murals
jon until; poor
jòop kiss
jòot-măi bplai tahng destination
jòp finish, end
jor-jair busy
jorng reservation; reserve
jor-ra-kây crocodile
jòrt park (verb)
jòt-măi letter; mail
jòt-măi ah-gàht aerogramme
jòt-măi long ta-bee-un registered letter
jùk-gra-yahn bicycle
jùk-sòo pâirt optician
jum dâi remember; recognize
jum-bpen necessary
jung ler-ee so
jung-wùt changwat, province
jùp catch; arrest
jùp bplah fishing
jùt arrange; bright; strong
jùt gahn organize

K

kăh leg
kâh kill; value
kăh kâo arrival
kâh bor-ri-gahn service charge
kâh bor-ri-gahn pi-sàyt supplement (extra charge)
kâh châo rent
kâh doy-ee săhn fare
kâh mút-jum deposit
kăh òrk departure
kâh pàhn tahng toll
kăh-gun-grai jaw
kâhm ta-lay crossing
kahng chin
kâhng beside; side

kâhng bon above, over; upstairs
kâhng lâhng downstairs
kâhng lŭng back; behind; rear
kâhng nâh in front (of); at the front
kâhng nai indoors; inside
kâhng nôrk outside
kahng toom mumps
kài egg
kâi temperature, fever; feverish
kăi sell
kăi gOOn-jair unlock
kâi jùp sùn malaria
kài mÔOk pearl
kâi wùt flu
kairk Indian; guest
kăirn arm
kăirn sêu-a sleeve
kair-nah-dah Canada; Canadian
kăirng solid; hard
kăirng rairng strong
kâirp narrow
ka-măyn Cambodian
ka-moy-ee steal; thief; burglar
ka-nà têe while
ka-nàht size; measurements
ka-nàht glahng medium-sized
ka-nòp-tum-nee-um tradition
káo he; him; she; her; they; them
kâo rice
kăo hill; mountain
kào message; news
kâo bpai go in
kâo jai understand
kâo jai láir-o I understand
kào-săhn information
ka-yà rubbish, litter, trash
kàyt district
kêe fÒOn dirt
kêe gèe-ut lazy
kèet sŏong sÒOt maximum
kĕe-un write
kem salty
kĕm needle
kĕm glùt sêu-a brooch
kĕm kùt belt
kĕm kùt ni-ra-pai seatbelt
kĕm mÒOt pin
kĕm-tít compass
ker-ee ever
kĕrn embarrassed; embarrassing
keun night; give back
keun la ... ... per night
kêun up
kêun bpai go up
keun née tonight; this evening
keun ngern refund
kêun rót may catch a bus
kew queue, line
kít think
klohn mud
klorng canal
kohm fai (fáh) lamp
koh-ték tampon
kŏhn classical masked drama
kòht hĭn rocky
kom sharp
kŏm bitter
kòm-kĕun rape
kon person; people
kŏn hair (on the body)
kon bâh idiot
kon bpah-gee-sa-tăhn a

Pakistani; Pakistanis
kon bplàirk nâh stranger
kon châo tenant
kon cha-rah senior citizen
kon dee-o just, only; alone, by oneself
kon dern táo pedestrian
kon fâo bpra-dtoo doorman; porter
kon fâo dèk baby-sitter
kon fa-rùng-sàyt a French person; the French
kon hǒo-a sǒong snob
kon jai yen calm
kon jeen a Chinese person; the Chinese
kon jùp bplah fisherman
kon ka-mǎyn a Cambodian; the Cambodians
kon kùp (rót) driver
kon kùp táirk-sêe taxi-driver
kon lao a Lao; the Laos
kon lée-ung doo dèk child minder
kon mâi gin néu-a vegetarian
kon nâirn crowded
kon new see-láirn a New Zealander; New Zealanders
kon ngôh fool
kon nún chap
kon pa-mâh a Burmese person; the Burmese
kon sa-górt a Scot; the Scots
kon sérp waiter; waitress
kon sèrp yǐng waitress
kon sôrm rorng táo shoe repairer
kǒn sùt wool
kon tai a Thai person; the Thais
kon tèep jùk-ra-yahn cyclist
kon tum ka-nǒm-bpung baker
kon ung-grìt an English person; the English; a Briton; the British
kon yêe-bpÒOn a Japanese person; the Japanese
kon yer-ra-mun a German; the Germans
kong (ja) probably
kôo pair
kôo meu num têe-o guidebook
kôo meu sǒn-ta-nah phrasebook
kôo mûn fiancé; fiancée
koo-ee chat
kÓOk prison
kOOn you
kOOn krúp (kâ) excuse me
kOOn-na-pâhp quality
koo-un ja should
kòo-ut bottle
kor neck; collar
kǒr please
pǒm (chún) kǒr I would like
kor bpòk sêu-a collar
kôr glào hǎh complaint
kǒr hâi dern tahng doy-ee bplòrt-pai! have a safe journey!
kor hǒy throat
kôr meu wrist
kǒr ... nòy can I have ...?
kǒr rórng request
kǒr sa-dairng kwahm yin dee! congratulations!
kôr sòrk elbow

kôr táo ankle
kôr tét jing fact
kórn hammer
kórng gong
kŏrng thing; of
kŏrng bplorm fake
kŏrng bpròht favourite
kŏrng fôOm feu-ay luxury
kŏrng káo his; her; hers; their; theirs
kŏrng kOOn your; yours
kŏrng kwŭn present, gift
kŏrng lên toy
kŏrng pŏm (chún) my; mine
... kŏrng pŏm (chún) ayng my own ...
kŏrng rao our; ours
kŏrng tee ra-léuk souvenir
kôrn-kâhng ja ... rather ...
kòrp-kOOn thank; thanks, thank you
kòrp-kOOn mâhk thank you very much
kŏr-tôht excuse me; sorry; I beg your pardon?
krai somebody
krai? who?
krai gôr dâi anybody
krao beard
kreem bum-rOOng pĕw moisturizer
kreem gohn nòo-ut shaving foam
kreem nôo-ut pŏm conditioner
kreem rorng péun foundation cream
kreem sa-măhn pĕw cold cream
kreem tah àhp dàirt suntan lotion
kreem tah nŭng dtah eye shadow
krêung half
krêung chôo-a mohng half an hour
krêung lŏh half a dozen
krêu-ung air air-conditioning
krêu-ung bàirp uniform
krêu-ung bin plane, airplane
krêu-ung bpào pŏm hairdryer
krêu-ung bplairng fai fáh adaptor (for voltage)
krêu-ung bpra-dùp ornament
krêu-ung bprùp ah-gàht air-conditioning
krêu-ung bpûn din pǎo pottery, earthenware
krêu-ung bun-téuk sĕe-ung tape recorder
krêu-ung chái sŏy equipment
krêu-ung chôo-ay fung hearing aid
krêu-ung dèum drink
krêu-ung dòot fOOn vacuum cleaner
krêu-ung dùp plerng fire extinguisher
krêu-ung gohn nòo-ut shaver
krêu-ung kít lâyk calculator
krêu-ung kOOm gum-nèrt contraceptive
krêu-ung lên pàirn sĕe-ung record player
krêu-ung lên tâyp kah-set cassette player
krêu-ung reu-un furniture
krêu-ung súk pâh washing machine

krêu-ung sŭm-ahng make-up
krêu-ung wee-dee-oh videorecorder
krêu-ung wút oon-na-ha-poom thermometer
krêu-ung yon motor; engine
krít Protestant
krít-dtung Roman Catholic
krít-sa-maht Christmas
kroo teacher
krôrp-kroo-a family
krúng time
krúng nèung once
krúp (kâ) yes
kum word
kûm dark
kum chern invitation
kum dtòrp answer
kum tăhm question
kun itch
kûn bun-dai step
kun gee-a gear lever
kun rêng accelerator
kun yôhk lever
kúp tight
kùp drive
kwăh right (not left)
kwahm bpra-préut behaviour
kwahm bun-terng entertainment
kwahm chéun humidity
kwahm chôo-ay lĕu-a help
kwahm dtai death
kwahm dtàirk dtàhng difference
kwahm fŭn dream
kwahm jèp bpòo-ay illness
kwahm jèp bpòo-ut pain
kwahm jing truth
kwahm kâo jai pìt misunderstanding
kwahm kít idea
kwahm lúp secret
kwahm ngêe-up silence
kwahm pìt fault; mistake
kwahm ray-o speed
kwahm rórn heat
kwahm rúk love
kwahm sŏong height
kwâhng throw
kwai water buffalo
kwûm upside down
kwun smoke

L

lah gòrn bye
láh sa-măi old-fashioned
lâhm interpreter
lăhn chai grandson; nephew
lăhn săo niece; granddaughter
láhng wash; develop (film)
lăi several
lâi shoulder
lai sen signature
láir and
lâirk bplèe-un exchange (verb: money)
... láir-o already
láir-o dtàir it depends (on); it's up to you
la-korn play
lâo alcohol
lay-kăh-nóo-gahn secretary
layn glôrng lens (of camera)
lée-o kwăh turn right
lée-o sái turn left

lèe-um sŏong cheeky
lék small, little, tiny
lèk iron
lék nóy only a few
lên play
lép meu fingernail
ler-ee bpai further; beyond
ler-ee bpai èek further on
lĕu-a gern jing jing shocking
léuk deep
leum forget
lêun slippery
lêu-ut blood
líf lift, elevator
likay popular folk theatre
lín tongue
lit litre
lŏh dozen
loh-hà metal
loh-hà sŭm-rít bronze
lôhk world; earth
lom wind
lom òrn òrn breeze
long get off
long bpai go down
long bpai! get down!
long mah! get down!
long ta-bee-un register
lôok child; children (one's own)
lôok born ball
lôok bpùt beads
lôok chai son
lôok gwàht sweets, candies
lôok kĕr-ee son-in-law
lôok ra-bèrt bomb
lôok săo daughter
lôok sa-pâi daughter-in-law
loong uncle (older brother of father or mother)
lôo-ung nâh in advance
lóp minus
lòr good-looking
lór wheel
lorng try; try out, test
lòrt fai fáh lightbulb
lum-tahn stream
lŭng after; back (of body)
lŭng jàhk nún then, after that
lŭng-kah roof

M

mah come
măh dog
máh horse
mah gèp ... collect
máh glàirp pony
mah nêe come here
mah tĕung arrive
ma-hăh-wít-ta-yah-lai university
mah-dtra-tăhn standard
mâhk a lot, lots; many; much; very; very much
... mâhk plenty of ...
mâhk (gern) bpai too much; excessive
màhk fa-rùng chewing gum
mâhk lĕu-a gern extremely
mâhk por sŏm-koo-un quite a lot
màhk róok chess
mâhn curtain
mai mile
măi silk
mái wood

mài new
mâi no; not
mâi ao ... no ...
mâi (ao) ... èek no more ...
mâi ao năi poor (quality); disgusting
mâi bòy seldom
mâi bpen rai don't mention it; it doesn't matter; never mind; that's all right
mâi bpen rêu-ung nonsense
mâi chêu-a! come on!, I don't believe you!
mâi dàirt sunburn
mâi dee bad
mái dtee racket (tennis)
mâi dtôrng sěe-a pah-sěe duty-free goods
mâi gin néu-a vegetarian
mái gwàht brush
mâi jing false
mâi jum-gùt ra-ya tahng unlimited mileage
mái kèet match
mâi ker-ee never
mâi kôy hardly
mâi lay-o it's not bad
mâi ler-ee not in the least
mâi mâhk not a lot, not much
mâi mâhk gwàh ... no more than ...
mâi mâhk tâo-rài not so much
mâi mao sober
mâi mee ... there isn't/ aren't ...; no ...
mâi mee a-rai nothing
mâi mee bpra-sìt-ti-pâhp inefficient
mâi mee krai nobody, no-one
mâi mee lôo-ut lai plain
mâi mee mah-ra-yâht rude
mâi mee tahng! no chance!, no way!
mâi nâh chêu-a amazing
mái nèep (pâh) clothes peg
mái pài bamboo
mâi pèt mild
mâi rêe-up bumpy
mâi ròrk! certainly not!
mâi sài without
mái sùk teak
mâi těung ... less than ...
mâi wâhng engaged, occupied
măi-lâyk number, figure
măir! well well!
máir dtàir ... even the ...
mâir (kŏrng) mother
mâir mái widow
mâir náhm river
máir wâh although
máir wâh ... even if ...
mâir-náhm kŏhng Mekhong River
mairng ga-prOOn jellyfish
mair-o cat
ma-lairng insect
ma-lairng gùt insect bite
ma-lairng sàhp cockroach
ma-lairng wun fly
mao drunk
ma-reun-née the day after tomorrow
mâyk kréum cloudy
may-săh-yon April
máyt metre
mee have
mee ... there is/are ...
mee ... mái? have you

got ...?; is/are there ...?
mee bpra-sìt-ti-pâhp efficient
mee bpra-yòht useful
mee chee-wít chee-wah lively
mee chee-wít yòo alive
mee chêu sěe-ung famous
mee fùk boo-a with shower
mee hàyt-pŏn sensible
mee kâh valuable
mee kwahm pìt guilty
mee lom òrn òrn breezy
mee-nah-kom March
mee pěw klúm dàirt suntanned
mee sa-này charming
mee sOOk-ka-pâhp dee healthy
mee torng pregnant
mêet knife
mêet gohn razor
mêet púp penknife
měn smell, stink
meu hand
mêu-a gòrn née once, formerly
mêu-a keun née last night
mêu-a rài? when?
mêu-a ray-o ray-o née lately, recently
mêu-a wahn née yesterday
měu-un similar, like
měu-un gun same
meu-ung city; town; country
meu-ung boh-rahn Ancient City
meu-ung gào old town
meu-ung lŏo-ung capital city
meu-ung tai Thailand (informal)
mí-cha-nún otherwise
mí-tOO-nah-yon June
mók-ga-rah-kom January
mŏo pig
moo-ay (săh-gon) boxing (international)
moo-ay tai Thai-style boxing
mòo-bâhn village
mòo-bâhn bon poo-kăo mountain village
mòo bâhn bpra-mong fishing village
mòo gòr in-dee-a dta-wun dtòk West Indies
môo-lêe blinds
mÓOng mosquito net
mòo-uk hat, cap
móo-un tâyp kah-set cassette
mŏr doctor
mòr ideal
môr saucepan
mŏr fun dentist
mòr sŏm suitable, appropriate
mòrk mist
mòrk long foggy
mŏrn pillow; cushion
mor-ra-sOOm monsoon
mor-sor scruffy
mòt láir-o empty
mòt sa-dtì unconscious
múk-kOO-tâyt guide, courier
mun it; it is; they; fat (on meat); rich
mun bpen it's
mûn engaged (to be married)
mun fa-rùng tôrt chips, French fries; crisps, (US) chips
mùt flea

N

năh thick
nah paddy field
náh uncle (younger brother of mother); aunt (younger sister of mother)
nâh face; front (part); page; season; next
nâh bèu-a boring
nâh dtèun dtên exciting
nâh fŏn rainy season
nâh glèe-ut ugly; horrible; disgusting
nâh năo winter
nâh nèu-ay nài tiring
nâh òk chest; bust
nâh rórn summer
nâh rung-gèe-ut unpleasant; revolting
nâh sĕe-a dai! what a shame!
nâh sêet pale
nâh sŏn jai interesting
nâh sŏng-săhn! what a pity!
nâh têung impressive
nâh tOO-râyt nasty
nâh-dtàhng window
nah-li-gah clock; watch
nah-li-gah bplÒOk alarm clock
nah-li-gah kôr meu watch
náhm water
nahm bùt business card
náhm dèum drinking water
nahm sa-gOOn surname, last name
nahm sa-gOOn derm maiden name
nahn a long time
nahng Mrs
nahng pa-yah-bahn nurse
nahng-săo Miss
nah-tee minute
nah-yók director, president
nah-yók rút-ta-mon-dtree prime minister
nai on; in; into; Mr
năi? which?
nai a-nah-kót in future
nai bpra-tâyt rao at home
nai lŏo-ung king
nai ra-wàhng during; among
nai têe sÒOt eventually, at last
nâir jai certain, sure
nâir norn of course, certainly, definitely
nâirn crowded, busy
năo cold; feel cold
née this; these
nêe ... this is ...
nêe a-rai? what's this?
nêe kŏrng krai? whose is this?
nêe krúp (kâ) there you are
nêe ngai here you are
nĕe-o sticky; sultry
nék-tai tie, necktie
nĕu-a north
nèu-ay tired
nèung one
nèung nai sèe quarter
néw inch
néw hŏo-a mâir meu thumb
néw meu finger
néw táo toe
ngah chánhg tusk
ngahm sa-ngàh elegant
ngahn job; work; carnival; festival

ngahn lée-ung party
ngahn sa-dairng sĭn-káh trade fair
ngahn sòp funeral
ngâi easy; simple
ngao shadow
ngăo lonely
ngao dàirt sunshade
ngêe-up quiet; silent
ngêe-up ngêe-up nòy! be quiet!
ngern money; silver
ngern bporn sterling
ngern deu-un salary
ngern dorn-lâh dollar
ngern dtàhng bpra-tâyt foreign exchange
ngern rĕe-un coin
ngern sòt cash
ngern típ tip
ngèu-uk gum
ngêu-un kăi bpra-gun insurance policy
ngôh stupid, silly, dumb
ngoo snake
ngoo hào cobra
ngôo-ung norn sleepy
ngót cancel
nîm soft
nít dee-o tâo-nún just a little
ní-tahn story
ní-tá-sa-gahn exhibition
nít-nòy a little bit
nít-ta-ya-săhn magazine
nók bird
nom milk
nŏo mouse; rat
nÒOm young; young man
nÒOm nÒOm săo săo young people
nòo-uk hŏo noisy
nôo-ut massage
nòo-ut moustache
nôrk jàhk apart from
norn lie down
norn lùp sleep
norn lùp yòo asleep
nôrng thigh
nŏrng swamp
nórng chai younger brother
nórng săo younger sister
nórng sa-pái younger sister-in-law
nòy some
nóy few
nóy gwàh ... less than ...
nóy têe sÒOt minimum
nùk heavy; serious
núk don-dtree musician
núk moo-ay boxer
núk rórng singer
núk sa-dairng chai actor
núk sa-dairng yĭng actress
núk sèuk-săh student
núk tôrng têe-o tourist
núm dtòk waterfall
núm hŏrm toilet water; perfume
núm kăirng ice
núm mun oil; petrol, (US) gas
núm mun gáht petrol, (US) gas
núm mun krêu-ung oil (motor oil)
núm mun rót dee-sen diesel (fuel)
núm mun tah àhp dàirt suntan oil

núm nùk weight
núm nùk gern excess baggage
núm póo fountain
núm tôo-um flood
núm yah àhp náhm bubble bath
núm yah láhng chahm washing-up liquid
nún that
nûn a-rai? what's that?
nûng sit
nŭng leather; film, movie
nŭng glùp suede
nûng si sit down!
núng-sĕu book
núng-sĕu dern tahng passport
núng-sĕu num têe-o guidebook
núng-sĕu pim newspaper
nút appointment

O

oh-gàht chance, opportunity
ong-săh degree
òo sôrm rót garage
oo-bùt-dti-hàyt accident
ôo-ee! ouch!
ôom carry
oo-mohng tunnel
oon-na-ha-poom temperature
òop-bpa-gorn equipment
òot fun filling
òot-săh-ha-gum industry
ôo-un fat
òrk bpai go out
òrk bpai hâi pón! get out!
òrk sĕe-ung pronounce
òrn weak (drink)
òrn-air weak (person)

pâh material, cloth
pah bpai take
pâh bpòo têe norn sheet; bed linen
pâh chét bpàhk napkin
pâh chét dtoo-a towel
pâh chét jahn tea towel
pâh chét meu napkin, serviette; tissues, Kleenex®
pâh chét nâh handkerchief; flannel
pâh hòm blanket
pâh kêe réw cloth, rag
pâh ôrm nappy, diaper
pâh pôhk sĕe-sà headscarf
pâh pun kor scarf (for neck)
pâh pun plăir bandage; dressing
pâh un-nah-mai sanitary towel, sanitary napkin
pâhk region
pâhk bung-kúp compulsory
pâhk dtâi southern region of Thailand
pâhk ee-săhn north-eastern region of Thailand
pâhk glahng central region of Thailand
pàhn through; via
pàhn bpai go through
pâhp kĕe-un painting; picture
pah-săh language

pah-săh tai Thai (language)
pah-săh tìn dialect
pah-săh ung-grìt English (language)
pah-sĕe duty; tax
pah-sĕe sa-năhm bin airport tax
pah-yóo storm
pah-yóo fŏn thunderstorm
pâi cards
páir goat; allergic to
páir dàirt heat stroke
pàirn slice
pàirn sĕe-ung record
pairng expensive
păirn-têe map
păirn-têe ta-nŏn road map, streetmap
pa-mâh Burma; Burmese
pa-nàirk dtôrn rúp reception; reception desk
pa-núk ngahn dtôrn rúp receptionist
pa-núk ngahn krêu-ung bin steward
pa-núk ngahn toh-ra-sùp operator
pa-nun gamble
pa-yah-yahm try; persevere
pay-dahn ceiling
pêe older brother/sister
pêe chai older brother
pêe săo older sister
pêe sa-pái older sister-in-law
pêrm increase
pèt hot, spicy
pét diamond
pét ploy jewellery
péun floor
yòo bon péun on the floor
pèun rash (on skin)
péun din ground
péun rorng táo sole (of shoe)
pêu-un friend
pêu-un bâhn neighbour
pêu-un rôo-um ngahn partner (in business)
pêu-un tahng jòt-măi penfriend
pĕw skin
pŏw klúm dàirt suntan
pĕw nŭng skin
pí-gahn disabled
pí-pít-ta-pun museum
pí-pít-ta-pun hàirng châht National Museum
pi-sàyt special; de luxe
pìt wrong; faulty
pìt gòt-măi illegal
pìt tum-ma-dah unusual
pìt wŭng disappointed
pi-tee dtàirng ngahn wedding
plăir bàht jèp injury
plăir gra-pór ulcer
plăir mâi burn
plăir porng blister
plăir wèr nasty
plăirng eccentric
playng song
playng póp pop song
plùk push
pŏm I; me; myself (said by a man); hair
pŏng súk fôrk soap powder
pŏn-la-mái fruit
pôo bplair translator
pôo doy-ee săhn passenger
pôo-chai boy; man

poo-gèt Phuket
pôo-jùt-gahn manager
poo-kăo mountain
poo-mi-bpra-tâyt scenery; landscape
pôot speak; talk
pôot èek tee repeat
pôot lên joke
pôo-uk group
pôo-uk née these
pôo-uk nún those
pôo-uk pôo-yĭng women
poo-ung mah-lai sái left-hand drive
poo-ung ma-lai kwăh right-hand drive
pôo-yài adult
pôo-yài bâhn village headman
pôo-yĭng woman; lady; girl
pôo-yĭng bah hostess (in bar)
pôo-yĭng ung-grìt English girl/woman
por enough
pôr father
pôr dtah father-in-law (of a man)
pôr dtah mâir yai parents-in-law (wife's parents)
por jai satisfied
por láir-o no more; that's enough
pôr mái widower
pôr mâir parents
pôr pŏo-a father-in-law (of a woman)
pôr pŏo-a mâir pŏo-a parents-in-law (husband's parents)
por sŏm-koo-un quite, fairly
pŏrm thin, skinny
pòt prickly heat
pót-ja-nah-nóo-grom dictionary
prá monk; priest
prá-ah-tít sun
prá-jâo God
prá-jun moon
prá-póot-ta-jâo Buddha
prá-póot-ta-rôop Buddha image
prá-rah-chi-nee queen
prá-râht-cha-wung palace
prá-tóo-dong mendicant monk
pree-o slim
préut-sa-jìk-gah-yon November
préut-sa-pah-kom May
prom carpet; rug
prôong née tomorrow
prór because
prórm ready
púk stay
pùk vegetables
púk krêung interval
púk pòrn rest
pun-ra-yah wife
pút fan (handheld)
pùt stir-fry
pút lom fan (mechanical)

R

ra-bee-ung patio; terrace; balcony
rah-kah cost; price
rah-kah tòok downmarket
ráhn shop, store

ráhn ah-hăhn restaurant
ráhn ah-hăhn jeen Chinese restaurant
ráhn gŏo-ay dtěe-o café; noodle shop
ráhn kăi dòrk-mái florist
ráhn kăi kŏrng chum food store
ráhn kăi kŏrng gào antique shop
ráhn kăi krêu-ung lèk hardware store
ráhn kăi krêu-ung pét ploy jeweller's
ráhn kăi lâo liquor store, shop selling wines and spirits
ráhn kăi núng-sĕu bookshop, bookstore
ráhn kăi pâhp kĕe-un art gallery
ráhn kăi pùk greengrocer's
ráhn kăi yah chemist's, pharmacy
ráhn kăi yah sòop tobacconist's, tobacco store
ráhn néu-a butcher's
ráhn sĕrm sŏo-ay beauty salon
ráhn súk hâirng dry-cleaner's
ráhn súk (sêu-a) pâh laundry
ráhn tum ka-nŏm-bpung bakery
râhng-gai body
rahng-wun prize
ra-hùt toh-ra-sùp dialling code
rai-gahn schedule
rai-gahn num têe-o tour
râirk first
rairng fai fáh voltage
ra-kung bell
rao we; us
ra-wàhng between
ra-wung! be careful!; look out!
ra-wung ná! look out!
ra-yá tahng distance
ray-o early; quick, fast; quickly
ray-o ray-o kâo! hurry up!
ray-o ray-o nòy! come on!
rêep rêep nòy! hurry up!
rêe-uk call; be called
ree-un learn
rêe-up smooth
rêe-up róy neat
rêrm begin, start
rĕu or
... rĕu ... either ... or ...
reu-a ship; boat
reu-a bpra-mong fishing boat
reu-a choo chêep lifeboat
reu-a hăhng yao long-tailed boat
reu-a kâhm fâhk ferry
reu-a pai rowing boat
reu-a ray-o speedboat
reu-a sŭm-bpûn sampan
reu-a sŭm-pao junk
reu-a yon motorboat
reu-a yórt yacht
rêu-ay rêu-ay so-so
reu-doo season
reu-doo bai mái plì spring
réu-doo bai-mái rôo-ung autumn, (US) fall
rêu-ung story
rêu-ung a-rai gun? what's going on?
rim fĕe bpàhk lip

rôhk disease
rôhk áyd Aids
rôhk bìt dysentery
rôhk bpòo-ut nai kôr rheumatism
rôhk gloo-a náhm rabies
rôhk hèut hay fever; asthma
rôhk hùt measles
rôhk hùt yer-ra-mun German measles
rôhk páir dàirt sunstroke
rôhk sâi dtìng appendicitis
rohng la-korn theatre
rohng ngahn factory
rohng nŭng cinema, movie theater
rohng pa-yah-bahn hospital
rohng rairm hotel
rohng ree-un school
rohng rót garage
rohng rúp jum-num pawnshop
rohng yim gym
rôm umbrella; parasol
nai rôm in the shade
rôm gun dàirt beach umbrella
roo hole
róo know
róo-a fence
rôo-a leak
roo-ay rich
róo-jùk know
rôOng dawn
rôOng cháo at dawn
rôop picture
rôop gàir sa-lùk carving
rôop lòr handsome
rôop-song figure
rôop tài photograph
rŏo-răh posh; luxurious; upmarket
róo-sèuk feel
róo-sèuk ja ah-jee-un feel sick
róo-sèuk kòrp-kOOn feel grateful
róo-sèuk mâi sa-bai feel unwell
roo-um include
roo-um yòo dôo-ay included
roo-um yôrt total
róp-goo-un disturb
ror wait
rórn hot; warm
rórng hâi cry
rórng playng sing
rorng táo shoe(s); boot(s)
rorng táo dtàir sandal(s)
rorng táo gee-lah trainer(s)
rorng táo ma-nóOt gòp flipper(s)
rót car; taste; flavour
rót air air-conditioned bus
rót bprùp ah-gàht air-conditioned bus
rót bun-tóOk lorry, truck
rót châo rented car
rót dtôo van
rót fai train
rót fai dòo-un express train
rót kĕn pushchair
rót kĕn sŭm-rùp kon bpòo-ay wheelchair
rót may bus
rót may bprùp ah-gàht air-conditioned bus
rót mor-dter-sai motorbike; moped
rót norn sleeping car
rót num têe-o coach trip

rót pa-yah-bahn ambulance
rót sa-bee-ung dining car
rót sa-góot-dter scooter
rót săhm lór trishaw
rót sa-năhm bin airport bus
rót too-a tour bus
rót yon car
rúk love
rûm roo-ay wealthy
rum tai Thai classical dancing
rum-kahn annoying; annoy
rum-wong ramwong dance (popular Thai folk dance)
rúp accept; receive
rút state
rút-ta-bahn government

S

sà pond; wash
sà pŏm wash one's hair
sà wâi náhm swimming pool
sa-àht clean
sa-bai well, in good health
sa-bai dee OK, all right
sa-bòo soap
sa-bòo gohn nòo-ut shaving soap
sa-bpay chèet pŏm hairspray
sa-dòo-uk convenient; comfortable
sa-dtahng satang (unit of currency)
sa-dtairm stamp
sa-dtree ladies' toilet, ladies' room
sa-gee náhm waterskiing
sa-górt táyp Sellotape®, Scotch tape®
sa-hà-rút a-may-ri-gah United States
săh-gon international
sâhk sa-lùk hùk pung remains, ruins
săh-lah pavilion
săhm three
săhm lee-um torng kum Golden Triangle
săh-mee husband
sâhp know
sàh-sa-năh religion
sàh-sa-năh póot Buddhism; Buddhist
săh-tah-ra-ná public
sai sand
sài put
sái left
săi late; telephone line; strap
săi fai fáh wire; lead
sài goon-jair lock
săi pahn fanbelt
săi rút fastener
săi yahng yêut elastic
sairng overtake
sa-lai slide
sa-lĕung salung (unit of currency)
sa-lùk nâh-dtàhng shutter
sa-mĕr always
sa-moh-sŏrn club, clubhouse
sa-moon prai herbs (medicinal)
sa-mòot notebook
sa-mòot bun-téuk bpra-jum wun diary
sa-móot măi lâyk toh-ra-sùp phone book
sa-mòot yay-loh páyt yellow pages

sa-năhm playing field; pitch
sa-năhm bin airport
sa-năhm gee-lah hàirng châht National Stadium
sa-năhm górp golf course
sa-năhm ten-nít tennis court
sa-năhm yâh lawn
sa-ngòp calm
sa-nòOk pleasant
sa-nòOk dee enjoyable, fun
sâo sad
săo young (girl)
sa-pahn bridge
sa-tăhn bor-ri-gahn rót châo car rental company
sa-tăhn gong-sOOn consulate
sa-tăhn lée-ung dèk lék nursery
sa-tăhn sùk-gah-rá shrine
sa-tăhn tôot embassy
sa-tăhn-na-gahn situation
sa-tăh-nee terminus; station
sa-tăh-nee dtum-ròo-ut police station
sa-tăh-nee rót fai railway station
sa-tăh-nee rót may bus station
sa-tăhn-têe place
sa-wàhng bright
sa-wít switch
sa-wít fai switch
sa-wùt dee hello
sa-wùt dee bpee mài! happy New Year!
sa-wùt dee kâ hello
sa-wùt dee krúp hello
sàyt sa-dtahng small change
sèe four
sĕe colour; paint
sĕe chom-poo pink
sĕe dairng red
sĕe dum black
sĕe kăo white
sĕe kĕe-o green
sêe krohng rib
sĕe lĕu-ung yellow
sĕe lêu-ut mŏo scarlet
sĕe môo-ung purple
sĕe néu-a beige
sĕe núm dtahn brown
sĕe núm ngern blue
sĕe òrn pale
sĕe sôm orange
sĕe tao grey
sĕe tao gairm lĕu-ung fawn
sèe yâirk crossroads, intersection
sĕe-a broken, faulty, out of order; polluted
sĕe-a jai sorry
sĕe-a láir-o damage; damaged
sĕe-o sharp
sèe-ung risky
sĕe-ung sound, noise; voice
sên line
sên dâi thread, cotton
sên lôo-ut wire
sèt ready; over, finished
séu buy
sêu dtrong honest
sêu-a chért shirt
sêu-a choo chêep lifejacket
sêu-a chÓOt dress
sêu-a fŏn raincoat
sêu-a gahng-gayng norn pyjamas
sêu-a glâhm vest (under shirt)
sêu-a gúk waistcoat

sêu-a klOOm coat, overcoat
sêu-a klOOm chóOt norn dressing gown
sêu-a nôrk jacket
sêu-a pâh clothes
sêu-a pâh chún nai underwear
sêu-a pôo-yĭng blouse
sêu-a sa-wet-dter sweater; sweatshirt
sêu-a yêut T-shirt
sëu-a yók sOng bra
sı-gah cigar
sîn sOOt end
sĭng-hăh-kom August
sĭn-la-bpà art
sĭn-la-bpà sa-măi mài modern art
sĭn-la-bpin artist
sìp ten; zip
sìp-hâh nah-tee quarter of an hour
sŏh-pay-nee prostitute
sòht single (unmarried)
sòk-ga-bpròk dirty
sôn rorng táo heel (of shoe)
sôn táo heel (of foot)
sòng send
sòng dtòr forward
sòng jòt-măi post, mail
sòng jòt-măi dtahm bâhn delivery
sòng tahng ah-gàht by airmail
sŏng-grahn Thai New Year
sŏng-krahm war
sòo towards
sŏo-ay beautiful
sòOk ripe
sòOk sòOk well-done (steak)
sòOk sòOk dìp dìp rare (steak)

sòOk-ka-pâhp health
sòOk-ka-pâhp mâi dee unhealthy
sòOk-ka-pâhp sŏm-boon fit, healthy
sôOm sâhm clumsy
sŏon zero
sŏon glahng centre
sŏong tall; high
sOOn-la-gah-gorn Customs
sOO-pâhp polite
sOO-pâhp bOO-ròOt gentleman
sOO-pâhp sa-dtree lady
sòop bOO-rèe smoke
sòOt bottom (of road)
sòOt tái last
sôo-um săh-tah-ra-ná public convenience
sòo-un part
sŏo-un garden
sòo-un dtoo-a private
sòo-un mâhk most (of)
sòo-un pa-sŏm mixture
sŏo-un săh-tah-ra-ná park
sŏo-un sùt zoo
sòo-ut mon pray
sôrm repair, mend; fork
sŏrn teach
sôrn hide
sorng pack, packet
sŏrng two
sŏrng ah-tít fortnight
sorng jòt-măi envelope
sŏrng krúng twice
sŏrng tâir-o van with two benches used as a bus
sòt fresh
sòt chêun refreshing
soy side street; lane; soi

sôy kor necklace, chain
súk wash
... **sùk nít nèung** a little ...
súk pâh wash clothes; laundry
sŭm-kun important; main
sŭm-lee cotton wool, absorbent cotton
sŭm-núk kào săhn núk tôrng têe-o tourist information office
sŭm-núk ngahn office
sŭm-núk ngahn kào săhn information office
sŭm-rùp for
 sŭm-rùp koon for you
sûn short
sŭn-châht nationality
sùng order
sŭn-yah promise
sŭn-yahn fay mâi fire alarm
sùp-sŏn complicated
sùt animal

T

ta-bee-un rót car registration number
tâh if
tâh reu-a docks; harbour, port; jetty; quay(side)
tâh yàhng nún then, in that case
tăhm ask
tahn (kâo) eat
tahng direction; path; route; way
tahng ah-gàht by air
tahng dern corridor
tahng dòo-un motorway, highway, freeway
tahng kâo entrance
tahng kóhng bend
tahng kwăh on the right
tahng lée-o turning
tahng lŏo-ung highway
tahng máh-lai pedestrian crossing
tahng òrk exit
tahng ôrm detour
tahng rót fai railway
tahng rót fai pàhn level crossing
tahng sái on the left
tahng yâirk junction; fork
tàht tray
tai Thai (adj)
tái tights, pantyhose
tài rôop photograph
táir genuine; original
tairm-porn tampon
tairn instead
 tairn têe ja ... instead of ...
tăir-o queue, line
ta-lay sea
ta-lay sàhp lake
ta-nah-kahn bank
ta-nai kwahm lawyer
ta-nŏn street; road
ta-nŏn yài main road
ta-nùt meu sái left-handed
táo foot
tâo-nún just; only
tâo-rài? how much?
tâyp nĕe-o Sellotape®, Scotch tape®
tee time
têe at

têe bâhn at home
têe bpèrt gra-bpŏrng can-opener
têe bpèrt kòo-ut bottle-opener; corkscrew
têe bpùt núm fŏn windscreen wipers
têe èun somewhere else
têe fàhk gra-bpăo left luggage, baggage check
têe fàhk kŏrng cloakroom
têe hâhm rót kâo pedestrian precinct
têe jâirng kŏrng hăi lost property office
têe jòrt rót car park, parking lot
têe jòrt rót tâirk-sêe taxi rank
têe jum-nài dtŏo-a ticket office
têe kèe-a bOO-rèe ashtray
têe láir-o last, previous
tee la nóy gradually
têe lĕu-a rest
tee lŭng afterwards; later, later on
têe năi somewhere
têe năi? where?
têe nêe here; over here
têe nôhn there; over there
têe norn mattress; berth
têe nûn there
têe nûng seat
têe nûng dtìt nâh-dtàhng window seat
têe nûng kâhng lŭng back seat
têe nûng rúp kàirk couch
têe pìt error
têe púk accommodation(s)
têe râhp lôOm plain
tee râirk at first
têe rúk darling
têe rút kĕm kùt seatbelt
têe sŏrng second (adj)
têe sòrp tăhm information desk
têe tum ngahn office
têe yòo address
têe-o visit; trip
têe-o bin flight
têe-o bin măo charter flight
têe-o hâi sa-nòOk! enjoy yourself!
têe-o sa-nòOk ná! have fun!, have a good journey!
tee-um imitation
tee-un candle
têe-ung keun at midnight
têe-ung wun midday
tee-wee TV
tén tent
ter you
tĕu carry
tĕung reach
tíng throw away
tíng wái leave behind
tôh! good heavens!
toh tahng glai long-distance call
toh-ra-lâyk telegram
toh-ra-sùp phone
toh-ra-sùp gèp ngern bplai tahng reverse-charge call, collect call
toh-ra-sùp săh-tah-ra-ná payphone
toh-ra-tút television
tong flag

too-a bus tour
tòo-a peanuts; peas; beans
tôo-a bpai everywhere
tôo-ay cup
tôo-ay chahm crockery
tóok every
tòok right, correct; cheap, inexpensive
tòok dàirt mâi sunburnt
tòok gòt-măi legal
tòok ka-moy-ee robbed; stolen
tóok kon everyone
tòok láir-o that's right
tóok yàhng everything
tòok-dtôrng accurate
... tôom ... p.m. (in the evening)
tŏong bag
tŏong bplah-sa-dtìk plastic bag
tŏong gra-dàht paper bag
tŏong meu gloves
tŏong norn sleeping bag
tŏong nôrng stocking(s)
tŏong táo sock(s)
tŏong yahng condom
tŏong yai boo-a tights, pantyhose
tóo-rá business
tóo-ra-gìt deal
tôr pipe
torng gold
tórng stomach
tórng pòok constipated
tórng sěe-a diarrhoea; upset stomach
tórp-fêe sweet(s), candy, candies
tôrt deep-fry
trah-wern ay-yen travel agency
tum make; do
tûm cave
tum dôo-ay meu handmade
tum hâi cause
tum hâi ôo-un fattening
tum kwahm sa-àht clean
tum lép manicure
tum ngahn work
tum têe bâhn home-made
tum-ma-châht nature; natural
tum-ma-dah normal; usually, normally; ordinary; plain
tum-mai? why?
tûn you
tun sa-măi fashionable; modern
tŭng bucket
tŭng dtàirk broke
tŭng ka-yà dustbin, trashcan
túng mòt all; altogether; completely
tŭng núm mun petrol tank, gas tank
túng sŏrng both of them
tun-tee at once, immediately; suddenly
tun-wah-kom December

U

um-per amphoe (sub-division of province)
un thing
un năi? which one?
un née this one

un nún that one
un-dta-rai harm; danger; dangerous
ung-grìt English (adj); British
un-nóo-yâht allowed
ùt-dta-noh-mút automatic
ùt-dtrah rate
ùt-dtrah lâirk bplèe-un exchange rate
ùt-ta-noh-mút automatic
ùt-ti-bai explain

W

wâh say
wăhn sweet
wahn seun née the day before yesterday
wahng put
wâhng empty; deserted
wâhng bplào empty, vacant
wâhng ngahn unemployed
wâi náhm swim
wáir stopover
wăirn ring
wâirn dtah glasses, (US) eyeglasses
wăirn dtàirng ngahn wedding ring
wâirn gun dàirt sunglasses
wăirn mûn engagement ring
wai-yah-gorn grammar
wâo kite
way-lah time
way-lah sòo-un mâhk most of the time
way-lah-nún then, at that time
wĕe comb
wee-sah visa
wèet rórng scream
wew view
wí-nah-tee second (in time)
wîng run
wí-sàyt incredible, tremendous
wí-sàyt jung ler-ee fantastic
wít-ta-yah-lai college
wít-ta-yah-sàht science
wít-ta-yóo radio
wít-tee method
wong don-dtree orchestra
wong glom circle
woo-a cow
wun day
wun ah-tít Sunday
wun gèrt birthday
wun gòrn ... the day before ...
wun jun Monday
wun lŭng jàhk têe ... the day after ...
wun ma-reun née the day after tomorrow
wun née today
wun pa-réu-hùt Thursday
wun póot Wednesday
wun prá Buddhist holy day
wun săo Saturday
wun săo ah-tít weekend
wun seun née the day before yesterday
wun sîn bpee New Year's Eve
wun sòok Friday
wun têe date
wun ung-kahn Tuesday
wun yòot holiday, vacation
wun yòot râht-cha-gahn public holiday

wung palace
wŭng hope
wút temple; monastery
wùt cold (illness)
wút-ta-na-tum culture

Y

yah medicine
yâh grandmother (paternal); grass
yàh! don't!
yah dùp glìn dtoo-a deodorant
yah glôrng pipe tobacco
yàh gun láir-o divorced
yah gun ma-lairng insect repellent
yah kâh chéu-a antiseptic
yah kâh chéu-a rôhk disinfectant
yah kOOm gum-nèrt contraceptive pill
yah kùt polish
yah kùt rorng táo shoe polish
yah kwin-neen quinine
yah láhng make-up remover
yah mét tablet
yah pít poison
yah ra-ngúp bpòo-ut painkiller
yah sà pŏm shampoo
yah sàyp-dtìt drug, narcotic
yah sĕe fun toothpaste
yah sòop tobacco
yah tah lotion; ointment
yah tah gun dàirt sunblock
yah tah lŭng àhp dàirt aftersun cream
yah tah lŭng gohn nòo-ut aftershave
yah tài laxative
yâhk hard, difficult
yàhk dâi want
yàhk (ja) I'd like to
yahng rubber
yahng a-lài spare tyre
yahng dtàirk puncture
yahng lóp rubber, eraser
yahng nai inner tube
yàhng née this way, like this
yàhng nóy at least
yahng rót tyre
yahng rút rubber band
yâht relatives
yai grandmother (maternal)
yài big, large
yài bêr-rêr enormous
yai sŭng-krór synthetic
yâir terrible, dreadful
yâir jung! too bad!
yâir long worse
yâir mâhk awful, terrible
yâir têe sÒOt worst
yâirk gun separate; separately
yao long
yêe hôr brand
yêe-bpÒOn Japan; Japanese
yeen jeans
yêe-um excellent, brilliant; visit
yêe-um ler-ee lovely, excellent
yêe-um yôrt fantastic
yen cold; cool
yen née this afternoon
yen prÔOng née tomorrow evening
yép sew

yer-ra-mun Germany; German
yeun stand
yèu-uk jug
yím smile
yin dee glad
yĭng rúp chái maid, chambermaid
yók wáyn except
yòo live; still; in, at home
káo mâi yòo he/she's not in
... yòo têe năi? where is ...?
yòo bon ... on top of ...; at the top of ...
yòo dtrong glahng in the middle
yòo dtrong nâh straight ahead
yòo glâi nearby
yòo kâhng bon at the top
yoong mosquito
yoo-rohp Europe; European
yòot stop
yòot pôot ná! shut up!
yóot-dti-tum fair, just
yôrt smashing, fabulous
yôrt! great!
yôrt yêe-um splendid, super
yung still; not yet
yung mâi sèt finish
yung-ngai? how?

Thai

→

English
Signs and Notices

Abbreviations

ป.อ. **bprùp ah-gàht** air-conditioned
อ. **um-per** Amphoe, district
ก.ท.ม. **groong-tâyp-ma-hăh-na-korn** Bangkok
พ.ศ. **póot-ta-sùk-ga-ràht** Buddhist Era (BE) (543 years ahead of AD)
ค.ศ. **krít-dta-sùk-ga-ràht** Christian Era (AD)
ช.ม. **chôo a mohng** hours
น. **nah li-gah** hours
ก.ม. **gi-loh-mét** kilometre
ช. **chai** men
จ. **jung-wùt** province
ถ. **ta-nŏn** road
ต. **dtum-bon** Tambon, sub-district
ญ. **yĭng** women

General signs

ระวัง **ra-wung** caution
อันตราย **un-dta-rai** danger
ห้าม ... **hâhm ...** ... forbidden
อย่า **yàh** ... do not ...
สอบถาม **sòrp tăhm** enquiries
โรงพยาบาลห้ามใช้เสียง **rohng pa-yah-bahn: hâhm chái sĕe-ung** hospital: no noise
ห้ามผ่าน **hâhm pàhn** no admission
ห้ามเข้า **hăhm kâo** no entry
ห้ามทิ้งขยะ **hâhm tíng ka-yà** no litter
ห้ามจอด **hâhm jòrt** no parking
ห้ามถ่ายรูป **hâhm tài rôop** no photographs
ห้ามสูบบุหรี่ **hâhm sòop boo-rèe** no smoking
กรุณาอย่าส่งเสียงดัง **ga-roo-nah yàh sòng sĕe-ung dung** please don't make a noise
โปรดถอดรองเท้า **bpròht tòrt rorng táo** please remove shoes
ตำรวจ **dtum-ròo-ut** police
โปรดเงียบ **bpròht ngêe-up** silence, please

Airport, planes

ที่ทำการบริษัทการบิน **têe tum gahn bor-ri-sùt gahn bin** airline company offices
ท่าอากาศยาน **tâh ah-gàht-sa-yahn** airport
ถึง **tĕung** arrives
ประชาสัมพันธ์

ท่าอากาศยานกรุงเทพฯ **bpra-chah sŭm-pun tâh-ah-gàht-sa-yăhn groong-tâyp** public relations, Bangkok Airport

ศุลกากร **soon-la-gah-gorn** Customs

สุขาชาย **sòo-kăh chai** gents' toilets, men's room

ชาย **chai** gents

ตรวจคนเข้าเมือง **dtròo-ut kon kâo meu-ung** immigration

ประชาสัมพันธ์ **bpra-chah sŭm-pun** information

สุขาหญิง **sòo-kăh yĭng** ladies' toilets, ladies' room

หญิง **yĭng** ladies

ออก **òrk** leaves

ฝากกระเป๋า **fàhk gra-bpăo** left luggage, baggage checkroom

ลิฟท์ **lif** lift, elevator

จุดนัดพบ **jòot nút póp** meeting point

ห้ามสูบบุหรี่ **hâhm sòop boo-rèe** no smoking

จุดตรวจค้นผู้โดยสาร **jòot dtròo-ut kón pôo doy-ee săhn** passenger check-point

เฉพาะผู้โดยสารและลูกเรือเท่านั้น **cha-pòr pôo-doy-ee săhn láir lôok reu-a tâo-nún** passengers and crew only

ตรวจหนังสือเดินทาง **dtròo-ut núng-sĕu dern tahng** passport control

ภัตตาคาร **pút-dtah-khan** restaurant

ตรวจสอบบัตรผู้โดยสารและกระเป๋า **dtròo-ut sòrp bùt pôo-doy-ee-săhn láir gra-bpăo** ticket and baggage check

ที่จำหน่ายตั๋ว **têe jum-nài dtŏo-a** ticket office

เวลา **way-lah** time

ผู้มาส่งผู้โดยสาร **pôo mah sòng pôo-doy-ee-săhn** visitors

ที่พักผู้มาส่งผู้โดยสาร **têe púk pôo mah sòng pôo-doy-ee-sahn** visitors' waiting area

ทางเข้า **tahng kâo** way in, entrance

ทางออก **tahng òrk** way out

Banks, money

บาท **bàht** baht

ธนาคาร **ta-nah-kahn** bank

ฝากประจำ **fàhk bpra-jum** deposit account, savings account

ฝากเงิน **fàhk ngern** deposits

อัตราแลกเปลี่ยนเงิน **ùt-dtrah lâirk bplèe-un ngern** exchange rate

อัตราแลกเปลี่ยนเงินตราต่างประเทศ **ùt-dtrah lâirk bplèe-un ngern dtrah dtàhng bpra-tâyt** foreign exchange rate

สอบถาม **sòrp tăhm** enquiries

แลกเปลี่ยนเงินตราต่างประเทศ **lâirk bplèe-un ngern dtrah dtàhng bpra-tâyt** bureau de change

เปิดบัญชีใหม่ **bpèrt bun-chee mài** new accounts

ถอนเงิน **tŏrn ngern** withdrawals

Bus travel

รถปรับอากาศ **rót bprùp ah-gàht** air-conditioned bus

ถึง **tĕung** arrives

ออก **òrk** departs

สุขาชาย **sòo-kăh chai** gents' toilets, men's room

ประชาสัมพันธ์ **bpra-chah sŭm-pun** information

สอบถาม **sòrp tăhm** information, enquiries

สุขาหญิง **sòo-kăh yĭng** ladies' toilets, ladies' room

รับฝากของ **rúp fàhk kŏrng** left luggage, baggage checkroom

ห้ามสูบบุหรี่ **hâhm sòop boo-rèe** no smoking

ห้องพักผู้โดยสาร **hôrng púk pôo doy-ee săhn** passengers' waiting room

ทางเข้าเฉพาะผู้ถือตั๋วโดยสาร **tahng kâo cha-pòr pôo tĕu dtŏo-a doy-ee săhn** passengers with tickets only

ที่จำหน่ายตั๋ว **têe jum-nài dtŏo-a** ticket office

กำหนดเวลาเดินรถ **gum-nòt way-lah dern rót** timetable, (US) schedule

รถทัวร์ **rót too-a** tour bus

Countries, nationalities

อาฟริกา **ah-fri-gah** Africa; African

อีก้อ **ee-gôr** Akha (hill tribe)

อเมริกา **a-may-ri-gah** America; American

เอเชีย **ay-see-a** Asia

ออสเตรเลีย **òrt-sa-dtray-lee-a** Australia; Australian

พม่า **pa-mâh** Burma,

Myanmar; Burmese
กัมพูชา gum-poo-chah Cambodia
แคนาดา kair-nah-dah Canada; Canadian
จีน jeen China; Chinese
ประเทศ bpra-tâyt country
อังกฤษ ung-grìt England; Britain; UK; English; British
ยุโรป yoo-rôhp Europe; European
ฝรั่งเศษ a-rùng-sàyt France; French
ประเทศเยอรมัน bpra-tâyt yer-ra-mun Germany; German
ชาวเขา chao kǎo hill-tribe person; hill-tribe people
แม้ว máy-o Hmong, Meo (hill tribe)
ฮอลแลนด์ horn-lairn Holland; Dutch
อินเดีย in-dee-a India; Indian
แขก kàirk Indian; Malaysian
อินโดนีเซีย in-doh-nee-see-a Indonesia; Indonesian
ไอร์แลนด์ ai-lairn Ireland
ประเทศอิตาลี bpra-tâyt ì-dtah-lee Italy
ญี่ปุ่น yêe-bpòon Japan; Japanese
กะเหรี่ยง ga-rèe-ung Karen (hill tribe)
เขมร ka-mǎyn Khmer; Cambodian
เกาหลี gao-lěe Korea; Korean
ลาว lao Laos; Lao
มาเลเซีย mah-lay-see-a Malaysia; Malaysian
นิวซีแลนด์ new see-lairn New Zealand
ไอร์แลนด์เหนือ ai-lairn něu-a Northern Ireland
ปากีสถาน bpah-gi-sa-tǎhn Pakistan
ฟิลิปปินส์ fin-lip-bpin Phillipines; Fillipino
สกอตแลนด์ sa-gort-lairn Scotland
สิงคโปร์ sǐng-ka-bpoh Singapore
ประเทศสเปน bpra-tâyt sa-bpayn Spain
ไทย tai Thai
เมืองไทย meu-ung tai Thailand (informal)
ประเทศไทย bpra-tâyt tai Thailand (formal)
สหรัฐอเมริกา sa-hà-rút a-may-ri-gah United States of America
เวียดนาม wêe-ut-nahm Vietnam; Vietnamese

เย้า yáo Yao (hill tribe)

Customs

ศุลกากร sŏon-la-gah-gorn Customs

มีของต้องสำแดง mee kŏrng dtôrng sŭm-dairng goods to declare

ตรวจคนเข้าเมือง dtròo-ut kon kâo meu-ung immigration

ไม่มีของต้องสำแดง mâi mee kŏrng dtôrng sŭm-dairng nothing to declare

เฉพาะหนังสือเดินทางไทย cha-pòr núng-sĕu dern-tahng tai Thai passport holders only

Days

วัน wun day

อาทิตย์ ah-tít week

วันเสาร์อาทิตย์ wun săo ah-tít weekend

วันจันทร์ wun jun Monday

วันอังคาร wun ung-kahn Tuesday

วันพุธ wun póot Wednesday

วันพฤหัส wun pa-réu-hùt Thursday

วันศุกร์ wun sòok Friday

วันเสาร์ wun săo Saturday

วันอาทิตย์ wun ah-tít Sunday

Entertainment

... บาท ... bàht ... baht

ถุงละ ... บาท toong la ... bàht ... baht per bag

ถ้วยละ ... บาท tôo-ay la ... bàht ... baht per cup

ชิ้นละ ... บาท chín la ... bàht ... baht per piece

บริการ ๒๔ ช ม. bor-ri-gahn yĕe-sìp sèe chŏo-a mohng 24-hour service

รอบ ๑๗.๐๐ น. rôrp 17.00 n(ah-li-gah) 5 p.m. show

บาร์ bah bar

โบว์ลิ่ง bohn-lîng bowling

ที่จำหน่ายตั๋ว têe jum-nài dtŏo-a box office

โรงภาพยนตร์ rohng pâhp-pa-yon cinema, movie theater

เร็วๆนี้ ray-o ray-o née coming soon

ดิสโก้ dít-sa-gôh disco

ทางเข้า tahng kâo entrance

ทางออก tahng òrk exit

เต็ม dtem full

อาบอบนวด **àhp òp nôo-ut** massage
รายการหน้า **rai-gahn nâh** next programme
อาทิตย์หน้า **ah-tít nâh** next week
ไนทคลับ **náit klúp** nightclub
ฉายวันนี้ **chăi wun née** now showing
ราคา **rah-kah** price
รอบ **rôrp** showing

Forms

ที่อยู่ **têe yòo** address
อายุ **ah-yóo** age
พ.ศ. **por sŏr** (year) ... BE (543 years later than AD)
สีตา **sĕe dtah** colour of eyes
สีผม **sĕe pŏm** colour of hair
เกิดวันที่ **gèrt wun-têe** date of birth
ชื่อ **chêu** first name
ตั้งแต่ ... ถึง ... **dtûng-dtàir ... tĕung ...** from ... until ...
ความสูง **kwahm sŏong** height
บ้านเลขที่ **bâhn lâyk têe** house number
ตรอก **dtròrk** lane
ซอย **soy** lane, soi
บันทึก **bun-téuk** memo
เดือน **deu-un** month
สัญชาติ **sŭn-châht** nationality
หมายเหตุ **măi-hàyt** note, n.b.
อาชีพ **ah-chêep** occupation
หนังสือเดินทางหมายเลข **núng-sĕu dern tahng măi-lâyk** passport number
จังหวัด **jung-wùt** province
เชื้อชาติ **chéu-a châht** race
อยู่ที่ **yòo têe** residing at
ถนน **ta-nŏn** road
เพศ **pâyt** sex
ลายเซ็น **lai sen** signature
ลงชื่อ **long chêu** signed
พักที่ **púk têe** staying at
นามสกุล **nahm sa-gOOn** surname
ตำบล **dtum-bon** Tambon, sub-district
หมู่บ้าน **mòo-bâhn** village
น้ำหนัก **núm nùk** weight
พยาน **pa-yahn** witness

Garages

บริการ ๒๔ ช.ม. **bor-ri-gahn yêe-sìp sèe chôo-a mohng** 24-hour service
บริการซ่อมรถ **bor-ri-gahn sôrm rót** car repairs
บริการล้างรถ **bor-ri-gahn**

láhng rót car wash
ดีเซล dee-sen diesel
เปลี่ยนหม้อกรอง bplèe-un môr grorng filters changed
อู่ òo garage
ห้ามสูบบุหรี่ hâhm sòop boo-rèe no smoking
เปลี่ยนน้ำมันเครื่อง bplèe-un núm mun krêu-ung oil changed
บริการอัดฉีด bor-ri-gahn ùt chèet pressurized air
ปะยาง bpà yahng punctures repaired
เครื่องอะไหล่ krêu-ung a-lài spare parts

Geographical terms

คลอง klorng canal
เมืองหลวง meu-ung lŏo-ung capital city
ชนบท chon-na-bòt countryside
ป่าดงดิบ bpàh dong dìp forest, jungle
เขา kăo hill
เกาะ gòr island
ป่า bpàh jungle, forest
ที่ราบลุ่ม têe râhp lôom plain
แม่น้ำ mâir-náhm river
ทะเล ta-lay sea
ชายทะเล chai ta-lay seaside
เมือง meu-ung town; city; country
หมู่บ้าน mòo-bâhn village

Hairdresser's, beauty salons

เสริมสวย sĕrm sŏo-ay beauty care
เครื่องสำอาง krêu-ung sŭm-ahng cosmetics
นวดหน้า nôo-ut nâh facial massage
ตัดผม dtùt pŏm hair cut
เป่าผม bpào pôm hair drying
ไดผม dai pŏm hair drying
สระผม sà pŏm wash
ตัดเล็บ dtùt lép manicure
ดัดผม dùt pŏm perm
เซทผม sét pŏm set
โกนหนวด gohn nòo-ut shave

Health

รถพยาบาล rót pa-yah-bahn ambulance

คุมกำเนิด koom gum-nèrt birth control
คลีนิค klee-ník clinic
ห้องคลอด hôrng klôrt delivery room
ทันตแพทย์ tun-dta-pâirt dentist
ทำฟัน tum fun dentist's
จำหน่ายยา jum-nài yah dispensary
แพทย์หญิง pâirt yĭng doctor (female)
พ.ญ. pâirt yĭng doctor (female)
น.พ. nai pâirt doctor (male)
นายแพทย์ nai pâirt doctor (male)
ตรวจสายตา dtròo-ut săi dtah eye test
ตรวจสายตา dtròo-ut săi dtah dtròo-ut săi-dtah eye-testing
โรงพยาบาล rohng pa-yah-bahn hospital
ฉีดยา chèet yah injections
นางพยาบาล nahng pa-yah-bahn nurse
ห้างขายยา hâhng kăi yah pharmacy, drugstore
ตรวจปัสสาวะ dtròo-ut bpùt-săh-wá urine test
เอ็กซเรย์ X-ray X-ray

Hiring, renting

ชั่วโมงละ ... บาท chôo-a mohng la ... bàht ... baht per hour
เดือนละ ... บาท deu-un la ... bàht ... baht per month
วันละ ... บาท wun la ... bàht ... baht per month
อพาร์ตเม้นท์ให้เช่า ah-paht-mén hâi châo apartment for rent
บาท bàht baht (unit of currency)
รถให้เช่า rót hâi châo car for hire, car to rent
เงินมัดจำ ngern mút-jum deposit
แฟลทให้เช่า flàirt hâi châo apartment for rent
ให้เช่า hâi châo for hire, to let, to rent
บ้านให้เช่า bâhn hâi châo house to let, house for rent
รถมอเตอร์ไซค์/รถจักรยานให้เช่า rót mor-dter-sai/rót jùk-ra-yahn hâi châo motorcycle/bicycle for hire
จ่ายล่วงหน้า jài lôo-ung nâh pay in advance
ค่าเช่า kâh châo rental, fee

ห้องให้เช่า hôrng hâi châo room for rent

Hotels

คอฟฟี่ช็อบ kòrp-fêe chórp café serving coffees, alcoholic drinks, snacks and meals

ห้องคู่ hôrng kôo double room

ห้องคู่ปรับอากาศ hôrng kôo bprùp ah-gàht double room with air-conditioning

ทางออก tahng òrk exit

ชั้น chún floor

เกสท์เฮาส์ gàyt háot guesthouse

สอบถาม sòrp tăhm enquiries

ห้องน้ำสตรี hôrng náhm sa-dtree ladies' toilet, ladies' room

หญิง yĭng ladies

ลิฟท์ líf lift, elevator

บริการรถรับส่ง bor-ri-gahn rót rúp sòng limousine service

ห้องน้ำบุรุษ hôrng náhm boo-ròot men's toilet, men's room

ชาย chai men

ห้ามสูบบุหรี่ hâhm sòop boo-rèe no smoking

แผนกต้อนรับ pa-nàirk dtôrn rúp reception

ห้องอาหาร hôrng ah-hăhn restaurant

ห้อง hôrng room

ห้องให้เช่า hôrng hâi châo rooms to let

บริการนำเที่ยว bor-ri-gahn num têe-o sight-seeing tours

ห้องเดี่ยว hôrng dèe-o single room

ห้องเดี่ยวปรับอากาศ hôrng dèe-o bprùp ah-gàht single room with air-conditioning

สระว่ายน้ำ sà wâi náhm swimming pool

สุขา sòo-kăh toilet

ห้องน้ำ hôrng náhm toilets

ห้องว่าง hôrng wâhng vacancies

ยินดีต้อนรับ yin dee dtôrn rúp welcome

Lifts, elevators

ลง long down

ชั้น chún floor

ลิฟท์ lif lift, elevator

ไม่เกิน ... คน mâi gern ... kon maximum load ... people

ห้ามสูบบุหรี่ hâhm sòop boo-rèe no smoking

ขึ้น kêun up

Medicines

หลังอาหาร **lŭng ah-hăhn** after meals

ทา **tah** apply (ointments)

ก่อนนอน **gòrn norn** before going to bed

ก่อนอาหาร **gòrn ah-hăhn** before meals

ยาอันตราย **yah un-dta-rai** dangerous medicine

วิธีใช้ **wí-tee chái** instructions for use

กินเกินขนาดเป็นอันตราย **gin gern ka-nàht bpen un-dta-rai** it is dangerous to exceeed the stated dose

ยา **yah** medicine

เม็ด **mét** tablet, pill

รับประทาน **rúp-bpra-tahn** take (orally)

ช้อนชา **chórn chah** teaspoon

วันละ … ครั้ง **wun la ... krúng** times ... times per day

วันละ … เม็ด **wun la ... mét** tablets ... tablets per day

Months

เดือน **deu-un** month

มกราคม **mók-ga-rah-kom** January

กุมภาพันธ์ **gOOm-pah-pun** February

มีนาคม **mee-nah-kom** March

เมษายน **may-săh-yon** April

พฤษภาคม **préut-sa-pah-kom** May

มิถุนายน **mí-tOO-nah-yon** June

กรกฎาคม **ga-rúk-ga-dah-kom** July

สิงหาคม **sĭng-hăh-kom** August

กันยายน **gun-yah-yon** September

ตุลาคม **dtOO-lah-kom** October

พฤศจิกายน **préut-sa-jìk-gah-yon** November

ธันวาคม **tun-wah-kom** December

Notices on doors

เฉพาะเจ้าหน้าที่ **cha-pór jâo-nâh-têe** authorized personnel only

กริ่ง **grìng** bell

หมาดุ **măh dòo** beware of the dog
ปิด **bpìt** closed
ทางเข้า **tahng kâo** entry
ทางออก **tahng òrk** exit
ห้ามจอดรถขวางประตู **hâhm jòrt rót kwăhng bpra-dtoo** no parking in front of the gate
เข้า **kâo** in
ห้ามเข้า **hâhm kâo** no entry
ไม่มีกิจห้ามเข้า **mâi mee gìt hâhm kâo** no entry to unauthorized persons
ห้ามจอด **hâhm jòrt** no parking
ห้ามกลับรถ **hâhm glùp rót** no turning
เปิด **bpèrt** open
ออก **òrk** out
กรุณาถอดรองเท้า **ga-roo-nah tòrt rorng táo** please remove your shoes
กรุณากดกริ่ง **ga-roo-nah gòt grìng** please ring
กด **gòt** press
ถนนส่วนบุคคล **ta-nŏn sòo-un bòok-kon** private road
ดึง **deung** pull
ผลัก **plùk** push
ระวังสุนัขดุ **ra-wung soo-núk dòo** beware of the dog

Numbers

ศูนย์ **sŏon** zero
หนึ่ง **nèung** one
สอง **sŏrng** two
สาม **săhm** three
สี่ **sèe** four
ห้า **hâh** five
หก **hòk** six
เจ็ด **jèt** seven
แปด **bpàirt** eight
เก้า **gao** nine
สิบ **sìp** ten
สิบเอ็ด **sìp-èt** eleven
สิบสอง **sìp-sŏrng** twelve
สิบสาม **sìp-săhm** thirteen
สิบสี่ **sìp-sèe** fourteen
สิบห้า **sìp-hâh** fifteen
สิบหก **sìp-hòk** sixteen
สิบเจ็ด **sìp-jèt** seventeen
สิบแปด **sìp-bpàirt** eighteen
สิบเก้า **sìp-gâo** nineteen
ยี่สิบ **yêe-sìp** twenty
ยี่สิบเอ็ด **yêe-sìp-èt** twenty-one
สามสิบ **săhm-sìp** thirty
สามสิบเอ็ด **săhm-sìp-èt** thirty-one
สี่สิบ **sèe-sìp** forty
ห้าสิบ **hâh-sìp** fifty
หกสิบ **hòk-sìp** sixty

เจ็ดสิบ **jèt-sìp** seventy
แปดสิบ **bpàirt-sìp** eighty
เก้าสิบ **gâo-sìp** ninety
หนึ่งร้อย **nèung róy** one hundred
หนึ่งพัน **nèung pun** one thousand
สองพัน **sŏrng pun** two thousand
หนึ่งหมื่น **nèung mèun** ten thousand
สองหมื่น **sŏrng mèun** twenty thousand
หนึ่งแสน **nèung săirn** one hundred thousand
สองแสน **sŏrng săirn** two hundred thousand
หนึ่งล้าน **nèung láhn** one million
หนึ่งร้อยล้าน **nèung róy láhn** one hundred million
๐ **sŏon** 0
๑ **nèung** 1
๒ **sŏrng** 2
๓ **săhm** 3
๔ **sèe** 4
๕ **hâh** 5
๖ **hòk** 6
๗ **jèt** 7
๘ **bpàirt** 8
๙ **gâo** 9
๑๐ **sìp** 10
๑๑ **sìp-èt** 11
๑๒ **sìp-sŏrng** 12
๑๓ **sìp-săhm** 13
๑๔ **sìp-sèe** 14
๑๕ **sìp-hâh** 15
๑๖ **sìp-hòk** 16
๑๗ **sìp-jèt** 17
๑๘ **sìp-bpàirt** 18
๑๙ **sìp-gâo** 19
๒๐ **yêe-sìp** 20
๒๑ **yêe-sìp-èt** 21
๓๐ **săhm-sìp** 30
๓๑ **săhm-sìp-èt** 31
๔๐ **sèe-sìp** 40
๕๐ **hâh-sìp** 50
๖๐ **hòk-sìp** 60
๗๐ **jèt-sìp** 70
๘๐ **bpàirt-sìp** 80
๙๐ **gâo-sìp** 90
๑๐๐ **nèung róy** 100
๑๐๐๐ **nèung pun** 1,000
๒๐๐๐ **sŏrng pun** 2,000
๑๐๐๐๐ **nèung mèun** 10,000
๒๐๐๐๐ **sŏrng mèun** 20,000
๑๐๐๐๐๐ **nèung săirn** 100,000
๒๐๐๐๐๐ **sŏrng săirn** 200,000
๑๐๐๐๐๐๐ **nèung láhn** 1,000,000
๑๐๐๐๐๐๐๐๐ **nèung róy láhn** 100,000,000

Phones

บาท bàht baht (unit of currency)
รหัส ra-hùt code
เหรียญ rěe-un coin
ต่อ dtòr extension
โทรศัพท์ทางไกล toh-ra-sùp tahng glai long distance telephone
เสีย sěe-a out of order
ตำรวจ dtum-ròo-ut police
ตู้โทรศัพท์สาธารณะ dtôo toh-ra-sùp săh-tah-ra-ná public telephone box
โทร. toh tel.
โทรศัพท์ toh-ra-sùp telephone
สมุดเบอร์โทรศัพท์ sa-mòot ber toh-ra-sùp telephone directory
เบอร์โทรศัพท์ ber toh-ra-sùp telephone number

Place names

อยุธยา a-yóot-ta-yah Ayutthaya
บางปะอิน bahng-bpà-in Bang Pa-In
กรุงเทพฯ groong-tâyp Bangkok
บางลำภู bahng-lum-poo Banglamphu
เชียงใหม่ chêe-ung-mài Chiangmai
อนุสาวรีย์ประชาธิปไตย a-nóo-săh-wa-ree bpra-chah-típ-bpa-dtai Democracy Monument
หาดใหญ่ hàht yài Hat Yai
หัวหิน hŏo-a hin Hua Hin
หัวลำโพง hŏo-a lum-pohng Hua Lampong
กาญจนบุรี gahn-ja-na-boo-ree Kanjanaburi
ขอนแก่น kŏrn-gàirn Khonkaen
เกาะสมุย gòr sa-mŏo-ee Koh Samui
สวนลุมพินี sŏo-un loom-pi-nee Lumpini Park
นครปฐม na-korn bpa-tŏm Nakhorn Pathom
พัทยา pút-ta-yah Pattaya
ภูเก็ต poo-gèt Phuket
ประตูน้ำ bpra-dtoo náhm Pratu Nam
แม่น้ำแคว mâir-náhm kwair River Kwai
สนามหลวง sa-năhm lŏo-ung Sanam Luang
สยามแสควร์ sa-yăhm

sa-kwair Siam Square
สงขลา **sŏng-klăh** Songkhla
สุโขทัย **sòo-kŏh-tai** Sukhothai
ธนบุรี **ton-boo-ree** Thonburi
อุบลราชธานี **oo-bon râht-cha-tah-nee** Ubonratchathani
อนุสาวรีย์ชัยสมรภูมิ **a-nóo-săh-wa-ree chai sa-mŏr-ra-poom** Victory Monument
เยาวราช **yao-wa-râht** Yaowarat (China Town area of Bangkok)

Post office

ผู้รับ **pôo rúp** addressee
ทางอากาศ **tahng ah-gàht** airmail
กรุงเทพฯ **groong-tâyp** Bangkok
ตู้จดหมาย **dtôo jòt-măi** letter box, mail box
ที่อื่น **têe èun** other places
พัสดุ **pút-sa-dòo** parcels
รหัสไปรษณีย์ **ra-hùt bprai-sa-nee** postcode
ที่ทำการไปรษณีย์ **têe tum gahn bprai-sa-nee** post office
ลงทะเบียน **long ta-bee-un** registered mail
ผู้ส่ง **pôo sòng** sender
ไปรษณียากร **bprai-sa-nee-yah-gorn** stamps
ทางเรือ **tahng reu-a** surface mail
โทรเลข **toh-ra-lâyk** telegrams
โทรศัพท์ **toh-ra-sùp** telephone

Public buildings

สนามบิน **sa-năhm bin** airport
ธนาคาร **ta-nah-kahn** bank
สนามมวย **sa-năhm moo-ay** boxing stadium
สถานีรถเมล์ **sa-tăhn-nee rót may** bus station
โรงภาพยนตร์ **rohng pâhp-pa-yon** cinema, movie theater
คลีนิค **klee-ník** clinic
วิทยาลัย **wít-ta-yah-lai** college
กรมศุลกากร **grom soon-la-gah-gorn** Customs Department
กรม **grom** department (government)
ที่ว่าการอำเภอ **têe wâh gahn**

um-per district office
กอง **gorng** division (government)
สถานทูต **sa-tăhn tôot** embassy
โรงพยาบาล **rohng pa-yah-bahn** hospital
โรงแรม **rohng rairm** hotel
กองตรวจคนเข้าเมือง **gorng dtròo-ut kon kâo meu-ung** Immigration Department
กรมแรงงาน **grom rairng ngahn** Labour Department
ศาล **săhn** law court
ห้องสมุด **hôrng sa-mòot** library
ตลาด **dta-làht** market
กระทรวง **gra-soo-ung** ministry
พิพิธภัณฑ์ **pí-pít-ta-pun** museum
สนามกีฬาแห่งชาติ **sa-năhm gee-lah hàirng châht** National Stadium
ร้านขายยา **ráhn kăi yah** pharmacy
สถานีตำรวจ **sa-tăhn-nee dtum-ròo-ut** police station
ไปรษณีย์ **bprai-sa-nee** post office
โรงเรียน **rohng ree-un** school
ร้าน **ráhn** shop, store
ศูนย์การค้า **sŏon gahn káh** shopping centre
ห้าง **hâhng** store, shop
องค์การส่งเสริมการท่องเที่ยวแห่งประเทศไทย **ong-gahn sòng sĕrm gahn tôrng têe-o hàirng bpra-tâyt** TAT – Tourist Organisation of Thailand
กรมสรรพากร **grom sŭn-pah-gorn** Tax Department
วัด **wút** temple
โรงละคร **rohng la-korn** theatre
สถานีรถไฟ **sa-tăhn-nee rót fai** train station
มหาวิทยาลัย **ma hăh-wít-ta-yah-lai** university

Public holidays

วันพระ **wun prá** Buddhist holy day
วันหยุดราชการ **wun yòot râht-cha-gahn** official public holiday
วันขึ้นปีใหม่ **wun kêun bpee mài** New Year's Day
วันสงกรานต์ **wun sŏng-grahn** Songkran Day (Thai New Year)

Rail travel

จองตั๋วล่วงหน้า **jorng dtŏo-a lôo-ung nâh** advance bookings
ถึง **tĕung** arrives
ออก **òrk** departs
แผนกสอบถาม **pa-nàirk sòrp tăhm** enquiries
สุขาชาย **sòo-kăh chai** gents' toilets, men's room
สุขาหญิง **sòo-kăh yĭng** ladies' toilets, ladies' room
รับฝากของ **rúp fàhk kŏrng** left luggage, baggage checkroom
ชานชาลา **chahn-chah-lah** platform, (US) track
ประชาสัมพันธ์ **bpra-chah sŭm-pun** public relations
สถานีรถไฟ **sa-tăh-nee rót fai** railway station, train station
ที่จำหน่ายตั๋ว **têe jum-nài dtŏo-a** ticket office
กำหนดเวลาเดินรถ **gum-nòt way-lah dern ròt** timetable, (US) schedule
รถไฟ **rót fai** train
ห้องพักผู้โดยสาร **hôrng púk pôo doy-ee săhn** waiting room

Regions, provinces etc

ชายแดน **chai dairn** border
เขต **kàyt** boundary; area
ภาคกลาง **pâhk glahng** central region
แม่น้ำเจ้าพระยา **mâir-náhm jâo pra-yah** Chao Phraya River
ประเทศ **bpra-tâyt** country
อำเภอ **um-per** Amphoe, district
แม่โขง **mâir-kŏhng** Mekhong River
ภาคอีสาน **pâhk ee-săhn** north-eastern region
ภาคเหนือ **pâhk nĕu-a** northern region
จังหวัด **jung-wùt** province
ภาคใต้ **pâhk dtâi** southern region
ตำบล **dtum-bon** Tambon, sub-district
บ้านนอก **bâhn-nôrk** up-country
ต่างจังหวัด **dtàhng jung-wùt** up-country

Restaurants, bars

บริการ ๒๔ ชั่วโมง **bor-ri-gahn 24 chôo-a mohng** 24-hour service

ห้องแอร์ **hôrng-air** air-conditioned room

ร้านอาหารโต้รุ่ง **ráhn ah-hăhn dtôh rôong** all-night restaurant

บาร์ **bah** bar

ชาม **chahm** bowl, dish

อาหารเช้า **ah-hăhn cháo** breakfast

คอฟฟี่ช็อบ **kórp-fêe chórp** café serving coffees, alcoholic drinks, snacks and meals

อาหารจีน **ah-hăhn jeen** Chinese food

อาหารเย็น **ah-hăhn yen** evening meal

อาหาร **ah-hăhn** food

อาหารญี่ปุ่น **ah-hăhn yêe-bpòon** Japanese food

อาหารกลางวัน **ah-hăhn glahng wun** lunch

อาหารมุสลิม **ah-hăhn móo-sa-lim** Muslim food

อาหารอีสาน **ah-hăhn ee-săhn** North-Eastern food

สวนอาหาร **sŏo-un ah-hăhn** open-air restaurant

ชามละ ... **chahm la ...** ... per bowl/dish

จานละ ... **jahn la ...** ... per plate/dish

จาน **jahn** plate, dish

ราคา **rah-kah** price

ภัตตาคาร **pút-dtah-kahn** restaurant

ร้านอาหาร **ráhn ah-hăhn** restaurant

ห้องอาหาร **hôrng ah-hăhn** restaurant

อาหารทะเล **ah-hăhn ta-lay** seafood

เชลล์ชวนชิม **chen choo-un chim** Shell® recommended, seal of approval, equivalent to Good Food Guide

อาหารปักษ์ใต้ **ah-hăhn bpùk dtâi** Southern food

อาหารไทย **ah-hăhn tai** Thai food

อาหารฝรั่ง **ah-hăhn fa-rùng** Western food

Road signs

ทางโค้ง **tahng kóhng** bend

ระวังทางข้างหน้าเป็นทาง

เอก ra-wung tahng kâhng nâh bpen tahng àyk caution: major road ahead
ระวัง ra-wung caution
อันตราย un-dta-rai danger
ทางเบี่ยง tahng bèe-ung diversion
ขับช้าๆ kùp cháh cháh drive slowly
๔๐ ก.ม. sèe sìp gi-loh-mét 40 kilometres
๔ ตัน sìi dtun 4 tons
หยุด ตรวจ yòot - dtròo-ut halt - checkpoint
โรงพยาบาลห้ามใช้เสียง rohng pa-yah-bahn hâhm chái sěe-ung hospital: no sounding horns
ชิดซ้าย chít sái keep left
ห้ามเข้า hâhm kâo no entry
ห้ามแซง hâhm sairng no overtaking, no passing
ห้ามจอดรถ hâhm jòrt rót no parking
ห้ามเลี้ยว hâhm lée-o no turning
ห้ามกลับรถ hâhm glùp rót no U-turns
ห้ามรถทุกชนิด hâhm rót tóok cha-nít no vehicles
ทางรถไฟ tahng rót fai railway
โรงเรียน rohng ree-un school
หยุด yòot stop
๓ ม. sahm mét 3 metres

Shopping

บาท bàht baht (unit of currency)
ลูกละ ... บาท lôok la ... bàht ... baht each (e.g. for large fruit)
ใบละ ... บาท bai la ... bàht ... baht each (e.g. for eggs, fruit)
ตัวละ ... บาท dtoo-a la ... bàht ... baht each (e.g. items of clothing)
โลละ ... บาท loh la ... bàht ... baht per kilo
คู่ละ ... บาท kôo la ... baht ... baht per pair (e.g. shoes)
ชิ้นละ ... บาท chín la ... bàht ... baht per piece/portion
สุขภัณฑ์ sòok-ka-pun bathroom accessories
ที่จ่ายเงิน têe jài ngern cash desk, cashier
พนักงานเก็บเงิน pa-núk ngahn gèp ngern cashier

แผนกเด็ก **pa-nàirk dèk** children's department
แผนกไฟฟ้า **pa-nàirk fai fáh** electrical goods
เครื่องเรือน **krêu-ung reu-un** furniture
ราคา **rah-kah** price
วิทยุทีวี **wít-ta-yóo - tee-wee** radio - TV
ลดราคา **lót rah-kah** sale; reduced
รองเท้า **rorng-táo** shoes
ลดพิเศษ **lót pi-sàyt** special reductions
อุปกรณ์กีฬา **òo-bpa-gorn gee-lah** sports equipment
ของเล่น **kŏrng lên** toys
นาฬิกา **nah-li-gah** watches

Sport

กรีฑา **gree-tah** athletics
มวย **moo-ay** boxing
ฟุตบอล **fóot-born** football
ประตู **bpra-dtoo** goal
กอล์ฟ **górp** golf
สนามกอล์ฟ **sa-năhm górp** golf course
สนามม้า **sa-năhm máh** race course
กีฬา **gee-lah** sport
สนามกีฬา **sa-năhm gee-lah** stadium
ว่ายน้ำ **wâi náhm** swimming
ทีม **teem** team
เทนนิส **ten-nít** tennis
สนามเทนนิส **sa-năhm ten-nít** tennis court
มวยไทย **moo-ay tai** Thai boxing

Streets and roads

ตรอก **dtròrk** lane (off a soi)
ซอย **soy** lane, soi
ถนน **ta-nŏn** road

Thai culture

เมืองโบราณ **meu-ung boh-rahn** Ancient City
กรมศิลปากร **grom sĭn-la-bpa-korn** Department of Fine Arts
ตลาดน้ำ **dta-làht náhm** Floating Market
พิพิธภัณฑ์ **pi-pít-ta-pun** museum
พิพิธภัณฑ์สถานแห่งชาติ **pi-pít-ta-pun sa-tăhn hàirng châht** National Museum

โรงละครแห่งชาติ **rohng la-korn hàirng châht** National Theatre
พระปฐมเจดีย์ **prá-bpa-tŏm jay-dee** Pra Pathom Jedi (Buddhist monument)
พระบรมมหาราชวัง **prá-ba-rom-ma-hăh-râtch-a-wung** Royal Palace
วังสวนผักกาด **wung sŏo-un pùk-gàht** Suan Pakkard Palace
วัด **wút** temple
วัดพระแก้ว **wút pra-kâir-o** Temple of the Emerald Buddha
มวยไทย **moo-ay tai** Thai boxing
รำไทย **rum tai** Thai dancing
วัดโพธิ์ **wút poh** Wat Po

Timetables

ถึง **tĕung** arrives
วันที่ **wun-têe** date
วัน **wun** day
ออก **òrk** departs
วันหยุด **wun yòot** holiday
นาฬิกา **nah-li-gah** hours
เวลา **way-lah** time
กำหนดเวลาเดินรถ **gum-nòt way-lah dern rót** timetable, (US) schedule
วันนี้ **wun née** today
พรุ่งนี้ **prôong née** tomorrow
วันเสาร์อาทิตย์ **wun săo ah-tít** weekend
เมื่อวานนี้ **mêu-a wahn née** yesterday

Toilets

ไม่ว่าง **mâi wâhng** engaged
บุรุษ **boo-ròot** gentlemen
ชาย **chai** gents
หญิง **yĭng** ladies
สตรี **sa-dtree** ladies
ผู้ชาย **pôo-chai** men
ช. **chor** men
ห้องน้ำ **hôrng náhm** toilet, rest room
สุขา **sòo-kăh** toilet, rest room
ว่าง **wâhng** vacant
ญ. **yor** women
ผู้หญิง **pôo-yĭng** women

Menu Reader:
Food

Contents

Essential Terms 246
Basic Foods 247
Basic Main Meals 247
Beef and Beef Dishes 248
Bread 248
Cakes and Biscuits, Sweet Pastries 248
Condiments and Seasonings, Herbs and Spices 248
Cooking Methods and Typical Combinations 249
Curries 249
Desserts 250
Eggs and Egg Dishes 250
Fish and Seafood 250
Fish and Seafood Dishes 251
Fruit 251
Meat 252
Menu Terms 252
Miscellaneous Dishes 252
Pork and Pork Dishes 253
Poultry and Poultry Dishes 253
Rice and Noodles 254
Salads 254
Snacks and Sweets 254
Soups 255
Vegetables and Vegetable dishes 255

Essential terms

bowl chahm ชาม
chopsticks dta-gèe-up ตะเกียบ
cup tôo-ay ถ้วย
dessert kŏrng wăhn ของหวาน
fish bplah ปลา
fork sôrm ส้อม
glass gâir-o แก้ว
knife mêet มีด
meat néu-a เนื้อ
menu may-noo เมนู
noodles gŏo-ay dtĕe-o ก๋วยเตี๋ยว
pepper prĭk tai พริกไทย
plate jahn จาน
rice kâo ข้าว
salt gleu-a เกลือ
set menu ah-hăhn chóot อาหารชุด
soup sóop ซุป
spoon chórn ช้อน
table dtó โต๊ะ

another ... èek ... nèung อีก ... หนึ่ง
excuse me! (to call waiter/waitress) koon krúp (kâ)! คุณครับ(ค่ะ)
could I have the bill, please? chék bin เช็คบิล

Basic foods

เนยสด **ner-ee sòt** butter
เนยแข็ง **ner-ee kǎirng** cheese
น้ำพริก **núm prík** chilli paste
กะทิ **ga-tí** coconut milk
น้ำปลา **núm bplah** fish sauce
แป้งสาลี **bpâirng sǎh-lee** flour
น้ำผึ้ง **núm pêung** honey
แยม **yairm** jam; marmalade
น้ำมันพืช **núm mun pêut** oil
น้ำมันมะกอก **núm mun ma-gòrk** olive oil
น้ำมันหอย **núm mun hǒy** oyster sauce
น้ำจิ้ม **núm jîm** sauce
น้ำซีอิ๊ว **núm see éw** soy sauce
น้ำตาล **núm dtahn** sugar
น้ำส้ม **núm sôm** vinegar
โยกัต **yoh-gut** yoghurt

Basic main meals

ข้าวผัดไก่ **kâo pùt gài** chicken fried rice
ข้าวมันไก่ **kâo mun gài** chicken rice
ข้าวผัดปู **kâo pùt bpoo** crab fried rice
บะหมี่แห้ง **ba-mèe hâirng** 'dry' egg noodles, served without soup
ก๋วยเตี๋ยวแห้ง **gǒo-ay dtěe-o hâirng** 'dry' noodles, served without soup
ข้าวหน้าเป็ด **kâo nâh bpèt** duck rice
บะหมี่น้ำ **ba-mèe náhm** egg noodle soup
ก๋วยเตี๋ยวผัดซีอิ๊ว **gǒo-ay dtěe-o pùt see éw** noodles fried in soy sauce
ก๋วยเตี๋ยวผัดราดหน้า **gǒo-ay dtěe-o pùt râht nâh** noodles with fried meat, vegetables and thick gravy
ก๋วยเตี๋ยวน้ำ **gǒo-ay dtěe-o náhm** noodle soup
ข้าวผัดหมู **kâo pùt mǒo** pork fried rice
ข้าวหมูแดง **kâo mǒo dairng** 'red' pork rice (pork soaked in a red marinade)
ข้าวคลุกกะปิ **kâo klóok ga-bpì** rice and shrimp paste fried together and served with pork and shredded omelette
ข้าวผัดกุ้ง **kâo pùt gôong** shrimp fried rice
ผัดไทย **pùt tai** Thai-style fried

noodles

ขนมจีนแกงไก่ **ka-nŏm jeen gairng gài** Thai vermicelli with chicken curry

Beef and beef dishes

เนื้อผัดน้ำมันหอย **néu-a pùt núm mun hŏy** beef fried in oyster sauce

เนื้อผัดพริก **néu-a pùt prík** beef fried with chillies

เนื้อผัดกระเทียมพริกไทย **néu-a pùt gra-tee-um prík tai** beef fried with garlic and pepper

เนื้อผัดขิง **néu-a pùt kĭng** beef fried with ginger

เนื้อสับผัดพริกกระเพรา **néu-a sùp pùt prík gra-prao** minced beef fried with chillies and basil

เนื้อเสต๊ก **néu-a sa-dték** steak

Bread

ขนมปัง **ka-nŏm-bpung** bread; roll

ปอนด์ **bporn** loaf

ขนมปังปิ้ง **ka-nŏm bpung bpîng** toast

Cakes and biscuits, sweet pastries

คุกกี้ **kóok-gêe** biscuit, cookie

ขนมเค๊ก **ka-nŏm káyk** cake

แป้งขนม **bpâirng ka-nŏm** pastry (dough)

ขนม **ka-nŏm** pastry, small cake

Condiments and seasonings, herbs and spices

ใบกระเพรา **bai gra-prao** basil

พริก **prík** chilli

ผักชี **pùk chee** coriander

ข่า **kàh** galangal (similar to ginger)

ขิง **kĭng** ginger

เครื่องเทศ **krêu-ung tâyt** herbs

ตะไคร้ **dta-krái** lemon grass

พริกไทย **prík tai** pepper

เกลือ **gleu-a** salt

Cooking methods and typical combinations

... ต้ม ... **dtôm** boiled ...
... ย่าง ... **yâhng** charcoal-grilled ...
... ทอด ... **tôrt** deep-fried ...
... ผัดหน่อไม้ ... **pùt nòr-mái** ... fried with bamboo shoots
... ผัดใบกระเพรา ... **pùt bai gra-prao** ... fried with basil leaves
... ผัดพริก ... **pùt prík** ... fried with chillies
... ทอดกระเทียมพริกไทย ... **tôrt gra-tee-um prík tai** ... fried with garlic and pepper
... ผัดขิง ... **pùt kĭng** ... fried with ginger
... อบ ... **òp** oven-cooked ...
... ผัด ... **pùt** stir-fried ...
... เปรี้ยวหวาน ... **bprêe-o wăhn** sweet and sour ...
ปิ้ง **bpîng** toasted

Curries

แกงเนื้อ **gairng néu-a** beef curry
แกงเขียวหวาน **gairng kĕe-o wăhn** beef curry made using green curry paste, made from green chilli peppers
ข้าวแกง **kâo gairng** curry and rice
แกงไก่ **gairng gài** chicken curry
พะแนง **pa-nairng** 'dry' curry (in thick curry sauce)
พะแนงเนื้อ **pa-nairng néu-a** 'dry' beef curry (in thick curry sauce)
พะแนงไก่ **pa-nairng gài** 'dry' chicken curry (in thick curry sauce)
พะแนงหมู **pa-nairng mŏo** 'dry' pork curry (in thick curry sauce)
แกงกาหรี่ **gairng ga-rèe** Indian-style curry made with beef and potatoes cooked in coconut milk with yellow curry paste
แกงมัสหมั่น **gairng mút-sa-mùn** 'Muslim' curry containing beef, potatoes and peanuts

แกงเผ็ด **gairng pèt** spicy curry

แกงจืด **gairng jèut** vegetable soup or stock (an accompaniment to curries)

แกง **gairng** 'wet' curry – meat cooked in coconut milk and served in a bowl full of liquid

Desserts

กล้วยบวชชี **glôo-ay bòo-ut chee** banana in sweet coconut-milk sauce

ของหวาน **kŏrng wăhn** dessert

ไอศครีม **ai-sa- kreem** ice cream

ข้าวเหนียวมะม่วง **kăo nĕe-o ma-môo-ung** sweet sticky rice, mango and coconut cream

ตะโก้ **dta-gôh** Thai-style jelly with coconut cream

Eggs and egg dishes

ไข่ต้ม **kài dtôm** boiled egg

ไข่ **kài** egg

ไข่พะโล้ **kài pa-lóh** egg stewed in soy sauce and spices

ไข่ยัดไส้ **kài yút sâi** filled omelette

ไข่ดาว **kài dao** fried egg

ไข่เจียว **kài jee-o** omelette

ไข่ลูกเขย **kài lôok kĕr-ee** 'son-in-law' eggs – hard-boiled eggs with various condiments

ไข่ลวก **kài lôo-uk** very soft boiled egg (eaten, or rather 'drunk' almost raw)

Fish and seafood

ปู **bpoo** crab

ปลา **bplah** fish

กุ้งใหญ่ **gôong yài** lobster

หอยแมงภู่ **hŏy mairng pôo** mussels

ปลาหมึกยักษ์ **bplah-mèuk yúk** octopus

หอยนางรม **hŏy nahng rom** oyster

อาหารทะเล **ah-hăhn ta-lay** seafood

หอย **hŏy** shellfish

กุ้ง **gôong** shrimp, prawn

ปลาหมึก **bplah-mèuk** squid

Fish and seafood dishes

กุ้งเผา **gôong păo** barbecued prawns
กุ้งทอดกระเทียมพริกไทย **gôong tôrt gra-tee-um prík tai** prawns fried with garlic and pepper
กุ้งผัดใบกระเพรา **gôong pùt bai gra-prao** shrimps fried with basil leaves
กุ้งผัดพริก **gôong pùt prík** shrimps fried with chillies
ทอดมันกุ้ง **tôrt mun gôong** shrimp 'tort mun', finely minced shrimps, fried in batter with spices
ปลาหมึกผัดพริก **bplah-mèuk pùt prík** squid fried with chillies
ปลาหมึกทอดกระเทียมพริกไทย **bplah-mèuk tôrt gra-tee-um prík tai** squid fried with garlic and pepper
ปลาเปรี้ยวหวาน **bplah bprêe-o wăhn** sweet and sour fish

Fruit

แอปเปิล **air-bpêrn** apple
กล้วย **glôo-ay** banana
มะพร้าว **ma-práo** coconut
น้อยหน่า **nóy-nàh** custard apple – green heart-shaped fruit with white flesh
อินทผาลัม **in-ta-păh-lum** dates
ทุเรียน **too-ree-un** durian – large green fruit with spiny skin, yellow flesh and a pungent smell
ผลไม้ **pŏn-la-mái** fruit
องุ่น **a-ngòon** grapes
ฝรั่ง **fa-rùng** guava – green-skinned fruit with white flesh
ขนุน **ka-noon** jackfruit – large melon-shaped fruit with thick, green skin and yellow flesh
มะนาว **ma-nao** lemon; lime
ลำไย **lum-yai** longan – like a lychee
ลิ้นจี่ **lín-jèe** lychee
มะม่วง **ma-môo-ung** mango
มังคุด **mung-kóot** mangosteen – round fruit with a thick, purplish-brown skin and white flesh

แตงไทย **dtairng tai** melon
ส้ม **sôm** orange
มะละกอ **ma-la-gor** papaya – green or yellow-skinned oblong-shaped fruit with reddish-orange flesh
ลูกพีช **lôok pêech** peach
ลูกแพร์ **lôok pair** pear
สับปะรด **sùp-bpa-rót** pineapple
ลูกพลัม **lôok plum** plum
ส้มโอ **sôm oh** pomelo – similar to grapefruit
เงาะ **ngór** rambutan – small fruit with reddish prickly skin and white flesh
ชมพู่ **chom-pôo** rose apple – red, pink or white strawberry-shaped fruit
ละมุด **la-móot** sapodilla – small brown-skinned fruit, similar in taste and texture to a pear
สตรอเบอรี่ **sa-dtror-ber-rêe** strawberry
แตงโม **dtairng moh** water melon

Meat

เนื้อ **néu-a** beef; meat
ไก่ **gài** chicken
เป็ด **bpèt** duck
เครื่องใน **krêu-ung nai** kidneys
ไต **tai** kidneys
เนื้อแกะ **néu-a gàir** lamb
ตับ **dtùp** liver
หมู **mŏo** pork
เนื้อหมู **néu-a mŏo** pork

Menu terms

อาหารจีน **ah-hăhn jeen** Chinese food
อาหาร **ah-hăhn** cuisine, cooking; meal; food
กับข้าว **gùp kâo** dish, meal
เมนู **may-noo** menu
รายการอาหาร **rai gahn ah-hăhn** menu
ราคา **rah-kah** price

Miscellaneous dishes

ทอดมัน **tôrt mun** deep-fried fish-cakes

ขนมจีบ **ka-nŏm jèep** 'dim-sum' – steamed balls of minced pork in dough
ปอเปี๊ยะทอด **bpor bpêe-a tôrt** Thai spring roll

Pork and pork dishes

หมูสับผัดพริกกระเพรา **mŏo sùp pùt prík gra-prao** minced pork fried with chillies and basil
หมู **mŏo** pork
เนื้อหมู **néu-a mŏo** pork
หมูผัดใบกระเพรา **mŏo pùt bai gra-prao** pork fried with basil leaves
หมูผัดพริก **mŏo pùt prík** pork fried with chillies
หมูทอดกระเทียมพริกไทย **mŏo tôrt gra-tee-um prík tai** pork fried with garlic and pepper
หมูผัดขิง **mŏo pùt kĭng** pork fried with ginger
หมูพะโล้ **môo pa-lóh** pork stewed in soy sauce
ซี่โครง **sêe krohng mŏo** spare ribs
หมูเปรี้ยวหวาน **mŏo bprêe-o wăhn** sweet and sour pork
หมูสะเต๊ะ **mŏo sa-dtáy** thin strips of charcoal-grilled pork

Poultry and poultry dishes

ไก่ย่าง **gài yâhng** barbecued or roast chicken
ไก่ **gài** chicken
ไก่ต้มข่า **gài dtôm kàh** chicken boiled in spicy stock
ไก่ผัดหน่อไม้ **gài pùt nòr-mái** chicken fried with bamboo shoots
ไก่ผัดใบกระเพรา **gài pùt bai gra-prao** chicken fried with basil leaves
ไก่ผัดเม็ดมะม่วงหิมพานต์ **gài pùt mét ma-môo-ung hĭm-ma-pahn** chicken fried with cashew nuts
ไก่ผัดพริก **gài pùt prík** chicken fried with chillies
ไก่ทอดกระเทียมพริกไทย **gài tôrt gra-tee-um prík tai** chicken fried with garlic and pepper
ไก่ผัดขิง **gài pùt kĭng** chicken fried with ginger

ไก่ผัดหน่อไม้ฝรั่ง gài pùt nòr-mái fa-rùng chicken with asparagus
เป็ด bpèt duck
เป็ดย่าง bpèt yâhng roast duck
ไก่ผัดเปรี้ยวหวาน gài pùt brêe-o wăhn sweet and sour chicken

Rice and noodles

ข้าวสวย kâo sŏo-ay boiled rice
หมี่กรอบ mèe gròrp crispy noodles
บะหมี่ ba-mèe egg noodles
ข้าวผัด kâo pùt fried rice
เส้นใหญ่ sên yài large (width of noodles)
ผัดราดหน้า pùt râht nâh noodles with fried vegetables and meat, served with a thick gravy
กวยเตี๋ยว gŏo-ay dtĕe-o rice-flour noodles
ข้าว kâo rice
ข้าวต้ม kâo dtôm rice porridge
เส้นเล็ก sên lék small (width of noodles)
ข้าวเหนียว kâo nĕe-o sticky rice
ขนมจีน ka-nŏm jeen Thai vermicelli
วุ้นเส้น wóon-sên transparent noodles
เส้นหมี่ sên mèe very small (width of noodles)

Salads

ส้มตำ sôm dtum papaya salad made with unripe green papaya, chillies, lime juice, fish sauce and dried shrimps
สลัด sa-lùt salad
ยำ yum Thai salad

Snacks and sweets

ช็อกโกเลต chórk-goh-let chocolate
มันฝรั่งทอด mun fa-rùng tôrt crisps, (US) potato chips
ไอศครีม ai-sa-kreem ice cream
ไอศครีมแท่ง ai-sa-kreem tâirng ice lolly

อมยิ้ม **om-yím** lollipop
ถั่ว **tòo-a** nuts; peanuts
ถั่วลิสง **tòo-a li-sŏng** peanuts
ทอฟฟี่ **tórp-fêe** sweets, candies
ลูกกวาด **lôok gwàht** sweets, candies

Soups

ต้มยำไก่ **dtôm yum gài** chicken 'tom yam' spicy soup
บะหมี่น้ำ **ba-mèe náhm** egg noodle soup
ต้มยำปลา **dtôm yum bplah** fish 'tom yam' spicy soup
ต้มยำโป๊ะแตก **dtôm yum bpó dtàirk** mixed seafood 'tom yam' spicy soup
ก๋วยเตี๋ยวน้ำ **gŏo-ay dtĕe-o náhm** noodle soup
ต้มยำกุ้ง **dtôm yum gôong** shrimp 'tom yam' spicy soup
แกงส้ม **gairng sôm** spicy vegetable soup

Vegetables and vegetable dishes

หน่อไม้ฝรั่ง **nòr-mái fa-rùng** asparagus
มะเขือ **ma-kĕu-a** aubergine, eggplant
หน่อไม้ **nòr mái** bamboo shoots
ถั่วงอก **tòo-a ngôrk** bean sprouts
กะหล่ำปลี **ga-lùm-bplee** cabbage
หัวผักกาดแดง **hŏo-a pùk-gàht dairng** carrot
ดอกกะหล่ำปลี **dòrk ga-lùm-bplee** cauliflower
พริก **prík** chilli
มันฝรั่งทอด **mun fa-rùng tôrt** chips, French fries
แตงกวา **dtairng-gwah** cucumber
ผัดผักบุ้งไฟแดง **pùt pùk bôong fai dairng** fried morning-glory (type of greens)
กระเทียม **gra-tee-um** garlic
ขิง **kĭng** ginger
พริกหยวก **prík yòo-uk** green pepper
ผักกาด **pùk-gàht** lettuce

ถั่วลันเตา **tòo-a lun-dtao** mange-tout
ผักบุ้ง **pùk bôong** morning-glory (type of greens)
เห็ด **hèt** mushrooms
หัวหอม **hŏo-a hŏrm** onion
ถั่ว **tòo-a** peas; beans; lentils
มันฝรั่ง **mun fa-rùng** potato
พริกหยวกแดง **príк yôo-uk dairng** red pepper
ผักคะน้า **pùk ka-náh** spring greens
ต้นหอม **dtôn hŏrm** spring onions
ข้าวโพด **kâo pôht** sweet corn, maize
มะเขือเทศ **ma-kĕu-a tâyt** tomato
ผัก **pùk** vegetables

Menu Reader: Drink

Contents: Drink

Essential Terms 260
Beer, Spirits, Wine etc 261
Coffee, Tea etc 261
Soft Drinks 261

Essential terms

beer bee-a เบียร์

bottle kòo-ut ขวด

another bottle of ..., please kŏr ... èek kòo-ut nèung ขอ ... อีกขวดหนึ่ง

coconut juice núm ma-práo น้ำมะพร้าว

coffee gah-fair กาแฟ

cup tôo-ay ถ้วย

a cup of ..., please kŏr ... tôo-ay nèung ขอ ... ถ้วยหนึ่ง

fruit juice núm pŏn-la-mái น้ำผลไม้

gin lâo yin เหล้ายิน

a gin and tonic, please kŏr yin toh-nik ขอยินโทนิค

glass gâir-o แก้ว

milk nom นม

mineral water núm râir น้ำแร่

soda (water) núm soh-dah น้ำโซดา

soft drink náhm kòo-ut น้ำขวด

sugar núm dtahn น้ำตาล

tea núm chah น้ำชา

tonic (water) núm toh-nik น้ำโทนิค

water náhm น้ำ

whisky lâo wĭt-sa-gêe เหล้าวิสกี้

wine lâo wai เหล้าไวน์

wine list rai-gahn lâo wai รายการเหล้าไวน์

another ... èek ... nèung อีก ... หนึ่ง

Beer, spirits, wine etc

เหล้า **lâo** alcohol, liquor
เบียร์ **bee-a** beer
ขวด **kòo-ut** bottle
เหล้าบรั่นดี **lâo brùn-dee** brandy
ค็อกเทล **kórk-layn** cocktail
แก้ว **gâir-o** glass
เหล้ายิน **lâo yin** gin
ยินโทนิค **yin toh-nik** gin and tonic
น้ำแข็ง **núm kăirng** ice
แม่โขง **mâir-kŏhng** Mekhong® whisky
เบียร์สิงห์ **bee-a sĭng** Singha® beer
วอดก้า **word-gâh** vodka
เหล้าวิสกี้ **lâo wít-sa-gêe** whisky, scotch
เหล้าไวน์ **lâo wai** wine

Coffee, tea etc

คาฟีน **kah-feen** caffeine
เย็น **yen** chilled
โกโก้ **goh-gôh** cocoa
กาแฟ **gah-fair** coffee
โอเลี้ยง **oh-lée-ung** iced black coffee
กาแฟเย็น **gah-fair yen** iced coffee
ชาใส่มะนาว **chah sài ma-nao** lemon tea
กาแฟผง **gah-fair pŏng** instant coffee
น้ำชา **núm chah** tea
ไม่ใส่นม **mái sài nom** without milk
ไม่ใส่น้ำตาล **mái sài núm dtahn** without sugar

Soft drinks

น้ำมะพร้าว **núm ma-práo** coconut juice
โค้ก **kóhk** Coke®
เครื่องดื่ม **krêu-ung dèum** drinks
ซ่า **sâh** fizzy, carbonated
น้ำส้มคั้น **núm sôm kún** fresh orange juice
น้ำแข็ง **núm kăirng** ice
น้ำผลไม้ **náhm pŏn-la-mái** juice
นม **nom** milk
น้ำมะนาว **núm ma-nao** lemonade
น้ำแร่ **núm râir** mineral water

น้ำส้ม **núm sôm** orange juice (bottled)
น้ำสับปะรด **núm sùp-bpa-rót** pineapple juice
น้ำโซดา **núm soh-dah** soda water
น้ำขวด **náhm kòo-ut** soft drink
นมกระป๋อง **nom gra-bpŏrng** tinned milk
น้ำมะเขือเทศ **núm ma-kĕu-a tâyt** tomato juice
น้ำ **náhm** water

How the Language Works

Pronunciation

Throughout this book Thai words have been written in a romanized system (see the Thai alphabet page 269) so that they can be read as though they were English, bearing in mind the notes on pronunciation below. There are, however, some sounds that are unlike anything in English. In this pronunciation guide, words containing these sounds are given in Thai script as well; ask a Thai to pronounce them for you.

Vowels

a	as in **a**live
e	as in t**e**n
i	as in s**i**n
o	as in **o**n
u	as in f**u**n
ah	as the **a** in r**a**ther
ai	as in Th**ai**
air	as in f**air**
ao	as in L**ao**
ay	as in h**ay**
ee	as in s**ee**
er	as in numb**er**
er-ee	as in the Thai word **ner-ee** เนย (butter); the **r** is not pronounced
eu	as in the Thai word **meu** มือ (hand); like the English exclamation **ugh!**
ew	as in f**ew**
oh	as the **o** in n**o**
oo	as in b**oo**t
OO	as in l**oo**k
oy	as in b**oy**

Consonants

bp	sharp **p** sound (don't pronounce the **b**). It occurs in the word **bpai** ไป (go)
dt	sharp **t** (don't pronounce the **d**). It occurs in the word **dtàir** แต (but)
g	as in **g**ate
ng	as in ri**ng**

When **k**, **p** and **t** are at the end of a word, it may sound almost as if these consonants are not being pronounced. Ask a Thai to say:

lâhk	ลาก	drag (verb)
lâhp	ลาบ	minced meat
lâht	ลาด	cover; spread (verb)

When a final **r** is followed by a vowel, the **r** is not pronounced:

ner-ee เนย butter

Bangkok Thai

Among some Bangkok speakers, when there are two consonants at the beginning of a word, the second consonant sound is often omitted:

bplah (fish) becomes **bpah**
gra-tee-um (garlic) becomes **ga-tee-um**

Sometimes, words beginning with a **kw** sound are pronounced as if they began with an **f** instead:

kwăh (right) becomes **făh**
kwahm sòok (happiness) becomes **fahm sòok**

Tones

Thai is a tonal language which means that the pitch at which a word is pronounced determines its meaning. The same combination of letters pronounced with a different tone will produce different words. In Thai there are five different tones: mid tone (no mark), high tone (´), low tone (`), falling tone (ˆ) and rising tone (ˇ). For example:

mai	ไมล์	(mid-tone)	mile	**mài**	ใหม่	(low tone)	new
mái	ไม้	(high tone)	wood	**măi**	ไหม	(rising tone)	silk
mâi	ไม่	(falling tone)	not				

In Thai, the tone is as important a part of the word as the consonant and vowel sounds.

To help you get a clearer idea of how the tones sound, Thai script equivalents are given for the words in this section. Ask a Thai speaker to read the words for you so that you can hear the tonal differences.

Mid-tone: e.g. **bpai** (go). This can be thought of as normal voice pitch. The following are words pronounced with mid-tone:

mah	มา	come	**mee**	มี	have
bpen	เป็น	is	**tum**	ทำ	do
nai	ใน	in			

High tone: e.g. **rórn** (hot). The voice has to be pitched slightly higher than normal. Tones are relative, though, and a Thai with a deep voice will have no problem producing a high tone, even though it will not be as 'high' in absolute terms as a child's high tone.

The following are words pronounced with high tones:

sái	ซ้าย	left	**rót**	รถ	car
cháo	เช้า	morning	**lék**	เล็ก	little
náhm	น้ำ	water			

Low tone: e.g. **nèung** (one). The voice should be pitched below the normal level:

yài	ใหญ่	big	**jàhk**	จาก	from
bpìt	ปิด	closed	**gài**	ไก่	chicken
tòok	ถูก	cheap			

Falling tone: e.g. **dâi** (can). The best way to convey a falling tone is to speak very emphatically, but this doesn't mean that Thai words with falling tones have to be shouted. English speakers tend to find this the most difficult tone and do not let the voice fall sufficiently. The secret is to start at a fairly high pitch in order to achieve a distinct fall:

têe	ที่	at	**mâi**	ไม่	not
hâh	ห้า	five	**mâhk**	มาก	much
chôrp	ชอบ	like			

Rising tone: e.g. **sŏrng** (two). The rising tone is like the intonation used when asking a question in English:

pŏm	ผม	I (said by a man)	**kŏr ...**	ขอ ...	may I ...
kwăh	ขวา	right	**lăi**	หลาย	several
mŏr	หมอ	doctor			

The relative positions of the five Thai tones can be represented graphically like this:

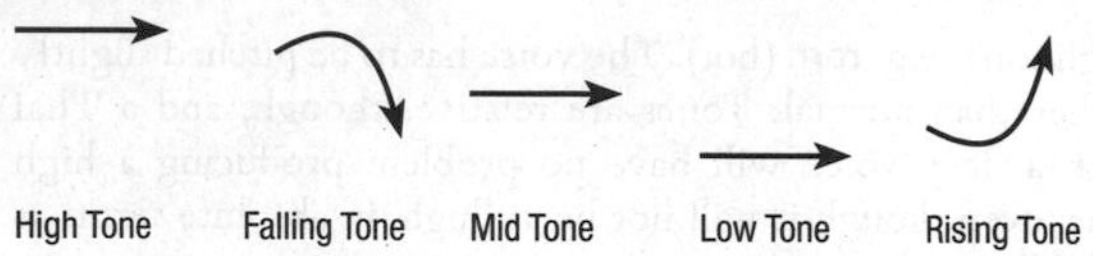

The Thai alphabet

Vowels

-อ	-or	เ-อะ	-er
-ะ	-a	เ-ะ	-e
-ั	-u-	เ-า	-ao
-ัว	-oo-a	เ-าะ	-or
-า	-ah	เ-ิ	-er
-ำ	-um	เ-ีย	-ee-a
-ิ	i	เ-ียะ	-ee a
-ี	-ee	เ-ือ	-eu-a
-ึ	-eu	แ-	-air
-ื	-eu	แ-็	-air
-ุ	-oo	แ-ะ	-air
-ู	-oo	โ-	-oh
เ-	-ay	โ-ะ	-o
เ-็	-e	ใ-	-ai
เ-ย	-er-ee	ไ-	-ai

Consonants

ก	g	ฑ	t
ข	k	ฒ	t
ค	k	ณ	n
ฆ	k	ด	d
ง	ng	ต	dt
จ	j	ถ	t
ฉ	ch	ท	t
ช	ch	ธ	t
ซ	s	น	n
ฌ	ch	บ	b
ญ	y	ป	bp
ฎ	d	ผ	p
ฏ	dt	ฝ	f
ฐ	t	พ	p

ฟ	f	ฦา	leu
ภ	p	ว	w
ม	m	ศ	s
ย	y	ษ	s
ร	r	ส	s
ฤ	reu	ห	h
ฤา	reu	ฬ	l
ล	l	อ	consonant that is not sounded
ฦ	leu	ฮ	h

Note

When appropriate, in the **How the Language Works** and **English-Thai** sections of this book, the phrases include two forms, the second of which is in brackets.

Where you have **pŏm (chún)** ('I' or 'me') in a phrase, **pŏm** should be used by a male speaker and **chún** by a female speaker.

There are also different polite particle forms for male and female speakers (see the **How the Language Works** section, page 282). Where you have **krúp (kâ)** or **krúp (ká)**, the form in brackets should be used by a female speaker.

Articles

There are no definite or indefinite articles in Thai. So, for example, **rót** (car) can mean either 'a car' or 'the car' depending on the context.

Nouns

Gender and Number

There is no gender in Thai and nouns have a single fixed form for both singular and plural. So, for example, **bâhn** means either 'house' or 'houses', depending on the context. In most cases, this is enough to make it clear whether it is a single item or more than one item that is being referred to. Even so, the Westerner has to learn to live with apparently ambiguous statements like **bpai gùp pêu-un** which can mean: 'I'm going with a friend' or 'I'm going with friends'.

You can be more specific in Thai by using a number with a noun. However, if you use a number or word denoting quantity, you also have to use a special 'counting' word known as a 'classifier'.

Classifiers

Every noun in Thai has a specific classifier which is used when counting or quantifying that noun. Some classifiers can be readily translated into English while others cannot. The classifier for all human beings, for example, is **kon** which means 'person' and the classifier for cars is **kun** which means 'vehicle'; **dtoo-a** literally means 'body' but is the classifier for animals.

The most common classifiers are:

bai	fruit, eggs, cups, bowls, small bits of paper such as tickets
cha-bùp	letters, newspapers, papers, documents
chín	pieces of cake, meat or cloth
dtoo-a	animals, chairs, tables, clothing
hàirng	places, buildings
hôrng	rooms
kon	people (excluding monks and royalty)
kòo-ut	bottles
kun	vehicles
lôok	round objects such as fruit or balls
lêm	books, knives
lŭng	houses

Uncountable nouns such as coffee, tea, beer etc are counted by the container in which they are sold. So food can be counted by the 'plate', coffee by the 'cup', beer by the 'bottle' etc.

When referring to more than one item the word order is as follows:

noun	number	classifier	
dtŏo-a	**hâh**	**bai**	five tickets
dtôm yum gài	**săhm**	**chahm**	three bowls of chicken 'tom yam'
cháhng	**sŏrng**	**dtoo-a**	two elephants
gairng néu-a	**sŏrng**	**jahn**	two plates of beef curry
pôo-yĭng	**săhm**	**kon**	three girls
bee-a	**sèe**	**kòo-ut**	four bottles of beer
rót	**sèe**	**kun**	four cars

When only one item is being counted the order of number and classifier is reversed:

noun	classifier	number	
dtŏo-a	bai	nèung	one/a ticket
măh	dtoo-a	nèung	one/a dog
pôo-chai	kon	nèung	one/a man
bee-a	koo-ùt	nèung	one/a bottle of beer
gah-fair	tôo-ay	nèung	one/a cup of coffee

For some nouns, the classifier is the same as the noun itself. For example, **hôrng** means 'room', and is also the classifier for rooms. However, the word **hôrng** is not repeated and only the classifier is used with the number:

sèe hôrng	**hôrng nèung**
four rooms	a room

Similarly, **kon** means 'person' and is also the classifier for people:

mee săhm kon	**kon nèung**
there were three people	a person, one person

Units of time and measurement are used in the same way as **hôrng** above; that is, the unit of time or measurement is the same as the classifer and is not repeated:

hâh wun	**sŏrng ah-tít**	**deu-un nèung**
five days	two weeks	one month

bpra-mahn yêe-sìp gi-loh-met
it's about 20 kilometres

Words such as 'all', 'every', 'many', 'several' and 'some' are also used with classifiers:

pêu-un	**tóok**	**kon**
friend	every/all	classifier

all my friends

kon ung-grìt	**lăi**	**kon**
English person	many	classifier
many English people		
rohng rairm	**bahng**	**hàirng**
hotel	some	classifier
some hotels		

If you can't think of the right classifier for something, use the general classifier **un**:

pŏm (chún) mâi dâi kŏr ao un née
I didn't ask for this (thing)

un la tâo-rài?
how much are they each?

èek un nèung
another one, the other one, the other thing

Adjectives and adverbs

Adjectives are always placed after the noun to which they refer:

pôo-yĭng sŏo-ay	**rót yài**	**ngern deu-un dee**
a beautiful girl	a large car	a good salary

Thai adjectives also function as verbs: **sŏo-ay** thus means both 'beautiful' and 'to be beautiful' and **yài** means both 'big' and 'to be big'. The above examples might therefore just as readily have been translated as 'the girl is beautiful', 'the car is big', and 'the salary is good'.

Note, however, that the Thai verb **bpen** (to be) cannot be used with adjectives and you cannot say:

pôo-yĭng bpen sŏo-ay* or **rót bpen yài***

*incorrect sentences

Comparatives

To form the comparative (more ..., ...-er), add **gwàh** after the adjective:

yài	large	**sŏo-ay**	beautiful
yài gwàh	larger	**sŏo-ay gwàh**	more beautiful
dee	good, nice		
dee gwàh	better, nicer		

To say 'more ... than ...' or '...-er than ...', the word order is as follows:

adjective + **gwàh ...**

grOOng-tayp yài gwàh chee-ung mài
Bangkok is bigger than Chiangmai

dee gwàh un née rŏu bplào?
is it better than this one?

bpai rót fai tòok gwàh bpai krêu-ung bin
going by train is cheaper than going by plane

Superlatives

To form the superlative, add **têe sòot** after the adjective:

yài	large	**dee**	good
yài têe sòot	(the) largest	**dee têe sòot**	(the) best

wút sŭm-kun têe sòot
the most important temple

tahng ray-o têe sòot
the quickest route

Adverbs

Adverbs are placed after the verb as in English. The adverb is the same as the adjective in Thai:

rót ray-o
a fast car

káo wîng ray-o
he runs quickly

pêu-un dee	**kăi dee**
a good friend	(it) sells well

Demonstrative Adjectives

The English demonstrative adjective 'this' is translated by **née**. 'That' is translated either by **nún** or **nóhn**. **nún** refers to something near the speaker and **nóhn** refers to something further away. Classifiers are also used with Thai demonstrative adjectives (see the section on Classifiers page 271):

noun	classifier	demonstrative	
dtó	**dtoo-a**	**née**	this table
gah-fair	**tôo-ay**	**nún**	that cup of coffee
dtum-ròo-ut	**kon**	**nóhn**	that policeman over there

Pronouns

Personal pronouns

There are many more personal pronouns in Thai than there are in English. The most useful pronouns are listed below. There is no distinction between subject and object pronouns in Thai:

pŏm (said by a man)	I, me
chún (said by a woman)	I, me
dee-chún (said by a woman)	I, me (more formal)
koon	you
káo	he, him; she, her; they, them
ráo	we, us
mun*	it

*Thais tend to avoid this as it is regarded as impolite in formal spoken Thai.

When appropriate, in the **How the Language Works** and **English-Thai** sections of this book, the phrases show both the male and female forms. Where you have **pŏm (chún)** ('I' or 'me') in a phrase, **pŏm** should be used by a male speaker and **chún** by a female speaker.

Frequently, pronouns are omitted altogether and it is only from the context that you will know who or what is being referred to. This sentence, for example,

doo	**nŭng**	**láir-o**	**glùp**	**bâhn**
see	film	already	return	home

could mean, 'after seeing a film, I/we/he/she/they went home'.

If you know a person's name, the polite way to address them or to speak about them is to use their first name and to place the word **koon** in front of it:

koon Chârt-chai mah jàhk năi?
where are you from?
where is Chartchai from?

koon Sŏm-chai séu a-rai?
what did you buy?
what did Somchai buy?

Possessives

The equivalent of possessive pronouns and adjectives in Thai is as follows:

noun + **kŏrng** + pronoun

The word **kŏrng** (of), however, is optional and frequently omitted:

pêu-un kŏrng káo or **pêu-un káo**
his/her/their friend

nûn kŏrng káo
that's his/hers/theirs

bâhn kŏrng pŏm or **bâhn pŏm**
my house

kŏrng chún
it's mine

Relative pronouns

There is only one relative pronoun in Thai – **têe** – which translates as either 'who', 'which', 'that' or 'where'. Here are some examples of how it is used:

kroo têe sŏrn pah-săh tai
the teacher, who teaches Thai

pŏn-la-mái têe rao séu
the fruit which we bought

órp-fit têe káo tum ngahn
the office where he works

Verbs

Verbs in Thai have a single fixed form. That is, unlike European languages, the form of the verb does not change according to the person or the tense. So, for example, **káo bpai** can mean 'he goes', 'he will go', 'he went' or 'he has gone'. Usually, the context in which you hear the verb will make it clear whether the speaker is referring to the past, present or future. But when it is important to be more specific, the context can be made clearer by placing a 'time-marker' word in front of or after the verb.

The most common and useful of these time-marker words are as follows:

ja
ja is placed immediately in front of the verb to indicate the future tense. For example:

chún ja bpai prÔOng née
I shall go tomorrow

rao ja séu rót mài
we shall buy a new car

ker-ee
ker-ee is placed in front of the verb to indicate the fact of having done something at least once in the past. It can also mean 'used to (do something)':

rao ker-ee bpai têe-o Chee-ung-mài
we have been to (visit) Chiangmai

káo ker-ee ree-un pah-săh tai
he used to study Thai

pŏm mâi ker-ee gin
I have never eaten it

láir-o

láir-o is placed at the end of a clause or sentence to indicate a completed action in the past:

káo gin kâo láir-o
he has eaten

chún doo láir-o
I've seen (it)

gum-lung

gum-lung is placed in front of the verb to indicate the continuous present or past:

káo gum-lung doo tee wee
he is watching TV or he was watching TV

These time-marker words are often omitted when the time context is specified or is otherwise obvious:

pŏm séu bpee gòrn
I bought (it) last year

rao bpai bpee nâh
we are going next year

Negatives

To form a negative sentence, place the word **mâi** in front of the main verb:

ah-hăhn a-ròy
the food is tasty

pŏm (chún) mee way-lah wâhng
I have some free time

ah-hăhn mâi a-ròy
the food is not tasty

pŏm (chún) mâi mee way-lah wâhng
I don't have any free time

Imperative

To make the imperative or command form, add **si** (pronounced **sí**, **see** or **sée**) after the verb:

doo sí
look!

ra-wung sí
look out!

bpìt bpra-dtoo sí
close the door!

For negative commands (don't ...), the word **yàh** is placed in front of the verb:

yàh tum	don't do it
yàh bpai	don't go
yàh gin	don't eat

Questions, answers, yes and no

... mái? questions

A statement can be made into a question by adding the question particle **mái** at the end of the sentence:

jèp (it) hurts	**jèp mái?** does it hurt?
bâhn yài the house is big	**bâhn yài mái?** is the house big?

To answer 'yes' to this type of question, you simply repeat the verb:

jèp mái? does it hurt?	**jèp** yes
bâhn yài mái? is the house big?	**yài** yes

If you want to say 'no', place the negative word **mâi** in front of the verb:

jèp mái? does it hurt?	**mâi jèp** no
bâhn yài mái? is the house big?	**mâi yài** no

... châi mái? questions

To form tag-questions in Thai, equivalent to the English 'isn't it?' or 'aren't they?' etc, add **châi mái?** to the end of a sentence:

káo mâi mah, châi mái?
he's not coming, is he?

soy săhm sìp săhm, châi mái?
soi 33, isn't it?

The **châi mái** question form is extremely useful for checking that you have understood what is going on. A 'yes' answer to a **châi mái?** question is **châi**. A 'no' answer is **mâi châi**:

bpai láir-o, châi mái?
he's gone, hasn't he?

châi/mâi châi
yes/no

... rĕu bplào? questions

Another common question form tags **rĕu blpào?** on to the end of a statement. Literally it means '... or not?', but it is not nearly as abrupt as such a translation suggests; it simply demands a straight answer:

kOOn bpai doo rĕu bplào?
are you going to see (it) or not?

mee rĕu bplào?
are there (any) or not?

If you want to say 'yes' to this, repeat the main verb – that is **bpai** in the first example, and **mee** in the second; if you want to say 'no', the answer is **bplào**.

Other question words: who? what? where? why? how? how much? how many?
Here are the remaining question words with examples; note that in almost every example the question word occurs at the end of the sentence.

krai
who?

kOOn bpai gùp krai?
who are you going with?

krai mâi bpai?
who isn't going?

a-rai
what?

nêe arai?
what's this?

kOOn pôot arai?
what did you say?

têe năi where?	**káo púk yòo têe năi?** where is he staying?
	hôrng náhm yòo têe năi? where's the toilet?
tum-mai? why?	**káo bpai tum-mai?** why is he going?
yung-ngai? how?	**kOOn ja tum yung-ngai?** how will you do (it)?
tâo-rài? how much?	**nêe tâo-rài?** how much is this?
gèe how many?	**bpai gèe krúng?** how many times did (you) go?

Polite particles: krúp, kâ, ká

An important way of making your speech sound polite in Thai is to use polite particles, which are untranslatable words placed at the end of a sentence. A male speaker should add the particle **krúp** to the end of both statements and questions to make them sound more polite, while a female speaker should add the particle **kâ** to the end of a statement and **ká** to the end of a question:

pŏm bpai prOOng née krúp
I am going tomorrow (said by a man)

chún mâi bpai kâ
I am not going (said by a woman)

káo bpai năi krúp?
where is he going? (said by a man)

kOOn tum a-rai ká?
what are you doing? (said by a woman)

It is important to get into the habit of using the appropriate polite particle at the end of every sentence and question. In the English-Thai section, most of the phrases have been given without these particles and the appropriate one should be added. Sometimes, depending on the situation and person addressed, it is acceptable to omit the polite particles, but, until you are more familiar with the Thai language, it is better to use them all the time.

Dates

Dates are expressed using the pattern:

wun (day) + ordinal number
+ month

Ordinal numbers are formed by placing **têe** in front of the cardinal number. A list of numbers is given on pages 286-287.

the first of July wun têe nèung ga-rúk-ga-dah-kom
วันที่หนึ่งกรกฎาคม
the twentieth of March wun têe yêe sìp mee-nah-kom
วันที่ยี่สิบมีนาคม
the twenty first of June wun têe yêe sìp èt mí-too-nah-yon
วันที่ยี่สิบเอ็ดมิถุนายน

Thais use both the Western Gregorian calendar and a Buddhist calendar – Buddha is said to have attained enlightenment in the year 543BC, so Thai dates start from that point: thus 1996 AD becomes 2539 BE (Buddhist Era).

Days

Monday wun jun วันจันทร์
Tuesday wun ung-kahn วันอังคาร
Wednesday wun póot วันพุธ
Thursday wun pá-réu-hùt วันพฤหัส
Friday wun sùk วันศุกร์
Saturday wun sǎo วันเสาร์
Sunday wun ah-tít วันอาทิตย์

Months

January mók-ga-rah-kom มกราคม
February goom-pah-pun กุมภาพันธ์
March mee-nah-kom มีนาคม
April may-săh-yon เมษายน
May préut-sa-pah-kom พฤษภาคม
June mí-too-nah-yon มิถุนายน
July ga-rúk-ga-dah-kom กรกฎาคม
August sĭng-hăh-kom สิงหาคม
September gun-yah-yon กันยายน
October dtoo-lah-kom ตุลาคม
November préut-sa-ji-gah-yon พฤศจิกายน
December tun-wah-kom ธันวาคม

Time

The Thai system of telling the time seems rather complicated at first because it uses different words for 'o'clock' depending on what time of day it is:

from 1 a.m. to 5 a.m. dtee
from 6 a.m. to midday mohng cháo
from 1 p.m. to 4 p.m. bài
from 5 p.m. to 6 p.m yen
from 7 p.m. to midnight tôom

Here, then, is how the hours are expressed in Thai:

1 a.m. dtee nèung ตีหนึ่ง
2 a.m. dtee sŏrng ตีสอง
3 a.m. dtee săhm ตีสาม
4 a.m. dtee sèe ตีสี่
5 a.m. dtee hâh ตีห้า
6 a.m. hòk mohng cháo หกโมงเช้า
7 a.m. jèt mohng cháo เจ็ดโมงเช้า
or mohng cháo โมงเช้า

8 a.m. bpàirt mohng cháo แปดโมงเช้า
or sŏrng mohng cháo สองโมงเช้า
9 a.m. gâo mohng cháo เก้าโมงเช้า
or săhm mohng cháo สามโมงเช้า
10 a.m. sìp mohng cháo สิบโมงเช้า
or sèe mohng cháo สี่โมงเช้า
11 a.m. sìp èt mohng cháo สิบเอ็ดโมงเช้า
or hâh mohng cháo ห้าโมงเช้า
midday têe-ung wun เที่ยงวัน
1 p.m. bài mohng บ่ายโมง
2 p.m. bài sŏrng mohng บ่ายสองโมง
3 p.m. bài săhm mohng บ่ายสามโมง
4 p.m. bài sèe mohng บ่ายสี่โมง
5 p.m. hâh mohng yen ห้าโมงเย็น
6 p.m. hòk mohng yen หกโมงเย็น
7 p.m. tôom nèung ทุ่มหนึ่ง
8 p.m. sŏrng tôom สองทุ่ม
9 p.m. săhm tôom สามทุ่ม
10 p.m. sèe tôom สี่ทุ่ม
11 p.m. hâh tôom ห้าทุ่ม
midnight têe-ung keun เที่ยงคืน

Note: There is no equivalent of 'it is ...' in Thai when stating the time; **săhm tôom** means both '9 p.m.' and 'it is 9 p.m.'.

To say 'half-past', use the word **krêung** (half). There is no special word for 'quarter past' or 'quarter to' the hour; these are translated by 'fifteen minutes (past)' and 'fifteen minutes (to)' the hour:

11.30 a.m sìp-èt mohng krèung สิบเอ็ดโมงครึ่ง
3.30 p.m bài săhm mohng krèung บ่ายสามโมงครึ่ง
11.30 p.m hâh tôom krèung ห้าทุ่มครึ่ง
1.15 p.m bài mohng síp hâh nah-tee บ่ายโมงสิบห้านาที
1.45 p.m èek sìp hâh nah-tee bài sŏrng mohng
อีกสิบห้านาทีบ่ายสองโมง

Note that when expressing minutes past the hour, the word order is:

hour time   number of minutes   **nah-tee** (minutes)

2.10 p.m bài sŏrng mohng sìp nah-tee บ่ายสองโมงสิบนาที
8.25 p.m sŏrng tôom yêe sìp hâh nah-tee สองทุ่มยี่สิบห้านาที

To express minutes to the hour, the word order is as follows:

èek (further, more)   number of minutes   hour time

4.50 p.m èek sìp nah-tee hâh mohng yen อีกสิบนาทีห้าโมงเย็น
10.55 p.m èek hâh nah-tee hâh tôom อีกห้านาทีห้าทุ่ม

what time is it? gèe mohng láir-o? กี่โมงแล้ว
hour chôo-a-mohng ชั่วโมง
minute nah-tee นาที
two minutes sŏrng nah-tee สองนาที
second wí-nah-tee วินาที
a quarter of an hour sìp hâh nah-tee สิบห้านาที
half an hour krêung chôo-a-mohng ครึ่งชั่วโมง
three quarters of an hour sèe sìp hâh nah-tee สี่สิบห้านาที

Numbers

0	sŏon ๐ ศูนย์
1	nèung ๑ หนึ่ง
2	sŏrng ๒ สอง
3	săhm ๓ สาม
4	sèe ๔ สี่
5	hâh ๕ ห้า
6	hòk ๖ หก
7	jèt ๗ เจ็ด
8	bpàirt ๘ แปด
9	gâo ๙ เก้า
10	sìp ๑๐ สิบ
11	sìp-èt ๑๑ สิบเอ็ด
12	sìp-sŏrng ๑๒ สิบสอง
13	sìp-săhm ๑๓ สิบสาม
14	sìp-sèe ๑๔ สิบสี่
15	sìp-hâh ๑๕ สิบห้า
16	sìp-hòk ๑๖ สิบหก
17	sìp-jèt ๑๗ สิบเจ็ด
18	sìp-bpàirt ๑๘ สิบแปด
19	sìp-gâo ๑๙ สิบเก้า
20	yêe-sìp ๒๐ ยี่สิบ
21	yêe-sìp-èt ๒๑ ยี่สิบเอ็ด
22	yêe-sìp-sŏrng ๒๒ ยี่สิบสอง
30	săhm-sìp ๓๐ สามสิบ
31	săhm-sìp-èt ๓๑ สามสิบเอ็ด
40	sèe-sìp ๔๐ สี่สิบ

50	hâh-sìp ๕๐ ห้าสิบ
60	hòk-sìp ๖๐ หกสิบ
70	jèt-sìp ๗๐ เจ็ดสิบ
80	bpàirt-sìp ๘๐ แปดสิบ
90	gâo-sìp ๙๐ เก้าสิบ
100	nèung róy ๑๐๐ หนึ่งร้อย
101	nèung róy nèung ๑๐๑ หนึ่งร้อยหนึ่ง
102	nèung róy sŏrng ๑๐๒ หนึ่งร้อยสอง
110	nèung róy sìp ๑๑๐ หนึ่งร้อยสิบ
200	sŏrng róy ๒๐๐ สองร้อย
201	sŏrng róy nèung ๒๐๑ สองร้อยหนึ่ง
202	sŏrng róy sŏrng ๒๐๒ สองร้อยสอง
210	sŏrng róy sìp ๒๑๐ สองร้อยสิบ
1,000	nèung pun ๑๐๐๐ หนึ่งพัน
2,000	sŏrng pun ๒๐๐๐ สองพัน
10,000	nèung mèun ๑๐๐๐๐ หนึ่งหมื่น
100,000	nèung săirn ๑๐๐๐๐๐ หนึ่งแสน
1,000,000	nèung láhn ๑๐๐๐๐๐๐ หนึ่งล้าน
100,000,000	nèung róy láhn ๑๐๐๐๐๐๐๐๐ หนึ่งร้อยล้าน

Ordinals

1st	têe nèung ที่หนึ่ง
2nd	têe sŏrng ที่สอง
3rd	têe săhm ที่สาม
4th	têe sèe ที่สี่
5th	têe hâh ที่ห้า
6th	têe hòk ที่หก
7th	têe jèt ที่เจ็ด
8th	têe bpàirt ที่แปด
9th	têe gâo ที่เก้า
10th	têe sìp ที่สิบ

Conversion Tables

1 centimetre = 0.39 inches
1 metre = 39.37 inches = 1.09 yards
1 kilometre = 0.62 miles = 5/8 mile

1 inch = 2.54 cm
1 foot = 30.48 cm
1 yard = 0.91 m
1 mile = 1.61 km

km	1	2	3	4	5	10	20	30	40	50	100
miles	0.6	1.2	1.9	2.5	3.1	6.2	12.4	18.6	24.8	31.0	62.1

miles	1	2	3	4	5	10	20	30	40	50	100
km	1.6	3.2	4.8	6.4	8.0	16.1	32.2	48.3	64.4	80.5	161

1 gram = 0.035 ounces

1 kilo = 1000 g = 2.2 pounds

g	100	250	500
oz	3.5	8.75	17.5

1 oz = 28.35 g
1 lb = 0.45 kg

kg	0.5	1	2	3	4	5	6	7	8	9	10
lb	1.1	2.2	4.4	6.6	8.8	11.0	13.2	15.4	17.6	19.8	22.0

kg	20	30	40	50	60	70	80	90	100
lb	44	66	88	110	132	154	176	198	220

lb	0.5	1	2	3	4	5	6	7	8	9	10	20
kg	0.2	0.5	0.9	1.4	1.8	2.3	2.7	3.2	3.6	4.1	4.5	9.0

1 litre = 1.75 UK pints / 2.13 US pints

1 UK pint = 0.57 l
1 US pint = 0.47 l

1 UK gallon = 4.55 l
1 US gallon = 3.79 l

centigrade / Celsius

°C = (°F - 32) x 5/9

°C	-5	0	5	10	15	18	20	25	30	36.8	38
°F	23	32	41	50	59	64	68	77	86	98.4	100.4

Fahrenheit

°F = (°C x 9/5) + 32

°F	23	32	40	50	60	65	70	80	85	98.4	101
°C	-5	0	4	10	16	18	21	27	29	36.8	38.3